AIN'T NOTHIN'
AS SWEET AS
MY BABY

Ain't Nothin' As Sweet As My Baby

The Story of Hank Williams' Lost Daughter

Jett Williams

WITH PAMELA THOMAS

HARCOURT BRACE JOVANOVICH, PUBLISHERS

SAN DIEGO   NEW YORK   LONDON

Copyright © 1990 by Cathy D. Adkinson and Fletcher Keith Adkinson

The song "Conceived in Love" by Milton L. Brown is quoted by permission of Bama Boy Music (BMI), Mobile, Alabama.

Library of Congress Cataloging-in-Publication Data
Williams, Jett, 1953–
   Ain't nothin' as sweet as my baby: the story of Hank Williams' lost daughter/by Jett Williams with Pamela Thomas.—1st ed.
      p.   cm.
   ISBN 0-15-104050-8
   1. Williams, Jett, 1953–   . 2. Country musicians—United States—Biography.   3. Williams, Hank, 1923–1953.   I. Thomas, Pamela, 1946–   .   II. Title.
ML420.W5515A3   1990
782.42'1642'092—dc20
[B]   90-35899

Design by Martha Roach

Printed in the United States of America

First edition
A B C D E

To
Hank Williams, Sr., & Bobbie Jett
for my heritage;

to
Wayne & Louise Deupree
for my values and my memories;

and

to
my husband,
Keith Adkinson,
for the love I never knew,
and without whom none of this
would have been possible

CONTENTS

Principal Characters   ix

Prologue   xv

1. MY BUCKET'S GOT A HOLE IN IT   1

2. HANK, THE MYTH   16

3. REAL LIFE   40

4. JUST WAITIN'   60

5. SWEET YVONE COMES HOME   72

6. BOBBIE   85

7. KEITH   107

8. THE PAPER CHASE   121

9. CROONIN' IN THE DISTRICT   136

10. NASHVILLE   145

CONTENTS

11.   READING THE RECORD   164

12.   LOVE AT LAST   185

13.   GOING PUBLIC   195

14.   DISCOVERY   212

15.   MY DAY IN COURT   236

16.   HANK, THE MAN   244

17.   THE WEARY BLUES   264

18.   HISTORY REPEATS ITSELF   276

19.   SETTING THE RECORD STRAIGHT   294

20.   JAMBALAYA   309

      Epilogue   319

      Chronology   323

      Acknowledgments   335

PRINCIPAL CHARACTERS

Jett Williams   I am the "lost daughter" born to Hank Williams and Bobbie Jett on January 6, 1953. At birth, I was named Antha Belle Jett by my natural mother. When I was adopted by Hank Williams' mother in 1954, my name was changed to Catherine Yvone Stone. When I was adopted by Wayne and Louise Deupree, I became Cathy Louise Deupree. After my marriage to Michael Mayer in 1975, I became Cathy Deupree Mayer. After my divorce from Michael in 1986, I took the stage name Jett Williams, but after my marriage to F. Keith Adkinson, I also became known as Cathy Adkinson, and occasionally, as B.J.— short for "Baby Jett."

F. Keith Adkinson   My husband, lawyer, and manager, whom I met in September 1984 and married in September 1986.

Roy Acuff   The patriarch of the Grand Ole Opry; former owner, with Wesley Rose, of Acuff-Rose Publishing Company, and one of the defendants in my lawsuit.

PRINCIPAL CHARACTERS

Billie Jean Jones Eshliman Williams Horton Berlin   Second wife of my father, Hank Williams, and one of the defendants in my lawsuit.

Jerry Bradley   A Nashville record executive and son of famed record producer Owen Bradley.

Owen Bradley   A member of the Country Music Hall of Fame and the producer of Patsy Cline, Loretta Lynn, Brenda Lee, and a host of other well-known singers. He took me under his wing and helped me with my singing.

Ilda Mae & James Henry Cook   My foster parents from March 1955 until February 1956. They loved and cared for me after Irene Williams Smith put me in an orphanage.

Wayne & Louise Deupree   My second adoptive parents, with whom I began living at age three.

Richard Emmet   A Montgomery County, Alabama, Circuit Court judge who presided over the 1967 and 1968 court proceedings, during which my existence first became public knowledge.

Helen Fountain   Louise Deupree's sister and my adoptive aunt.

Stanley Fountain, Jr.   Son of Helen Fountain and my adoptive cousin.

Drayton Hamilton   A Montgomery, Alabama, attorney who was appointed as my guardian ad litem and represented my interests in a 1955 dispute over my grandmother's estate and in the 1967–68 proceedings.

Marie McNeil Glenn Harvell   My grandmother's niece and Hank Williams' first cousin.

Don Helms   The steel guitar player in Hank Williams' Drifting Cowboys band during the height of Hank's success. He now plays steel for "Jett Williams and the Drifting Cowboys Band."

Bob & Connie Helton   Hank Williams' close friends. Bob Helton provided key testimony in my paternity trial.

Antha Pauline Jett   My grandmother on my mother's side.

Bobbie Webb Jett   My mother.

Ocie Belle Jett   My great-grandmother on my mother's side; she raised my mother.

Willard Jett   My mother's uncle and the patriarch of the Jett family.

Patsy Jett   Willard's wife; she was present when Hank Williams picked up my pregnant mother and took her away with him.

David Cromwell Johnson   A Birmingham, Alabama, attorney who worked with Keith on my paternity trial and my estate claims.

John F. Keenan   A United States District Court judge who presided over my claims to a child's portion of the copyright renewal revenues generated by my father's songs.

Mark Kennedy   A Montgomery County Circuit Court judge who presided over my paternity trial and ruled that Hank Williams is my father. He is now a justice on the Alabama Supreme Court.

Michael Mayer   My first husband. We were married in 1975 and divorced in 1986.

Neil "Pappy" McCormick   One of Hank Williams' oldest friends. He gave Hank Williams one of his first jobs as a musician and provided key testimony at my paternity trial.

Joseph Phelps   A Montgomery County, Alabama, Circuit Court judge who was originally assigned to my case when I sued for my adoption records. He later recused himself.

PRINCIPAL CHARACTERS

Jerry Rivers The fiddle player in Hank Williams' band. He now plays fiddle with "Jett Williams and the Drifting Cowboys Band."

Fred Rose Co-founder of Acuff-Rose Publishing Company who played a key role in shaping the career of Hank Williams. All of Hank Williams' songs were published by Acuff-Rose.

Wesley Rose Son of Fred Rose; former owner, with Roy Acuff, of Acuff-Rose Publishing Company; and one of the defendants in my lawsuit.

Milton A. Rudin Well-known copyright lawyer whom Keith brought in to spearhead my claim to a child's portion of the copyright renewal revenues generated by my father's songs.

Irene Williams Smith Lillian Williams Stone's daughter, Hank Williams' sister, and my aunt. She turned me over to the state of Alabama after the death of her mother in 1955.

William Wallace Stone My grandmother's second husband, and my first adoptive father.

Lillian Skipper Williams Stone Hank Williams' mother and my grandmother. She began a two-year effort to adopt me within days of Hank's death, and died two months after completing the process.

Jo Jett Tanguay Bobbie Webb Jett's first child and my half sister.

Audrey Mae Sheppard Guy Williams First wife of Hank Williams. She was the mother of Randall Hank Williams.

Elonzo Huble Williams Father of Hank Williams and first husband of Lillian Skipper Williams Stone. They were divorced in the early 1940s.

Hiriam "Hank" Williams   My father, who died on January 1, 1953, five days before my birth.

Hank Williams, Jr. (or *Randall Hank Williams*)   My half brother, born May 26, 1949, and one of the defendants in my lawsuit.

PROLOGUE

This is the story of an adopted child. Like many tales of adopted children, it doesn't begin at the beginning; it starts in the middle—when the adopted child wakes up standing on the brink of adulthood and realizes that he or she can't really get on with life until the mystery of the past is solved. Also, like many such stories, it is the tale of an obsessive and often frightening quest, which only ended when the skeletons of the past were confronted head-on.

This is my story, and my name is Jett Williams. As with my quest, I came to my name at mid-life, not at the beginning. At birth, I was called Antha Belle Jett, and for a host of complicated reasons over the years, I was known at various times as Catherine Yvone Stone, Cathy Louise Deupree, Cathy Deupree Mayer, Cathy Deupree Adkinson, and, to one very special person—and several not so special people—Baby Jett.

After having answered to so many names for so long, I finally decided I had better pick one of my own, and I decided on "Jett Williams" as a tribute to both my birth parents. My natural mother was a beautiful, lively woman from a fine Nashville, Tennessee, family, and her name was Bobbie Webb Jett. My natural father was a gifted musician from Montgomery, Alabama, a legend in his own time and for all time. And his name was Hank Williams.

Often during my search for my natural parents I found myself feeling almost "outside" myself. As I will mention several times in this book, I experienced my life as running along two tracks, one that I knew about and one I did not. After I understood what had gone on along that "other" track, I found myself saying (among other things): "This is a fascinating story!" I would often think about it, look at it, analyze it, and tell it to others as though it were somebody else's fantastic yarn. It seemed that incredible to me.

Yet when I came to actually writing about it, I realized that the importance of my "saga" was not so much the tale of an adopted child who learns that one of her natural parents was, in fact, a celebrated person. Ultimately, the real meaning of my story concerns the plight of adopted children. In my case, my origins were deliberately hidden from me by people associated with my natural parents whose motives had nothing to do with my feelings or well-being. To complicate matters, my adoptive parents, particularly my adoptive mother, could not cope emotionally with me, let alone with my search for my roots. For years, I felt inhibited and afraid to track down my biological parents for fear of hurting my adoptive ones.

Many people believe that all adopted children should be informed about their origins and, if they so choose, be permitted to search for their natural parents. I know from my own experience that adopted children want and need the support of their adoptive families in such a pursuit—and I think that the adoptive family should be responsive to that need. In return, I believe adopted children must also be sensitive to and considerate of the feelings of their adoptive parents. Indeed, they need to acknowledge that the adoptive parents are the "real" parents. Nevertheless, I believe it is the right of the child to look, and the responsibility of the adoptive parents to help the child in the search—at least emotionally, if not in fact.

However, I also believe every case is unique and each adopted child must make his or her own decision. What is right for one may not be right for another. Pursuit of the past may be fine for one adopted child, while avoiding it at all costs may be equally appropriate for another. One thing is certain, it is not to be undertaken lightly. Rejection is always a possibility, and the reality of the past may be unpleasant.

The feelings of natural parents who make the heart-wrenching decision to put a child up for adoption have to be considered, too. The laws are such that natural parents are insulated from contact and future emotional or financial demands, but generally, I believe natural parents should give serious consideration to a reunion. If they are contacted and refuse to meet, they compound their early abandonment of the child with current rejection.

Thus, many people think that natural parents have a responsibility to meet with their child if they are contacted. I am very fortunate because members of my natural family—at least on my mother's side—welcomed me, and accepted me with open arms and open hearts. I don't believe it is an obligation of family members (other than the natural parents) to accept the natural child, but, I can say from my own experience, it has made my life sweeter.

Finally, I believe that adoption agencies, whether public or private, should permit adoptees access to their entire adoption records (especially if both natural parents have died) and should provide help in contacting lost parents. They should be open and honest with adult adopted children. Moreover, given the problems I faced, agencies should take special care that adopted chilren are encouraged to obtain all necessary legal counsel, depending upon the situation.

Since my story is about my own adoption experience, I certainly hope this book will be read and enjoyed by all adopted children, adoptive parents—and natural parents.

For adopted children, the smallest details regarding their natural parents become very important, and, in my case, one little incident led me to the title for this book—*Ain't Nothin' as Sweet as My Baby*.

PROLOGUE

Late one night in the fall of 1989, Jerry Rivers, the fiddler from my daddy's old band, shared with my husband and me scores of old transcription discs made by my father for an early-morning radio show that aired on Station WSM in Nashville in 1951. Although these shows usually aired live, since Hank and his band had engagements on the road and were often unable to be in the studio at showtime, over 50 of them were prerecorded. These were the transcriptions that Jerry played for us.

These discs included over 150 songs, many of which were never put on record by my father. One of those songs concerned a blond-haired, blue-eyed baby girl and was titled "There's Nothing as Sweet as My Baby." As Hank introduced the song on his radio show, he explained that he was going to sing "a new one he wrote." Then, adding the sort of emphasis that made Hank's shows so especially warm and personal, he said quite forcefully: ". . . ain't nothin' as sweet as my baby." Somehow, this really touched me.

Since my situation is unique in that my father never put me up for adoption, never intended that I be adopted—and, in fact, made provisions to care for me himself—I'd like to think that had he lived, this song, "There's Nothing as Sweet as My Baby," would have had special meaning for us, that it would have been "our song." That's why I selected it as the title of my book.

Having said all this, I will now stop preaching and return to my original comment: When I look at my life story objectively, I can't help but shake my head in wonder and say, "That is amazing!" Believe me, it is a great story—replete with lust, passion, greed, betrayal, fraud, rejection, terror, lying, cheating, deceiving, tears, loneliness, despair—and most of all, love lost and love found. In other words, it contains all those wonderful human dilemmas we all know about, and all those fascinating human emotions that my daddy spent his life putting so profoundly into song.

In fact, my life is rather like a country song, except for one thing: It starts in the middle.

Ain't Nothin' as Sweet as My Baby

1

MY BUCKET'S GOT A
HOLE IN IT

Most people I know have a family picture book of some kind filled with photographs of family celebrations and landmark occasions. There is usually one marking the birth of each child captioned "First Day Home," with Mama holding the newborn and Daddy standing nearby, beaming with pride. There was such a book in the house where I grew up, and in it, a standard-issue picture of me labeled "First Nite Home." But this particular picture was kind of unusual. First of all, I am not an infant. In fact, I look to be something bigger than toddler-sized, and I'm sitting alone on an ottoman, dressed in a little bathrobe. Mama is not holding me, and given the "I'm trying to accommodate" look on my face, I suspect she was operating the camera. Daddy is sitting in a chair behind me, smiling, but not with the assurance and intimacy of a man who has lovingly changed four thousand diapers. He looks happy, but since he did not scoop me up in a big hug for the sake of posterity, I can only assume he didn't know quite what to do with his newly adopted daughter.

Most adopted children are placed with their adoptive families as infants, but I was three years old on that "First Day Home" with Wayne and Louise Deupree, the people I would grow up calling Mother and Daddy. I had always been called Cathy; and now, in my new family, I became Cathy Louise Deupree. While I don't remember having my picture taken on that memorable day, I always had hazy memories of certain other events. I recall riding in the back seat of a car, knowing I was being taken to Mobile, Alabama, to live with my new "mama" and "daddy." I had a vague memory that just prior to that time I had been living on a farm with a wonderful woman named Mama Cook and her family. I also knew I had lived somewhere else before I went to Mama Cook's house, but I didn't know who those people were or where they lived. I also don't remember who explained the events of my first three years to me—or when. I just knew and accepted them.

Later, my mother would tell me that on the afternoon of that "First Day Home," she had walked me around and around the block until, as she put it in her slow, south-Alabama drawl, I "could walk no more." I don't remember that walk, but I vaguely recall an exchange that took place later that evening. As my new mother was getting me ready for my "First Bath Home," she tried to help me unbutton my blouse. I turned away and said, very politely, "No, thank you, ma'am. I can do that myself."

I came to the Deuprees fully aware that I was not their natural child. No one would ever have to sit me down at the age of five or six and tell me the awful truth—that I was adopted—an occasion that is often fraught with pain and anxiety for both the adoptive parents and the adopted child. I knew I was adopted, and by the age of three I apparently believed that it was dangerous for me to get too attached to anybody. I had come to the conclusion that if I was going to get along in life, I'd pretty much have to do it myself, thank you, ma'am.

Like many adopted children, I often fantasized about where I might have come from. I would weave tales for myself about the probable fate of my natural parents, stories that usually involved a tragic plane crash or automobile accident. Years later, a journalist would give me a book about the feelings of adopted children, and I learned that the adopted child's scenario of the "tragic plane crash" is a common one. As I would come to understand only too well, there is a very good reason for this fantasy: It removes the possibility of rejection. If my mama and daddy have died through no fault of their own, it proves that they didn't choose to give me away.

I also sometimes imagined that I was some sort of extraterrestrial. (I later discovered that the "outer space" theory is also standard fare for young adopted children.) I, of course, remembered the car ride to the Deuprees' and a bit about the Cook family, but when I was little I wondered if perhaps somewhere, sometime, I'd been plucked out of a burning spacecraft in a field out in the Alabama countryside. I figured some kind, brave soul—Mama Cook perhaps?—might have decided to do this baby Martian a good turn and place her with the childless Deuprees.

Given my later, often problematic and troublesome life with Wayne and Louise, this fabrication was not too surprising. I looked and acted nothing like them. Wayne was a rugged, tough individualist; I was tiny, talkative, and outgoing. Mother was dark, sultry, and very beautiful; I was towheaded, blue-eyed, and effervescent. Louise liked to dress up in the latest fashion and always had "one foot in the road," as they say in Alabama. (In other words, she liked to go out on the town.) Me, well, I never thought I looked the part of a Southern belle; I liked to wear cutoff jeans, play ball, and hang out with my friends. I would try to help around the house, but I never did learn how to fold a towel right or pick the perfect moment to vacuum the living room. I loved sports, and I was very proud of the many awards I won, particularly for volleyball, but my parents showed no interest and never once came to a game.

Occasionally, as I was growing up, I would ask Mother or Daddy if they had any idea where I had come from. In our family, you didn't analyze things too much anyway, and this particular question made my parents very uneasy. They would always answer very quickly: "We don't know anything." Yet, I suspected that they knew at least a bit more than they admitted. Once when I was about eight years old, I was rummaging around in one of my mother's bureau drawers and found a packet of official-looking documents together with some scraps of paper that seemed meaningless. Buried inside was a photograph of a young woman, and on the back of the picture it said: "To Cathy, the sweetest little girl in the world. May you always be happy and never forget me as long as you live. Always remember that Jewel loves you and God bless you."

I asked Mother about this photo, and she said she thought Jewel was probably one of the kids in the foster home. (By then, I had learned that Mama Cook had been my foster mother.) Besides, Mother said, "You shouldn't be lookin' where you shouldn't be lookin'." End of conversation. But that inscription made a difference in my life. When things got rough, I would remember that somebody named Jewel would always love me. I swore to myself that when I grew up I would find Jewel, because she would know where I came from.

I did have another piece of physical evidence that a life had existed for me before the age of three. On my right wrist, I had a wicked-looking scar, shaped like a sea horse, which my parents told me had been there when I came. Today, that scar is about three inches long, but it must have extended up my entire fore-arm when I was a baby. I would think, "My God, I must have been in some terrible accident!" But I had no conscious memory of a fall or a crash; although I did have a faint recollection of spurting blood. I would sit and stare at that scar, but only one image would flicker through my mind: I am a baby, sitting in the back seat of another car— not the car that had brought me to the Deuprees— and a warm, large woman— a woman with no waist— is holding me and trying to comfort me. That thought would bubble up again and again, but it was so fleeting, so vague, that I finally concluded it was only a dream.

Despite this well of blurriness and lack of concrete information about my true identity, I was, at least on the surface, a reasonably happy kid. My parents, though emotionally neglectful in many ways, provided for me well. They dressed me beautifully, sent me to good schools, gave me dancing lessons (because Louise wanted me to take them) and guitar lessons (because I wanted them). Daddy was particularly generous with presents, and while often he couldn't give me things in a forthright way— like a new car on my sixteenth birthday, for example—for fear that Mother would get upset, he would hitch it around a bit and make sure I got special things sooner or later. They both had fine senses of humor, which I appreciated, and at times their silly or absurd views on people or situations would make us all laugh and bring us closer together, at least for a while. My mother, particularly, could be quite comical in her own way, and I enjoyed her in those moments.

But both my parents drank too much, and my mother suffered not only from alcoholism but also from addiction to prescription drugs, and was prone to dark depressions that at times disabled her completely. She could not cope with life, let alone with a little girl who was not at all her notion of a dream child. (In fact, for my mother a dream child was just that—a dream.) They were older when they adopted me—Daddy was forty-six and Mother was thirty-three—and basically I had to work my way into the life that they had already established for themselves. Some parents alter their lives to accommodate their children, but I felt that my parents viewed me as a nice, respectable asset, like a big car or something, and that I was not to question anything or disturb their status quo. And I didn't. I suppose I feared they'd trade me in.

We played out this life in front of a curtain of secrecy—the mystery of my background—for eighteen years, until the eve of my twenty-first birthday. Being accepting and accommodating by nature and breeding, I guess I assumed this would be my life, that I would never know who my real parents had been or what had occurred during those first three years of my life. And then, for reasons that would take years for me to untangle, my parents lifted a corner of that curtain. They allowed me to peek behind and catch a glimpse of something truly astonishing. They told me who my real father might be.

As I would come to understand, most adopted children are ambivalent, if not downright frightened, about discovering their true parentage, and most adoptive parents, if they know the truth, are reluctant to tell. For the child, it means facing the reality of his birth, which is often painful. For the adoptive parents, it means coming eyeball-to-eyeball with the fact that no matter how much they loved their child, that child is not blood of their blood.

In most cases, however, the natural parents are just "real" people. The father might be seventeen-year-old John Smith, garage mechanic, who falls madly in love with Mary Jones, girl-next-door. Or maybe the mother is a young college girl from Ohio who travels to Venice and allows a flirtation with an Italian boy to go too far. For these people, the birth of a baby could ruin their lives, so they end up having an abortion, or giving the baby up to people better able to provide care.

But in my case, the story had some spin on it. This man rumored to be my father was not a garage mechanic or an Italian boy with a twinkle in his eye. He was a singer and a songwriter, a man whose name, voice, and music were known throughout the world. He was the king of country music. He was a legend. He was, according to my very agitated mother on the eve of my twenty-first birthday, Hank Williams.

Christmas was never a particularly joyful holiday for me. Mother was usually depressed, and both my parents tended to drink even more than usual during those weeks. And you could always count on a major family "fallin' out" to develop at some point during the season. I had just finished the first semester of my junior year at the University of Alabama, Tuscaloosa, where I was majoring in therapeutic recreation. I came home a few days before Christmas, but spent most of my time with my old friends from Mobile, friends I'd known since grade school. I'd visit over at their houses during the day, and then in the evenings we'd go out to some local bars to talk, laugh, and listen to music.

As usual, we had a big turkey dinner at my Aunt Helen's house on Christmas Day, a decidedly tense occasion. Helen Fountain was my mother's sister and she and her family lived a few blocks from us. If you were to ask her today, Helen would say she and my mother couldn't have been closer throughout their lives. But the fact of the matter is that their relationship was as turbulent as any other that my mother had. Mother and Aunt Helen were either speaking or they weren't speaking. On this particular Christmas, they were speaking.

Aunt Helen's husband, Uncle Stanley, was the federal marshall for the southern district of the state of Alabama. They had one son, Stanley Boy (or Nanley Boy), whom I liked well enough. When I was a little child, say four or five years of age, I adored him. He was five years older than I, and he was occasionally kind enough to let me ride his bike or play cards with me. (His favorite card game was 52 Pickup; I picked up.) As we got older, our relationship petered out.

I don't really remember now, but I suspect I spent New Year's Eve with friends and then drove back the two hundred miles to Tuscaloosa on Wednesday or Thursday of that week. My birthday fell on the following Sunday, January 6, 1974, and it would be my twenty-first. I was about as enthusiastic about my birthday as I was about the Christmas holidays. Everyone was pretty much celebrated out—if you can call our Christmas holidays "celebrating"—by the time January 6 rolled around, so my birthday was never a festive occasion for me or anybody else.

Oddly enough, the day after I got back to school, I received a call from my parents saying that they were going to come up to Tuscaloosa for the weekend to celebrate my birthday. I say "oddly enough" because Mother and Daddy had never come to visit me at school during the entire three years I'd been there. I also say "oddly enough" because they had not mentioned that they were thinking of coming up during the two weeks I'd been at home—and I'd just gotten back the day before. I was very surprised. And especially touched.

They arrived late Saturday morning, and we spent the afternoon touring the campus and meeting my friends at the Alpha Delta Pi sorority house where I lived. We decided to have my birthday dinner at Nick's, a local restaurant that served great steaks and Zombies, those big, pink, silent-killer drinks that come in brandy snifters. They said they wanted to rest a bit before dinner, so we went back to their motel before the big celebration. Once we got into their motel room, Daddy suddenly decided that he wanted to go for a walk. I thought that was a little strange because Daddy never took walks, but since this entire situation was odd, I didn't think much of it.

Once mother and I were alone, I noticed that she was becoming particularly agitated. I was just sitting on the bed, but she had begun pacing up and down the room, smoking cigarette after cigarette. Suddenly she began talking, and telling me things that would take days—or years—for me to absorb.

"Cathy," she said, in her wonderfully slow manner, "there's something we have got to talk about."

"Yes, ma'am," I said, wondering what on earth was troubling her.

"I talked this week with a lady at Pensions and Security. That's the adoption agency, the adoption agency where we got you."

I didn't say anything. I just sat on the bed and watched her pacing back and forth, back and forth, up and down that room. I couldn't imagine what she was trying to say.

"We think we know who your daddy may have been. Your real daddy, that is. Do you know who he was, Cathy?"

"No, ma'am, I don't," I answered, totally confused. Did she think that I had actually known all these years who my real parents were?

"Well, your daddy may have been a very famous person—a famous man from Alabama. Do you know who he is?" she said.

"No, ma'am, I don't," I said, still confused and wondering why I was being subjected to this game of twenty questions.

"But he was a famous man, Cathy, a famous musician from Montgomery, Alabama. Who do you think he was?"

Now I was starting to get apprehensive—even scared—so I tried to break the tension by saying the first name that came to my mind, a name that fit her description.

"Nat King Cole!" I said.

We both laughed nervously.

"Cathy, be serious," she said in her inimitable way. "Who do you think I'm talking about?"

"Well, the only other person I can think of is Hank Williams," I answered.

"Well . . ."

I was almost struck dumb. Just being told that I had a blood father was shocking. But that my father might be Hank Williams? Hank Williams! Why, everybody knew Hank Williams. He was a legend, especially in Alabama.

"Mother," I said, "what are you saying? Why are you telling me this?"

She was still pacing up and down the room, nervous as a cat. I was beginning to see why Daddy had decided to take a walk. She kept on pacing, but she managed to tell me the rest.

"You've been left a little bit of money from a lady named Lillian Stone. I believe she was Hank Williams' mother. We think it's about two thousand dollars, something like that. They have it down at the courthouse in Montgomery—a check. This money was put aside for you, a little money from her estate or something, and you are to have it when you turn twenty-one."

This information was not completely penetrating my mind. For a brief, almost-unacknowledged moment, I saw the shadowy form of the woman, the woman holding me in the back seat of the car when I had cut my arm. But the memory vanished into the air as quickly as it came. I didn't know what to make of it. I didn't know what kind of questions to ask. I didn't even think about asking questions.

"Now, Cathy," Mother went on. "There is absolutely no proof of this. I have to tell you that."

It was as though she had doused me with ice water. Set me on fire, then drowned me in ice.

"Proof of what?" I asked.

"Well, this thing about Hank Williams, of course. Five or six years ago, there was a trial. Somebody called us then. Your existence came up—something about you possibly being the daughter of Hank Williams. Everything was decided—there really wasn't any money involved. And there was no proof that Hank Williams really was your father anyway. No proof at all."

First she had said that she thought she knew who my father was, that my father was Hank Williams. Then she said she had no proof. No proof at all. It barely made sense to me.

"All I can tell you is that this money at the courthouse has something to do with Hank's mother, Mrs. Lillian Stone, and you're to go pick it up in Montgomery. Now, Uncle Stanley's gonna go with you, just in case somebody says something to you."

"Like what?" I asked.

"Well, because of this trial, there might be some reporter or somebody following up on the story. We don't know. But we talked it over, and we thought it would be best if Uncle Stanley went with you."

I wasn't able to make sense of what she was saying at the time, but later I would see that my parents were more worried about publicity than they let on to me, so they had arranged for Uncle Stanley to go with me for safety's sake, I guess.

A few minutes later, Daddy returned from his walk, but he didn't mention anything about Hank Williams or Lillian Stone or a free-floating two-thousand-dollar check. We didn't discuss it again that weekend—which was pretty typical behavior in our family. We just went out to Nick's and had ourselves those big steaks and quite a few Zombies. The next morning I met them for breakfast, they wished me happy birthday, I waved them off in the early afternoon, and then I headed straight for the library. I needed to find out a little bit more about this guy who might be my father. This singer everybody knew—Hank Williams.

I was as stunned as any adopted child would be to have a hint as to who my real daddy might be. And for anyone to even suggest that he might be Hank Williams was quite frightening to me really—Hank Williams was bigger than life. I could slip a dime into any jukebox in the state of Alabama and listen to him sing. I could walk over to any record store in town and choose from scores of his albums. I could actually go to the public library and find a book on his life, which is exactly what I did.

I felt as though I was walking slowly through a dream or on a stage acting out somebody else's life story. I sat in the library for an hour or so that Sunday afternoon skimming through a book entitled *Sing a Sad Song: The Life of Hank Williams* by Roger M. Williams. There, buried in the back of the book, I found a reference to "the child, a girl . . . born a couple of months after Hank's death." From the book, I learned that Hank had died pitifully on the night of December 31, 1952, in the back seat of a car on his way to a singing engagement in Canton, Ohio. I was born on January 6, 1953. That was not a couple of months, that was six days. I learned that "the mother was a brunette in her

late twenties whom Hank had apparently met in Tennessee."
Well, as far as I could make out, Hank Williams had dark hair,
and the book said this woman had dark hair, so how did I get to
be blond? These facts didn't sound too promising.

But then it said, "Lilly Stone virtually acknowledged her
son's paternity by caring for the woman before the birth and for
the child afterward, until the local welfare agency found an
adopted home. However, the entire matter remained a family
secret until it came out in a court hearing in 1967." Mother had
just said there had been a trial and my name had come up. That
sounded right.

I read that Lillian Stone had died in February 1955, and I
knew I had not gone to the Deuprees until February 1956. Well,
I vaguely remembered Mama Cook, so I figured I must have
been in the foster home for at least a year, but I couldn't tell
from this book whether I'd stayed with Lillian Stone for just a
few days after I was born, or for two years until she died. And
then there was the matter of this check, money that was evidently from her estate. The book said that Lillian Stone "virtually acknowledged her son's paternity," and I now knew I was
going to get a little bit of money. Could I dare to assume that
she had actually cared about me?

On Monday morning, January 7, I got in my car and drove the
hundred and some-odd miles over to Montgomery. Montgomery,
Alabama's capital, is right in the heart of the state, and I'd driven
the interstates and highways that go up, around, and through
the city a time or two, but I'd never stopped off in the city itself.
If I'd been asked, I would have said that I'd never been to Montgomery, but, if I was to believe what my mother was telling me,
that I was "the child, a girl" I'd read about the afternoon before,
I reasoned that I must have been born there.

It could be said that Montgomery is the quintessential
Southern American city—both for its importance during the "War
for Southern Independence" and for its place in the history of
the civil rights struggle. As every schoolchild raised in Alabama
knows, Jefferson Davis was inaugurated president of the Confederate States of America on February 18, 1861, on the portico

of the State Capitol Building that still sits majestically at the top of Dexter Avenue, Montgomery's main street. Before the Civil War, Montgomery was an important cotton center, and many of the beautiful antebellum houses, once owned by the "cotton kings," still line the quiet streets.

Montgomery is also known as a focal point for many of the events that sparked the civil rights movement of the late 1950s and 1960s. The Reverend Dr. Martin Luther King, Jr., was the pastor of the Dexter Avenue King Memorial Baptist Church from 1954 to 1960, and from this church he directed several pivotal civil rights actions.

Like many American urban centers, the heart of the city has suffered from urban blight. Gray-looking parking lots, broken-down warehouses, and seedy-looking fast-food franchises have replaced what were once lovely department stores, pretty shops, and bustling cafés. At the same time, Montgomery has not lost its innate sense of dignity. Today, Montgomery's most important "business" is government, and a few sleek-looking office buildings and well-tended parks give the city a sense of beauty. And Montgomery citizens still take great pride in their natives, who include Zelda Sayre Fitzgerald (the wife of writer F. Scott Fitzgerald), Nat King Cole, and, of course, Hank Williams.

I met Uncle Stanley at noon at a new hotel—part of Montgomery's rejuvenation—near the center of the city. We had a leisurely, pleasant lunch in the hotel, but in true family tradition, we just chatted about Aunt Helen, Stanley Boy, Mother, and school. Nothing, absolutely nothing, was mentioned about why we were sitting there together in Montgomery, Alabama, about to walk down the street to the courthouse and pick up a check for me from the estate of one Lillian Stone, who just happened to be Hank Williams' mother.

After lunch, we crossed over Dexter Avenue and walked up to Montgomery's courthouse building. As we crossed Dexter Avenue, I could see the stately white State Capitol Building sitting on top of the hill, and I thought to myself, "My, that's grand!" When we got to the courthouse, we walked down a broad, echoing corridor and found the designated room. We opened the door and found ourselves face-to-face with a man, a classic bureaucratic sort, sitting at a desk. Uncle Stanley explained to him that we were there to pick up a check set aside for me from the estate of Lillian Stone.

"What name are you going by?" he asked, looking at me.

Given the circumstances, I thought that was an interesting question. I wondered if I couldn't wheedle a bit more information out of him.

"Why, what choices do I have?" I asked, thinking he might give me a clue about my real name.

"The name on your driver's license," he said quickly, clearly annoyed with my question.

"Cathy Louise Deupree," I answered politely, and handed him my license. He then reached into his desk and pulled out a big checkbook, wrote out a check to me for a little over two thousand dollars, using the name on my driver's license, signed it himself, and handed it to me. He didn't mention Hank Williams or Lillian Stone. He didn't hum a few bars from "Hey, Good Lookin'" or "I'm So Lonesome I Could Cry." He didn't eye me curiously, or act nervous because I was—I might be— the child of Montgomery's favorite son. Nothing.

When Uncle Stanley and I got back out into the corridor, hordes of reporters weren't elbowing each other out of the way to get a good look at me. No flashbulbs were popping. No one was shoving a microphone in my face to get a statement. Nobody was falling all over themselves, thrilled with the notion that the long-lost daughter of the famous Hank Williams had been found at last. I had started out that morning all excited, sure that I would leave that building knowing more about my mysterious past than when I went in. But nothing happened. Picking up this check had been no more eventful than applying for a fishing license. Uncle Stanley and I just walked back out to the street into the gray January light. He got into his car and drove back on down to Mobile. I got into mine and drove back to Tuscaloosa, back to my real life.

For the next few years, I tucked this little fact—the "fact" that Hank Williams might be my father—in the back of my mind. I didn't talk about it with Wayne and Louise because any discussion of my "real" parents upset them, and disturbing them was frightening to me. What's more, evidently there wasn't any proof.

Occasionally, I would start to examine these weird "facts" by myself, but after a couple of minutes of contemplation, I'd start to go nuts. I could make a "case" for Hank Williams being my father. (I had received money from his mother's estate; I had come up in a trial involving his family.) And just as easily, I could make a "case" against it. (There is just no proof; a judge had evidently said so.) I couldn't go find Hank and ask him face-on—he was dead. "We just don't know anything." That's what my parents had always said to me the few times I mustered up the courage to bring up the subject. "We don't know anything else. It's a dead issue." So, naturally, I figured there wasn't much else I could do.

But one thread kept tickling me, and it wasn't one I cared to pull on in any significant way. I now knew that there had been no car or plane crash. After all was said and done, I hadn't arrived, child-sized, in a spaceship on the Deupree lawn. I'd been born of a woman. But what about her, this nameless woman with the brunette hair from Tennessee who had carried me? Who was she? But I would get only so far into that line of thinking when it would occur to me that it was Hank's mama who had cared for me until I'd been turned over to the foster home. The only rational conclusion a sane mind could draw was that my own mama had given me away. Beyond that, the only rational question I could ask was "Why?"

Those conclusions and questions were unbearable for me at age twenty-one. I couldn't face them. Besides, I had a real life going on, a real life that involved finishing school, setting up a career, and maybe getting married. What's more, I would always come back to Mother's statement that there was no proof—it was a dead issue. I also could tell that Mother and Daddy weren't too interested in probing these questions. Their response of "We don't know anything" had an edge to it. I truly believe they didn't know too much. But more, I was their little girl, and despite their sometimes erratic behavior, I could see they didn't much want to share me with the ghost of Hank Williams and some brunette woman from Tennessee.

So I let it be. But instead of disappearing, the obsession grew. As time passed, I realized that this revelation wasn't the end of the story, it was just the beginning, the first hint I had that my life had actually been running along two tracks since the day I was born. Unknown to me, those tracks had crossed and tangled several times over the years since my birth, and later, both with and without my knowledge, would crisscross again and again.

On one of those tracks, I had been riding along, basically trying to put together a nice life for myself. On the other track rode a group of people who were very interested in checks much larger than the one I had picked up at the courthouse in Montgomery. I would eventually learn that they had gone to great lengths to hide information from me and my adoptive parents because my very existence posed a very big problem for them.

Within weeks of my uneventful sojourn to the courthouse with Uncle Stanley, a prominent lawyer from Montgomery, Alabama, would send a letter to another important attorney in Nashville, Tennessee, telling him that a certain "Baby Jett" had picked up her check from the Stone estate. I wouldn't know about this letter for more than a decade, by which time lawyers would be arguing that by collecting that check, I had inadvertently set the clock ticking on an extremely interesting "statute of limitations."

Looking back, I am amazed that my two-thousand-dollar check ever saw the light of day. What's more, I've always thought it was curious that those people riding the other track—the folks with their secrets and their highfalutin legal maneuvers—yes, I thought it was fascinating that they allowed that check to leak out at all.

2
HANK, THE MYTH

On the day after my twenty-first birthday, as I drove back to Tuscaloosa from Montgomery, I began thinking about Hank Williams. I certainly knew he was a famous country singer. In fact, I was under the impression that he was the most renowned country singer who ever lived. Of course, I also knew Hank was from Alabama, a piece of information engraved on the mind of any native-born Alabamian. Also, like virtually everybody in the state who was of sound mind and could afford a ticket to the movies, I'd seen the film *Your Cheatin' Heart*, starring George Hamilton as Hank, which was the source of most of my information about him.

The movie, touted as the "true story of Hank Williams' life," was originally made around 1964, but it had been rereleased several times, especially in Alabama. Originally, I had gone to see it with my friend Sally when I was about fourteen—at the adamant insistence of my adoptive father, who, in retrospect, I feel certain must have had his suspicions about my relationship to Hank when he sent us off to the theater. My friend and I loved it, and like most people we bawled our eyes out when Hank died in the end. What's more, I accepted this accounting of Hank's life as gospel.

I knew Hank was famous for "lonesome," "lovesick" songs, and had a low, sorrowful voice. I was aware that he'd sung—and maybe written—a few old standards like "Hey, Good Lookin' " and, of course, "Your Cheatin' Heart," and that his music had been popular during the years just prior to the arrival of Elvis Presley and rock and roll. I was also certain that some of Hank's songs had been recorded by various pop artists like Tony Bennett and Joni James in the late 1940s and early 1950s. Later, I would come to appreciate that Hank truly was not only one of the greatest country singers and songwriters of all time, but one of the few whose songs crossed over into the popular genre—not once or twice, but repeatedly.

The Hank Williams I conjured up in my mind was a tall, skinny fellow who wore a big, white cowboy hat and carried one fine-looking guitar. I didn't doubt that somewhere, sometime, I must have seen a photograph of him, or maybe I just remembered George Hamilton's Hank.

I realized almost immediately that getting to know Hank Williams was very scary to me, and my fears had everything to do with my adoptive parents and their adamant refusal to discuss the subject. On one or two occasions, after their revelation on my 21st birthday, I had tried to ask them about their knowledge of the Williams family, but they—especially Mother—made it clear that any interest I might have in Hank was a betrayal to them. As a result, I was afraid to read up on Hank, even without their knowledge. Occasionally, over the next few years, my fascination would overtake my fears, and I would glance at an article about Hank or listen to one of his records, but I never shared my thoughts and feelings with anyone, certainly not Wayne and Louise.

In any case, as I would later learn when I felt free to steep myself in the life story of Hank Williams, much of the information I could have collected was more or less the stuff of legend rather than fact. Many of the "Hank stories" were homogenized, cleaned up by his mother, his wife Audrey, some of his friends, and the powers-that-be at the Grand Ole Opry, all people who for reasons of their own wanted Hank's memory to live on, untarnished.

So the Hank Williams legend was born and cultivated. Some of the facts are hard and unalterable, others are patently false. Some of the stories have been spun out so many times that nobody knows the truth, but the essence of these anecdotes is probably true enough and often imparts something significant about Hank's artistic and personal development. In any case, the story of Hank Williams' life most often available for public consumption goes something like this:

Hank Williams was born on September 17, 1923, in a tiny community called Mt. Olive, Alabama, located in the center of Butler County, about sixty miles south of Montgomery. He was named Hiriam Williams ("Hiriam" was probably someone's spelling error), and he was called Hiram (or Harm or Skeets) until he reached adolescence, when he decided he wanted to be called something a little manlier and landed on "Hank."

Hank's parents, Elonzo Huble Williams and Jessie Lillie Belle (or Lillian) Skipper Williams, were natives of south and central Alabama; Lon from Lowndes County, where he grew up on a farm, and Lillie from Butler County, where the men in her family had been blacksmiths, farmers, and loggers, all endeavors common to that part of the state. Although, according to the local pecking order, the Skippers were considered to be a bit "above" the Williamses, both families had known nothing but hardscrabble poverty for generations. These were poor people, but hardworking, God-fearing, and proud, qualities that they would pass on to their son.

When Hank was born in 1923, his parents had been married for about seven years and already had another child, a girl named Irene who had been born just the year before. Lon and Lillie had moved to Mt. Olive, probably from another equally small town nearby, shortly before Hank was born. They had leased a classic Alabama farmhouse, built like two three-room shoe boxes shoved together; opened a small country store on one side; and lived in the other. They had also bought three acres of workable land and planted strawberries with the hope of establishing a berry business. Supporting a family off a strawberry patch requires tough, backbreaking work, but no different from the small-farm labor they both had always known and most of their neighbors shared.

From birth, Hiram was thin and frail, physical attributes that would never change. He was also known as a child who liked to "go his own way." In *Sing a Sad Song*, Roger Williams quotes J. C. McNeil, Hank's cousin, as saying Hank was "a real loner. He never was a happy boy, in a way. He didn't laugh and carry on like other children. It seemed like somethin' was always on his mind." At the same time, he had a certain macho toughness to him, both physically and emotionally. He loved to fish and hunt (he always adored guns), and was proficient at both. Even at a very young age, he was self-assertive, resourceful (one legend has him selling peanuts at a logging camp at the age of three), and, in an odd sort of way, astonishingly self-contained, qualities he inherited from his mother.

Stories of Lillian Williams' toughness are legion. Lillie was tall, imposing (she weighed around two hundred pounds), and strong. If her loud haranguing didn't pull her husband and children into line, she wouldn't think twice about whipping them with a pine switch or hauling off and "whomping" them over the head. Her hardiness was matched by Lon's inexplicable weakness. Given the jobs he held, Lon was not a weak man physically. His problems seemed to be emotional, which Lillian attributed to shell shock he received while in battle in Europe during World War I.

Throughout Hank's early childhood, the Williamses moved frequently, always, apparently, to find more lucrative work—or perhaps any work at all. Money was scarce—and would become scarcer when the Depression hit—and people had to scratch out a living however they could with the resources at hand. The Williamses lived in several towns in and around Butler County—Garland, Chapman, and McWilliams—and Lon worked variously as a farmer, a logger, and a locomotive driver for a lumber camp. (Hank was always fascinated by trains, perhaps due to memories of his dad's days as a trainman, and romantic images of life on the rails show up repeatedly in his songs, from early pieces like "Pan American" to "The Log Train," released long after his death, to one of his most sophisticated pieces, "Ramblin' Man.")

In 1930, when Hank was seven, Lon checked himself into a veterans hospital in Biloxi, Mississippi, where he stayed, off and on, for the next ten years. Apparently, his already-fragile emotional makeup had broken down completely and as work became scarcer and the demands of family life tougher, Lon just couldn't take it anymore. If Lillie was not already the driving force in the family—which she probably was—from this moment on, she now became the central stabilizing figure. Somewhere along the line, Lillian divorced Lon, and Lon exerted virtually no influence over his children ever again.

By 1934, Lillian, Irene, and Hank had moved to Georgiana, the second-largest town in Butler County, where Lillie got a job at a WPA cannery. Eventually, Lillie also opened her first boardinghouse there and, in part, fed the family and her tenants by cultivating a large garden. Snide, appalling tales of Lillie's bullying are always qualified by compliments for her hard work, diligence, and responsibility on behalf of her children. Invariably, she found ingenious ways to hold body and soul together, and sweat blood bringing her ventures to fruition—whether it was a vegetable garden, a boardinghouse, or her son's career.

By now it was the height of the Depression, and despite Lillie's efforts, it was necessary for both Irene (age eleven or twelve) and Hank (age ten or eleven) to help earn money. In a decidedly Lillian-sounding scheme, Irene and Hank set up a little business where Irene roasted peanuts and packed them in small sacks; Hank went out every afternoon after school and sold them on the street. He also carried shoe polish and a rag, so if someone didn't want peanuts—or even if he did—Hank might also sell him a shine.

One famous tale has it that on Hank's first day out, he made thirty cents, and with it he bought stew fixings. He took the food home and asked his mother to make gumbo, a special favorite of his. Lillie was thrilled. The next day he made another thirty cents, but, in a gesture not at all surprising for an eleven-year-old boy, spent the money on firecrackers and caps. Years later, Lillian relished telling how she discovered where the peanut money had gone. She paddled Hank so hard, she claimed, that the caps went off.

During the couple of years the Williamses lived in Georgiana, Hank's first serious interest and talent for music emerged. Legend has it that when he was only three or four years old, he would sit entranced by his mother's side while she played the organ in the Baptist church back in Mt. Olive. The village still displays the bench where Hank supposedly sat each Sunday.

By the time he was eleven, Hank was known as a boy who liked to sing and play the guitar. Many people claim credit for buying him his first guitar and teaching him to play. The most famous tale was told by Frank Thigpen, who owned the local Ford dealership in Georgiana. He claimed to have recognized Hank's superior gifts and bought him a guitar outright. The notion of a shrewd businessman buying a scruffy street kid a new guitar seems pretty farfetched, whereas his mother's version strikes a chord of reality: She claimed she ordered an inexpensive guitar for him by mail from a Sears Roebuck catalog.

The source of Hank's early musical instruction was also fertile ground for tall tales, including stories told by his own mother. Hank's mother may well have paid for a couple of guitar lessons, but since money was tight—and Lillian was tightfisted—Hank probably had to pay for guitar lessons himself if he wanted them. More than likely, like any kid fascinated with a particular art form, be it playing the guitar or pitching a ball, Hank picked up his knowledge wherever he could find it.

Hank himself attributed the greatest part of his musical education to a black street singer named Rufe Payne, known locally as Tee-tot. There were several black street singers in the area, but Tee-tot was the most famous. He lived up the tracks from Georgiana in Greenville, the county seat, but he "worked" both towns, hitching rides back and forth on the train a couple of days a week. Later, when the Williamses moved to Greenville, Hank's relationship with Tee-tot would grow stronger.

Around 1934, Hank spent several months living at the home of his cousins, the McNeils, in Fountain, Alabama, a small town about eighty miles west of Georgiana. The McNeils wanted their daughter to attend high school in Georgiana, so while their daughter lived with Lillian and Irene, Hank stayed for almost a year at the McNeils'.

The McNeils lived in a logging camp in what was known as a "camp car," or one or more railroad cars hitched together to form a house. As primitive as this arrangement sounds, the camp cars made reasonably pleasant living establishments, and the camps themselves were happy, sociable places. (In fact, Hank may well have been exposed to much back-country music in Fountain, since weekly dances were a standard form of entertainment at the camps.) The men had steady, paying jobs, and while the families were far from rich, they were secure with the knowledge of a regular paycheck and food on the table. Beyond these considerations, the McNeils offered Hank a more conventional family life. Hank's uncle provided the male influence lacking in Hank's own family, and his cousin J.C., a boy about Hank's age, offered brotherly companionship.

Apparently, Hank was also drinking some by the time he was eleven. At the logging camp in Fountain, Hank would have been exposed to some hard-drinking men, and somehow it seems credible that a skinny, fatherless boy would gravitate toward an easy way to express his manhood. Actually, drinking was not unusual for boys in the rural South in those days, since beer, wine, and moonshine were easily available and country kids, especially preadolescent boys, just naturally took a few nips. In any case, rumors of Hank's drinking sprees began early and stuck to him all his life.

In 1935, Lillian moved the children up the railroad tracks to Greenville, a city four times the size of Georgiana. She set up another boardinghouse, found odd jobs for herself like nursing and sewing, and put Hank and Irene back to work selling peanuts and shining shoes.

In Greenville, Hank's devotion to music really took hold. His relationship with Tee-tot flourished, and through Tee-tot Hank developed a style of guitar playing and singing that he used for the rest of his life. From Tee-Tot, he may have learned several old-time country songs like "My Bucket's Got a Hole in It," tunes that had been staples in rural America for decades, and surely he picked up a number of black spirituals and gospel songs. Tee-tot was known for his "bluesy" or "jazzy" style, and elements of blues and jazz would show up in Hank's later music, both in the religious songs and the more popular tunes.

Tee-tot was the first professional to show Hank how to present a song to an audience—to put a song across. Tee-tot earned his living singing on the street, and in order to seduce a passerby (who, in 1935, probably wasn't too flush himself) to part with a nickel or a dime, he had to be pretty good. Even at eleven or twelve, Hank seemed to possess a natural confidence and poise as an entertainer. In *Sing a Sad Song*, Roger Williams relates a story told by Taft Skipper about Lillie's "wanting us to listen to Hank sing and play," one evening while the Williamses lived in Greenville. As Taft put it, "We did, and he was pretty good." Through Tee-tot, Hank learned how to create a certain intimacy with the audience with a straightforward look-in-the-eye, a smile, and a joke. He even figured out—or else knew instinctively— how to add subtle sexual undertones to his performance. Later, Hank would develop these qualities into an art form, making him, on his best days, a superb stage entertainer.

The Williamses moved to Montgomery, Alabama, in July 1937. Montgomery was then a city of 75,000 residents, the third-largest city in the state after Mobile and Birmingham. They settled first at 114 South Perry Street, where Lillian again established a boardinghouse. Although the family would move to various homes around the city several times over the next fifteen years, they would forever after call Montgomery home. It would appear that in the past, all of Lillie's moves had been to find places to earn a more substantial living, and her move to Montgomery was no exception. Now, however, it seemed that she was beginning to get the notion that perhaps Hank's singing might pay off.

About the time he moved to Montgomery, Hank traded in his old mail-order guitar for a brand-new sunburst Gibson. He heard about an amateur night competition at the local Empire Theater, and wearing cowboy boots and a cowboy hat, toting his Gibson, he stood up and sang a ditty he had written himself, a song called "The WPA Blues." He took first prize, fifteen dollars cash, more money than he'd ever had—let alone earned—in his life.

Hank followed up his Empire Theater success by auditioning for a singing spot on the local radio station, WSFA, and almost instantly, he landed a twice-a-week, fifteen-minute program of his own. Dubbed "The Singing Kid" (he was only fourteen), he strummed his guitar, sang country songs, and took home fifteen dollars per week—which sure beat selling peanuts.

Hank's radio show created a demand for "show dates," or appearances at school dances, church socials, hoedowns, barbecues, and roadhouses or honky-tonks. Although Hank worked alone on his radio show, for show dates he needed a backup band. Hank had no trouble putting together a group—lots of guys around Montgomery were interested in singing—and with a good friend named Smith "Hezzy" Adair, Hank formed a group he called Hank and Hezzy and the Drifting Cowboys. Decked out in what was fast becoming Hank's signature attire—a cowboy hat and the best boots they could afford—Hank and Hezzy and the Drifting Cowboys began appearing in small towns throughout south Alabama. The year was 1938.

Lillian, of course, quickly turned herself into Montgomery's answer to a Hollywood stage mother. She'd book Hank and the boys into a party or dance, drive them over, and even take tickets. She insisted that everyone pay admission, even the ubiquitous Skipper and Williams relations. Lillian undoubtedly wanted to capitalize financially on Hank's abilities, but she was also a proud woman, and delighted in proving that a Williams could make something of himself.

Hank quickly became more and more accomplished as a performer, a real professional. He learned to play the rudiments of other instruments like the fiddle, and with his natural, down-to-earth poise, he became a skilled master of ceremonies, able to maintain a friendly chatter between songs and hold the audience's attention. The Drifting Cowboys sang all matter of music— folk songs, bluegrass, and popular country songs that came out of Nashville. One of Hank's favorite performers was Roy Acuff, a star at the Grand Ole Opry whose songs, like "Wabash

Cannonball" and "Big Speckled Bird," were big hits in the late 1930s. Hank apparently had seen Acuff perform in Montgomery and surely had listened to him on the radio, and adopted some aspects of Acuff's style, like the "sob" in his voice during the sad songs, and the tremendous energy for the upbeat numbers.

One popular show place was Thigpen's Log Cabin, a honky-tonk located near Georgiana and owned by the same Frank Thigpen who took credit for buying Hank his first guitar. Hank and the Drifting Cowboys performed there many times in the late thirties and early forties, and Thigpen's was one of the places where Hank learned the hard realities of performing at the tougher dance halls.

Of course, the main problem with the honky-tonks was booze. Much of Alabama was legally "dry," so whiskey was not served in public. Nevertheless, at the honky-tonks, liquor was smuggled in, folks got drunk—and fights started—sometimes even before an evening's entertainment really got going. Hank was often the target of fights, both because he was commanding attention as the leader of the band and because he was already something of a celebrity in south Alabama as a result of his radio show.

One story that still flies in Fort Deposit and is colorfully told in *Sing a Sad Song* concerned a drunken farmer who came up to Hank at the local roadhouse and picked a classic fight. Roger H. Williams tells it like this:

"I told my wife to quit yammering about what a great singer Hank Williams is," the farmer said to Hank. "I'm going to knock her brains out the next time I hear her listening to your bellowing on the radio."

"I don't blame you, friend," Hank supposedly answered, hoping to placate the man.

"On second thought," the farmer said, "stand up and I'll knock your brains out."

Without another word, Hank bashed the guy over the head with his Gibson.

This story sounds funny, but often the fights got serious, and the appearance of guns and knives was not uncommon. One Drifting Cowboy was stabbed so severely that they feared for his life. During another fight, a man bit a piece of Hank's eyebrow right off his face. When Don Helms joined the Drifting Cowboys in 1941, the first thing Hank did was buy him a blackjack.

Hank had just turned fourteen when he began playing on the radio and touring with the Drifting Cowboys, and he kept up a full professional performing schedule for the next five years. He was singing live on the radio two or three mornings a week— and morning shows came on very early, often 5:30 or 6:00 A.M. to accommodate the farmers. Hank and the boys also worked show dates, if they were lucky, two or three times per week, which meant that the boys—and they were still boys—might well be up all night. This schedule did not leave much time or energy for schoolwork.

Hank graduated from Abraham Baldwin Junior High School in Montgomery and went on to Sidney Lanier High School, but quit in the fall of 1942, when he turned nineteen. Because he had missed so much school—and since he didn't much care about things like Algebra or World Civilization—he was only about to begin the tenth grade.

But for a Southern boy of his time, age nineteen was considered manhood. What's more, World War II had started the preceding winter, and surely, most of the local boys were going off to war. Hank apparently tried to join the army, but couldn't get in because of a bad back. His radio show and the show dates must have seemed old-hat after five years, and according to his mother, Hank felt his career was going nowhere. Or, more likely, his mother thought his career was going nowhere and insisted that he get a "real" job.

In any case, Hank took a job as a welder at the Alabama Drydock and Shipbuilding Company in Mobile, Alabama. Some think he took the job to escape his mother's control, although Lillie wrote in her little biography of her son, *Our Hank Williams*, published shortly after his death, that he hadn't been gone three weeks before she'd booked him into two months' worth of lucrative show dates—and saved his career. The truth is, he put his music career more or less on hold, and worked in Mobile for two years, until the fall of 1944.

What brought him back to Montgomery is anybody's guess,

but it may well have had something to do with a woman he had met. Although the date and circumstances of their meeting varies depending on who is telling the story, Hank met Audrey Mae Sheppard sometime in the early forties while he was appearing at a medicine show in Banks, Alabama.

Audrey, who grew up on a farm just outside of Banks, was a tall, good-looking blonde, and was married—but separated—at the time she met Hank to a local fellow named Erskine Guy with whom she had a baby daughter, Lycrecia. Hank always liked a pretty girl (in *Sing a Sad Song,* his cousin J.C. is quoted as saying "Hank was a go-getter. He'd go after anybody's gal."), and apparently his infatuation with Audrey was instant and particularly intense. At twenty-one, he was probably trying to put an adult life together for himself—which would include a wife and children—and Audrey, who shared his interest in music, may well have encouraged his return to a singing career. In any case, they were married on December 15, 1944, ten days after her divorce from Erskine Guy. The wedding took place at a gas station in Andalusia, Alabama, and was witnessed by Hank's life-long friend, Don Helms.

Hank and Audrey moved into Lillie's boardinghouse in Montgomery. In no time, Hank put together another band, still called the Drifting Cowboys. Audrey quickly took over many of the duties that formerly had been Lillian's domain, although Lillie never disappeared completely from the scene. Audrey arranged show dates, took tickets, handled the finances, and occasionally sang with the group or filled in on guitar. Hank and the boys began performing frequently, and Hank took to writing more seriously than he ever had in the past. They were rolling.

In September 1946, Hank and Audrey traveled to Nashville, to try to make contact with Fred Rose, the well-known songwriter and co-owner of the Acuff-Rose music publishing company. Fred and his son, Wesley, were playing Ping-Pong during their lunch hour at Nashville's WSM radio studio when Hank and Audrey walked in and asked if they might sing some songs. The Roses agreed to listen, but only because they had nothing better to do. Hank sang several of his own songs, including "When God Comes and Gathers His Jewels," "Six More Miles to the Graveyard," and "My Love for You Has Turned to Hate."

Fred Rose was mildly impressed and, in what is probably an apocryphal story, decided to test Hank's songwriting ability by requesting that he compose a tune on the spot. Rose conjured up a classic situation, a story about a girl who marries the rich boy in town instead of the poor boy, who truly loves her. Hank supposedly labored for a half hour and came up with "A Mansion on the Hill," which became one of his early hits.

It is doubtful that Fred Rose ever gave Hank this sort of stress test; however, Rose could smell talent a mile away. He agreed to take the six songs that Hank had sung, and quickly signed Hank to a standard songwriting contract, which allowed three cents for each copy of sheet music sold and 50 percent of all record royalties.

Fred Rose was about forty-eight years old at the time he met Hank. Born in Evansville, Indiana, he had taught himself to play the piano, was playing professionally by the time he was ten, and started writing songs when he was in his mid-teens. For several years he hosted his own radio show, "Fred Rose's Song Shop," in Chicago. Listeners would phone up and give him an idea, and Fred would compose songs spontaneously. Some of his songs became not only instant hits but standards, including "Red Hot Mama," "Honest and Truly," and "Tears on My Pillow."

During the Depression, Rose began singing and touring with a group, and somehow ended up in Nashville. Some of his contemporaries say he was burned out as a songwriter by the time he relocated to Nashville, but he obviously had additional talents on his side. In 1942, he formed Nashville's first music publishing company with Roy Acuff, and by 1946, when Hank signed with Acuff-Rose, the stable already included Pee Wee King and Redd Stewart, who wrote "Tennessee Waltz," and others who were already or would become lucrative professionals.

Although Rose first considered Hank a songwriter, he did not completely dismiss him as a performer. Three months later, when Sterling Records was looking for a country singer, Fred and Wesley Rose remembered Hank, and brought him up to

Nashville's WSM studios, where he made his first recordings: "Calling You," "Never Again," "Wealth Won't Save Your Soul," and "When God Comes and Gathers His Jewels"—all Hank's own songs. These records sold so well that within weeks, Hank was asked to record again. This time they chose "My Love for You Has Turned to Hate," "I Don't Care If Tomorrow Never Comes," "Honky Tonkin'," and "Pan American." According to George William Koon, in *Hank Williams: A Bio-Bibliography*, Hank was paid a flat fee of $82.50 for each of the recording sessions.

Not long after Hank completed his sessions for Sterling Records, Rose heard that MGM was forming a new record label, and he negotiated a contract for Hank. MGM and Fred agreed that all the recordings would be made in Nashville without supervision from MGM. Then Rose would send records to New York with instructions as to which songs to release and when, and MGM would then supervise all the promotion.

Within six months of interrupting Fred Rose's lunchtime Ping-Pong game, Hank Williams had his first national hit record, "Move It On Over," a wonderfully witty song about a guy who has a fight with his wife, so he moves in with the dog.

Fred Rose quickly assumed the role of manager/father for Hank. He immediately recognized that in order for Hank to make it big, he needed to be established as a top-drawer performer. Although Hank had been entertaining publicly for years, he was known only in and around south Alabama. What's more, despite Hank's "street smarts," his presentation was still amateurish and he needed a vehicle, a more professional place to practice and grow. In the spring of 1948, Fred learned that radio station KWKH in Shreveport, Louisiana, was establishing a replica of Nashville's Grand Ole Opry, a show called the Louisiana Hayride. Like the Opry, the Hayride was a live country music program where performers sang before an audience while the show was simultaneously broadcast by radio to cities and towns throughout the South. While the Hayride was never as important as the Opry, it was very popular in the late forties and fifties, and would eventually become known as a sort of farm team for Opry stars.

Hank's deal with the Hayride was similar to the arrangement the Grand Ole Opry offered the bigger stars. He was required to appear on the weekend shows, he got a radio program of his own on station KWKH in Shreveport, and he was booked for personal appearances in cities throughout the South. Only now, instead of playing honky-tonks in Fort Deposit or Georgiana, Hank was appearing at civic auditoriums in Birmingham, Baton Rouge, Texarkana, and even New Orleans.

Hank and Audrey moved to Shreveport in May 1948. Hank put together yet another Drifting Cowboys band and began a more rigorous touring schedule than he had ever known before. His hours were long—virtually endless, since he worked seven days a week—and, as Fred Rose had recognized, the bigger towns demanded a more polished presentation. Hank realized that this was his moment to push—and to shine—and he did. Although he was always relaxed and easy on stage, during practice hours he could be abrupt and a perfectionist about his own music and the performance of the band. He was, and he always would be, generous with time, money, and allowing others to display their talents—but he wanted it done right. And he got it.

Part of the mystique of country music stars is their appearance of an impeccable personal life. In fact, success at the Louisiana Hayride—not to mention the Grand Ole Opry—depended on it. Over the years in Alabama, Hank had established quite a reputation for unreliability, which had everything to do with his drinking. Apparently Hank was the sort of drinker who could manage to stay sober for weeks if he chose to do so, but after only a couple of drinks would become out of control. Every so often he would just take off, drink himself into oblivion, and not return for days.

Even in his early teens back in Montgomery, Hank would sometimes get resistance from clubs, who would book him only reluctantly for fear that he would hare off on a binge and not show up. In fact, when Fred Rose and others from Nashville came down to Alabama to check Hank out, they heard, in no uncertain terms, that this was a nice boy with lots of talent— but not a kid to be counted on.

Nevertheless, from 1946—when Hank first ventured to Nashville—to 1950 or so, although he had occasional lapses,

Hank was able to keep his drinking under control. From the moment the Louisiana Hayride signed him on, Hank knew he was destined for greatness. Always a professional, he now worked with particular diligence. And even after he made it to the Opry, he kept his drinking in check. For a while.

While Hank and Audrey were living in Shreveport, Randall Hank Williams was born on May 26, 1949. This new baby served as the ultimate symbol of good and simple family life, that quality so prized by country music fans and encouraged by the country music establishment. It looked like Hank and Audrey were doing everything right.

In his book *Hank Williams: From Life to Legend,* Jerry Rivers asserts that Hank learned the song "Lovesick Blues" from his old friend and musical mentor Tee-tot. If so, this fact makes for a nice roundness to Hank's life, since "Lovesick Blues" was the song that catapulted him to international fame. "Lovesick Blues" was written in the early 1920s, and had been recorded by several artists, but had never been a big hit. Although it was more complex and bluesy than most of the other songs Hank had recorded up until that time, it was an ideal song for him. It requires a soulful "sob" in the voice and expert yodeling, and yet must stay swingy and upbeat. Nobody combined those qualities better than Hank Williams.

Hank recorded "Lovesick Blues" in late 1948, and by the following March it had rocketed to the top of the country charts. With its success, some of his other recordings, "Wedding Bells" and "Mind Your Business" among them, were pulled onto the charts as well. By the end of 1949, "Lovesick Blues" was voted Best Hillbilly Record of the Year by *Cash Box,* the journal that measured jukebox success, and Hank ran second to Eddy Arnold as Top Selling Folk Artist in *Billboard.* With the success of "Lovesick Blues," both Hank and Fred Rose believed Hank was ready for a position at the top of the country music establishment, the Grand Ole Opry.

The Grand Ole Opry is the longest-running show in the history of radio, and for those who know country music, it embodies the pinnacle of success. The Grand Ole Opry made its first radio broadcast in 1925, less than two months after WSM, the station that has always carried it, went on the air, and it has been broadcast every Saturday night since. Like its offspring, the Louisiana Hayride, the Opry is performed before a live audience as it is being broadcast over the airwaves. Its stars read like a who's who of twentieth-century country music: Roy Acuff, Ernest Tubb, Webb Pierce, Faron Young, Ray Price, Minnie Pearl, Hank Snow, Chet Atkins, Johnny Cash, Loretta Lynn, Patsy Cline, Dolly Parton—the list is virtually endless.

The Opry is difficult to crack for any artist, and Hank was no exception, especially since, despite his hard work in Shreveport, his reputation for unreliability preceded him. Yet Fred Rose knew that Hank could give a fantastic performance, and managed to book him for a guest appearance on June 11, 1949.

Hank's performance that Saturday night made Opry history. "Lovesick Blues" was high on the charts, and, although the name Hank Williams rang only dim bells, when he broke into that song the audience went wild. They jumped up, clapped their hands, stamped their feet, and asked for encore after encore— six in all—a reception never witnessed at the Opry before or since.

The Opry signed him on instantly. Although he was overshadowed at first by Roy Acuff, Red Foley, and Eddy Arnold— all enormous country stars on a national and international scale— by the end of 1949 Hank Williams was bigger than any of them.

When Hank arrived at the Opry, he again needed to put together his own band, and he knew precisely who he wanted to back him. He easily convinced Bob McNett, his lead guitar player from the Hayride, to move to Nashville. He pressed his old friend Don Helms, a gifted steel guitar player who had played with the Drifting Cowboys back in Alabama, to join up. He picked up a Nashville-area man, Hillous Butrum, on bass. And, after a memorable audition, he took on a nineteen-year-old kid named Jerry Rivers on fiddle. (In 1950, Bob McNett left the band to open a country music park in Pennsylvania and was replaced by Sammy Pruett, another former Drifting Cowboy from Hank's Alabama days. About the same time, Hillous Butrum was replaced by Howard Watts, a bass fiddle player known professionally as Cedric Rainwater.)

For the next three years, Hank Williams and the Drifting Cowboys led an even more rigorous professional life than Hank had known in Shreveport—if that was possible. Hank and the band had a five-day-a-week, 7:15 A.M., radio show on WSM; they appeared at the Opry every Friday and Saturday night; and finally, they were out on the road at cities throughout the country during the rest of the week.

After years of struggle, Hank's superstardom arrived overnight. In three short years (although they probably didn't seem so short to Hank), he had secured the Acuff-Rose publishing contract, the MGM recording contract, the WSM radio show, and star billing at the Grand Ole Opry. He had had a handful of hit records and one blockbuster, "Lovesick Blues," and after 1949, every song he recorded went to the top of the charts.

Hank's recording schedule was particularly intense. Between December 1946 and December 1948, when he recorded "Lovesick Blues," Hank had worked nine sessions, recording fourteen songs, most of which he had written himself. Between March 1949, his first recording session after the success of "Lovesick Blues," and his last recording session, in September 1952, he worked more than twenty-five recording sessions, or about one every six weeks. During this period, he recorded over eighty songs (or different arrangements of previously recorded songs) and, of these, more than sixty were composed by Hank himself.

Hank had written songs since he was a boy, but during his halcyon years he was astonishingly prolific, in part due to the encouragement and expertise of Fred Rose. When he wasn't performing or recording, he was writing. In all, Hank Williams wrote over 140 songs that were ultimately recorded and released (many after he died) and probably innumerable songs that for one reason or other were lost or unused. Apparently he could write anywhere—riding along in the back of a car, in bed, during a jam session, anywhere. The legend that he wrote "Mansion on the Hill" in thirty minutes after Fred Rose gave him a "story line" is probably a myth. But myths grow from kernels of truth, and

Hank was such a genius that undoubtedly he did write very quickly and could be inspired by the tiniest image.

Fred Rose, who knew a thing or two about turning out a song himself, always believed Hank's greatest gift was songwriting. Rose also thought that many of Hank's songs could cross over into the so-called pop market, and assigned his son, Wesley, to promote Hank's music in that area. Wesley started with "Cold, Cold Heart." He beat on any number of doors, and finally convinced Mitch Miller, an A & R man with Columbia Records, to help. Miller placed "Cold, Cold Heart" with a young singer named Tony Bennett, and Bennett's version of it sold over a million copies, became number one on the pop charts, and launched Bennett's career. Other stars, like Frankie Laine, Jo Stafford, and Rosemary Clooney, would also enjoy great success in the pop market with Hank's songs.

Many of the songs Hank wrote during the last four years of his life turned out to be not only big hits at the time of their release, but classics in the country music genre, including "Honky Tonk Blues," "I'm So Lonesome I Could Cry," "Cold, Cold Heart," "I Can't Help It If I'm Still in Love With You," "Hey, Good Lookin'," "Ramblin' Man," "Your Cheatin' Heart," "Jambalaya," "Kaw-liga," and "I'll Never Get Out of This World Alive," which ironically was high on the charts the day Hank died.

Most people associate Hank with sad songs like "Cold, Cold Heart" and "I'm So Lonesome I Could Cry," but, no question about it, he had a marvelous sense of irony, humor, and fun. "Honky Tonkin' " and "Hey, Good Lookin' " are both tunes about going out and having a good time. "Kaw-liga" is a tale of a broken-hearted lover, always an important Hank Williams theme, but Kaw-liga is a wooden Indian who yearns for the Indian maid "over in the antique store" and loses her because his heart is "made of knotty pine."

Hank also did a fair amount of recording under the pseudonym Luke the Drifter. Hank obviously had a penchant for romantic songs, but as Luke the Drifter he could indulge a taste for extremely sentimental numbers, including maudlin recitations about tragic or fallen lives, such as "Pictures From Life's Other Side," "Men With Broken Hearts," and "I Dreamed About

Mama Last Night," or old-fashioned, gimmicky songs like "I've Been Down That Road Before." According to George William Koon, in *Hank Williams: A Bio-Bibliography*, the decision to release certain songs under the name Luke the Drifter had to do with marketing. Jukebox concessionaires "would take everything by Hank, but skip anything by Luke because the latter was more suitable for radio and retail sales than for the juke joints."

Hank's performing schedule was as intense as his recording work. Now, however, instead of driving an old heap from Andalusia, Alabama, to Troy, he was cruising in a big Cadillac from Dallas, Texas, to Louisville, Kentucky, or from New Orleans to Cincinnati. What's more, he knew it was imperative that he return to Nashville for the Friday and Saturday night Opry shows, so he and the boys would beat it back there every weekend.

Most show dates were booked in the South or Southwest, but ultimately he appeared throughout the United States and made two remarkably successful trips to Canada. In late 1949, he even went to Germany to appear at American army bases with Roy Acuff, Minnie Pearl, Little Jimmy Dickens, and others from the Opry. This was a boy who only two years before had never been out of the state of Alabama, or if he had, it was to De-Funiak Springs, Florida, or a quick trip to Louisiana.

One of the most famous events of Hank's career was the Hadacol Caravan tour, a blowout Hollywood version of an old-fashioned medicine show, the sort that Hank had worked a hundred times in south Alabama. During the summer of 1951, Dudley J. LeBlanc, the inventor of Hadacol, a popular patent medicine of the time, hired a luxurious seventeen-car train and put America's biggest entertainment stars on tour throughout the South and Midwest. Some of the stars, like Bob Hope, Milton Berle, Jack Benny, and Jimmy Durante, would join the troupe in major centers such as Atlanta or Houston, but most of the entertainers, including Hank, lived on the train and did one-night stands in scores of towns. Hank and the Drifting Cowboys performed second-to-last on the docket, just before megastar Bob Hope. Nevertheless, this was "Hank Williams country," and night after night the audience cheered so loud and long for Hank that finally the mildly perturbed Bob Hope decided he had to publicly recognize this phenomenon. One night he doffed a cowboy hat, loped out on the stage, and said: "Good evenin', folks, this is Hank Hope."

The lifestyle of a professional entertainer is notoriously tough on a marriage and family life, but Hank and Audrey, despite their youth, put a good face on it. As they had done in Alabama early in their marriage, they occasionally performed together both on stage and on records. They seemed to enjoy all the accoutrements of Hank's success. They bought a big house on Franklin Road in Nashville; a farm outside the city, where Hank kept a couple of horses; several big cars, which were Hank's passion; and even invested in a clothing store that featured Western gear. The Opry encouraged the notion of "the good loving marriage and family," and Hank and Audrey—especially after the birth of Randall, who Hank referred to as Little Bocephus after a puppet used by a comedian on the Opry— fit the image. Audrey's daughter by her first marriage, Lycrecia, though never adopted by Hank, helped round out the picture of the perfect Opry family.

Nevertheless, Hank's success and the pressures of his work were taking their toll. In December 1951, Hank had an operation on his bad back. He was bedridden at home in Nashville for many weeks, but the back injury and the resulting pain—which must have been excruciating—were exacerbated by the escalation of his drinking.

By spring and summer of 1952, Hank's drinking problem began to show up even while he was performing. He began missing dates and, like the old days, disappearing for days on end. As the months passed, he would even appear on stage looped. At first, his fans accepted the obvious drunkenness—they loved Hank and they'd take him any way they could get him. But quickly, audiences began to feel resentful and cheated, and on at least one occasion people walked out of a theater demanding their money back.

In late 1952, Hank was booked for a New Year's Day show in Canton, Ohio. Apparently Hank spent the Christmas holidays in Montgomery with his family, and on the thirtieth the weather turned cold and snowy, making air travel impossible. Hank hired a local boy named Charles Carr to drive him in his now-famous blue Cadillac from Montgomery to Canton, where he would link up with his band.

Canton, Ohio, is some 750 miles north of Montgomery, a fifteen- or twenty-hour drive even in good weather. On December 30, 1952, the weather was not only bad in Montgomery, but got progressively worse as they traveled each mile north. Carr drove as Hank lay stretched out in the backseat, sleeping on and off and, according to Carr, occasionally taking a few nips of beer or whiskey. They stopped in Knoxville, Tennessee, and a doctor was called to give Hank an injection to relieve his unrelenting back pain. Carr drove on for a couple more hours, but began to get concerned when Hank made no movement whatsoever. Finally, in Oak Hill, West Virginia, Carr stopped at a gas station and reached back to touch Hank's hand. It was cold. He then drove quickly to the Oak Hill hospital, where Hank was pronounced dead on arrival just before dawn on January 1, 1953.

Hank's funeral was held on Sunday, January 4, in Montgomery. More than 25,000 people from all over the United States converged on the city for the service that was held in the municipal auditorium on Perry Street. At 2:30 P.M. the service began with Ernest Tubb singing "Beyond the Sunset." Later, Roy Acuff, Red Foley, Carl Smith, and Webb Pierce sang "I Saw the Light," backed by a chorus. The pastor of the Highland Avenue Baptist Church gave the eulogy, stating humbly, "I can't preach Hank's funeral—he preached it himself in song."

The casket was then taken to the Oakwood Cemetery, where thousands watched as Hank Williams, aged twenty-nine years and four months, was placed into the earth.

This was more or less the story of Hank Williams' life as it was handed down, passed around, written, and told, and basically the version of his life presented in the film *Your Cheatin' Heart*. Years after I first learned that Hank Williams might be my father—when I finally felt free enough to read the serious Hank

Williams biographies—I would discover that his story was far more complicated and tragic than the legend implied. Although I wouldn't understand the full meaning of those complexities for many years more, I ultimately realized that they had a direct impact on me. In fact, I was one of the complexities, or perhaps, more to the point, I was part of the tragedy.

For starters, Hank and Audrey's marriage was not the vision of joy the keepers of the legend wanted everyone to believe. In reality, the marriage was a mess, and always had been. In fact, Hank and Audrey had divorced in May 1952. Within a few months, Hank had "fallen in love" with a beautiful nineteen-year-old girl named Billie Jean Jones Eshliman, and they were married—not once, but twice—in a big public carnival in New Orleans on October 19, 1952. A little more than two months later, Hank was dead.

From the moment the first clod of earth was dropped onto Hank's silver casket, the lines of battle were drawn. At first, Lillian Stone, Irene Williams Smith, Hank's sister, and Audrey Williams combined forces to fight off Billie Jean's claims of widowhood. After Lillian died in February 1955, Irene Williams Smith took over as administratrix of the Hank Williams estate, whereupon she and Audrey began their own not-so-cold War. In the mid-1960s, Audrey sued Irene for selling the copyright renewals to Hank's songs to Acuff-Rose, the original publisher, sixteen years before they came due and for far too little money.

It was at this 1967 trial that all the Williams family secrets were hung out on the line for the world to see, and the most interesting piece of "laundry" was the sudden appearance of a certain little girl child. Apparently, two days after Hank's funeral, on January 6, 1953, a mysterious woman, who had been staying with Mrs. Stone during her pregnancy, checked into St. Margaret's Hospital in Montgomery and gave birth to a child, a girl. For some reason, the baby was given over to Mrs. Stone, and according to the Montgomery papers, Lillian had taken care of the little girl until the local welfare agency had found the baby a good home.

At the 1967 trial, the existence of this baby, now fourteen

years old, finally came to light. Irene Smith, Roy Acuff, Wesley Rose (Fred Rose had died in 1955), Audrey Williams, and Randall Hank Williams were at each others' throats, but they paused just long enough to make sure this teenager didn't join in their fight.

3
REAL LIFE

I believe that everyone is shaped by a combination, probably fairly equally divided, of genes and upbringing. Inherited gifts and tendencies are blended with the knowledge, attitudes, and experience gleaned through the people who raise you. This is no less true for me, except that, unlike most children, the people who donated the genes were different from the people who provided the experience. If my blood came from Hank Williams and a lady from Tennessee, my upbringing—and my view of the world— was shaped, to a large extent, by Wayne and Louise Deupree.

Like all adopted children, I have had to integrate my inherited self with my "living" self. This hasn't been easy for me; I'm sure it is not a simple task for any adopted child. But unlike most adoptees who are placed with their adoptive parents at birth, I didn't arrive on the Deupree doorstep until I was three years old. Most psychologists agree that a child's psyche is pretty well formed by the age of three—and apparently mine was, too. I can only think that my genes must have been pretty good, and

that during those first three years of my life I was loved by some
people a whole lot. For, although I hate to say it—I feel intense
guilt and ambivalence saying it—and I say it, believe it or not,
with a heart full of love: Life with Louise and Wayne Deupree
was not easy.

I'm sure the Alabama State Department of Pensions and Security thought it had found me a good home. By all outward appearances, the Deuprees looked to be a stable, affluent, attractive
couple. Wayne ran a successful business and made a good living.
They owned a nice new house on Forest Hill Road, a quiet street
in a middle-class suburb of Mobile, and although the house wasn't
large, it was comfortable and well furnished. They deeply wanted
a child, especially a girl. If there was any problem at all, it was
that Wayne and Louise were considered a little old to be new
parents. But then, I was considered to be a little too old to be a
new child. In fact, Mother didn't hesitate to tell me that they
had to accept a three-year-old instead of an infant because Daddy
was in his mid-forties by the time they applied to adopt. I was
shocked many years later when I learned that most adopted children are told that they are "special" because they are "chosen"
children. I was led to believe, from the beginning, that I was
your basic "fire sale" item.

Wayne Deupree was born on February 23, 1910, in New
Orleans, Louisiana, although he spent most of his growing-up
years in Meridian, Mississippi. Daddy was the third of seven
children, six boys and a girl who died at age two, so basically he
grew up in the midst of a passel of rowdy boys. His father, Leroy
Madison Deupree, was a train conductor on the New Orleans
and Northeastern Railroad line that ran between Meridian and
New Orleans, coincidentally the same line where Jimmie Rodg-
ers, "the father of modern country music," had worked for many
years. His mother died of cancer shortly after the birth of her
last child when Daddy was seven, and he was raised by his father's sister, who he always said was just like a mother to him
and the other boys.

Daddy and his brothers remained fairly close and loving

throughout their lives. A couple of Daddy's brothers lived in Mobile (including one who also had an adopted daughter), and they— and the others—would visit us fairly often.

Daddy told me many times that he never went beyond the third grade in school; however, despite his lack of formal education, he was one of the best-read people I've ever known. He read books and newspapers constantly and grilled me on events and personalities, and thought it was important that people be knowledgeable about the world around them.

I'm not quite sure how Daddy ended up living in Mobile, but he got married in the mid-1930s to a woman who lived there. When World War II started, he enlisted in the army and spent several years in the South Pacific, supervising the buying and selling of supplies and equipment.

He used the knowledge he gained in the army to start a surplus business, the Gulf Machinery Company, when he returned from the war. Originally, he dealt in army surplus— things like trucks, machinery, and heavy construction equipment—which he would buy up in large lots, refurbish, then resell to, say, a Central American transport firm, or a small boat company. As the years passed and the aviation business became more and more important, he dealt in supplies necessary for airlines.

As far as personality goes, Daddy was a real interesting mixture. On one hand, he was absolutely a man's man kind of guy— dark and muscular—and very tough in business. He also had a great sense of humor, and liked to go drinking and partying. In other words, he worked hard and he played hard.

On the other hand, he had a warm, sentimental side, and was extraordinarily generous to everyone—family, employees, friends. Men who worked for him adored him. Once, the wife of a guy who worked down at the shop died suddenly. Daddy stepped in and made all the arrangements, and then took care of the burial. A few days after Daddy died, another man who had worked for Daddy for years came by to visit with Mother and me and he said: "Mr. Deupree was better to me than my own father." He was crying like a baby.

Mary Louise Sims Deupree was born on August 21, 1922,

in Mobile. Her parents, Comer and Josephine Sims, divorced when she was about six and her sister, Helen, was ten, and eventually her mother remarried a wealthy man from New Orleans named Henry Barrett. In later years, neither Mother nor Aunt Helen spoke much about their childhood, but it was clear that their parents' divorce was painful for both of them.

Mother's family was different from Daddy's. His family, though poor, exhibited evidence of real caring, while her family showed very little love and security. Aunt Helen and Mother were bounced from pillar to post and remained at odds with their family and even with each other for the rest of their lives. After their parents' divorce, Mother and Aunt Helen were placed for a year or two in the Convent of Mercy in Mobile while Josephine took off for New Orleans and Comer tried to put his life back together in Mobile. After Comer remarried, Aunt Helen went to live with her father and his new bride, while Mother went to live with their grandmother in Mount Vernon, Alabama, a small town about twenty miles north of Mobile.

Apparently both girls were unhappy. Aunt Helen escaped from her father's house as fast as she could by getting a job in a laundry. Eventually she married a man named Stanley Fountain, who worked in law enforcement, and they had one son, Stanley Junior.

Mother attempted to make her own escape by a more conventional route—she got married during her senior year in high school. Or at least this was one of the stories she told me. She also told me that she got married on December 7, 1942—exactly one year to the day after Pearl Harbor—which would have made her twenty years old, too old to be in high school. It was typical of my mother to shade the truth or to tell a number of different versions of a story, depending upon her audience or her mood.

Mother was an extraordinarily beautiful woman—I used to think she was more beautiful than Elizabeth Taylor. She had rich dark hair, vivid green eyes, and a voluptuous figure. What's more, she was high-spirited, mercurial, and lots of fun.

For Mother, her looks were synonymous with her personality. Her physical appearance was of primary importance to her. She loved beautiful clothes, and always dressed to the nines, whether she was going to a Mardi Gras ball or out to the stoop to pick up the newspaper. For her, "looks" also extended to how her behavior and family appeared to the outside world. Her house had to look a certain way, her background—at times—had to seem to be something it wasn't, her child—me—had to behave in a particular manner. But, of course, this attitude ultimately and inevitably got her into trouble. If things weren't "looking" quite the way she wanted them to, she would abruptly change them, disassociate herself from them, or ignore them. But Mother had a brain and a conscience. At certain times in her life, she found it impossible to reconcile the reality of things with the way she wanted them to be. And this made her crazy.

Her first marriage "looked" pretty good. Her husband came from one of the most prominent families in Mobile. She was the beauty queen—at least in her own mind—and he was the captain of the football team as well as wealthy and socially connected. But the marriage didn't last. World War II broke out, her young husband shipped out overseas, and Mother, never one to sit at home knitting socks, was eager to have a good time. Mobile was an important port during the war, and sailors were coming and going constantly. For my mother, this was like bees to honey. The moment her husband got back, she served him divorce papers.

After her divorce, Mother moved over to New Orleans, and lived for a couple of years with her mother and her mother's second husband, Henry Barrett, and worked as a typist. While living in New Orleans, she experienced a trauma that would prove to be one of her "irreconcilable realities." It would haunt her the rest of her life, and would also have a resounding effect on me. She had an affair with a married man and got pregnant. In the mid-1940s, abortion was, of course, illegal, and Mother ended up having a back street hack job. Several times Mother told me that she believed that the reason she and Daddy couldn't have a child was because God was punishing her for having the abortion.

As best I can figure it, she moved back to Mobile shortly after the end of her traumatic affair, and through Aunt Helen and Uncle Stanley met Daddy, who was by then also divorced from his first wife. They were married on September 26, 1948.

For the next several years, Daddy and Mother put together a pretty nice life for themselves. Mother was not only a crack-erjack typist, she also had a very good head for business— and she enjoyed being involved in Daddy's growing company. How-ever, as with most other things in her life, she wanted to work on her own terms, and she had married a man who would cater to her whims. Daddy allowed her to come work when she was in the mood, or go shopping or visiting with Aunt Helen when she was not. He also hired a maid, Mary Lee Glover, to clean, cook, do the laundry.

Mary Lee, a trim, handsome, energetic woman who was about Mother's age, worked for Daddy and Mother for a couple of years before I arrived on the scene. She and Mother developed an interesting friendship that would continue even after Mary Lee left us when I was twelve. In a sense, Mary Lee became a sort of "mother figure" for Mother. Mary Lee was the only per-son who could always speak frankly to her— a position not shared by Daddy or Aunt Helen— and certainly not by me.

When Mother would get out of hand and scream or cuss at some person or situation, Mary Lee would say to her: "You ought to be ashamed of yourself." Sometimes Mother would just ignore her, but often she'd say, "You're right, Hon." Mary Lee says that years later, right before Mother's last illness, she stopped in to visit. Mother must have been reminiscing, because she said to Mary Lee: "You know, I've been real mean in my day, haven't I?" Mary Lee just responded in her typical matter-of-fact way. "You wasn't the meanest," she told Mother, "but you was mean enough."

Mother could be mean, it was true, but she could also be loads of fun. She loved to socialize, and she and Daddy belonged to the country club— not so much for the golf, but for the social life. Daddy was also very much involved in one of the secret men's societies that planned the festivities surrounding Mardi Gras.

In Mobile, the focal point of the year is Mardi Gras. In

many ways, Mobile is like a little New Orleans, with a strong French heritage and history; beautiful homes, churches, and other buildings designed in the French manner and decorated with tooled wrought-iron trim; and most of all, a great love for Mardi Gras. Each year, scores of grand balls are planned, not only for "Fat Tuesday" itself, but for the entire weekend preceding it. Beginning on Saturday, all business stops, and the gaiety begins. There are parades every day with floats, costumes, and masked revelers throwing souvenirs to people in the streets. Parties and balls are held all over the city, with the high point being the crowning of the King and Queen of Mardi Gras.

The ladies of Mobile plan their ball gowns months in advance, and each one is more fabulous than the next. (The men are equally well turned out in white ties and tails.) Needless to say, dressing up in a "drop dead" evening dress suited Mother just fine. Every years, she would order a special gown made by the best dressmaker in town. Often she would clip out a photograph of a designer dress from a fancy magazine and insist that her dressmaker duplicate it.

Yet, despite this comfortable life—or perhaps because of it—Mother still wanted to have a child. By the mid-1950s, Daddy and Mother were a nice, middle-class couple and the only thing missing from this perfect picture was a baby—preferably a blond, curly-haired, Shirley Temple look-alike, who would never cry, track in dirt, or utter a word. Since Mother couldn't physically conceive such a child, they decided to adopt. Adopting was not an easy task for a middle-aged couple who liked to party, but in early 1956, their wish was granted.

One day in February 1956, Mother asked Mary Lee to stay late at the house until they returned about five-thirty or six o'clock in the evening from a quick trip to Montgomery. Louise told Mary Lee that she was bringing home a surprise.

"I didn't know what it was," Mary Lee says. "All she'd told me was that she had a surprise. I heard the car drive in and I opened the door, and there you were comin' up the steps wearing these little brown pedal pushers. You had your little guitar on your back. Then, Mrs. Deupree says, 'Look what I got,' and I picked you up and sat you down on the kitchen table."

I'm sure a guitar-totin' toddler in brown pedal pushers sitting on the kitchen table was not Mother's vision of Baby Beautiful. For my part, I know I felt that I'd been uprooted one more time, and I wasn't about to let myself get too close to these people. I was going to take care of myself. For Mother's part, I guess she thought she had been presented with a self-sufficient little girl whom she couldn't completely control. Her response to me was a sort of cold, hurtful rejection. Mary Lee confirms this.

"As soon as you was there for a while, Mrs. Deupree didn't want people to hold you," she remembers. "Mr. Deupree never could hold you, either. When Mr. Deupree would pick you up in his arms, Mrs. Deupree would curse so. I never saw Mrs. Deupree hold you. If she did pick you up, you would have had a heart attack."

For very different reasons, neither Mother nor Daddy could deal with a child. Oddly enough, I believe their marriage was a good one. Sure, they would regularly become annoyed and angry with one another, but I think each genuinely appreciated and loved the other. I also think they loved me in their own ways, but the day-to-day care of a child was another story.

Child rearing was an impossible and alien task for Mother. I think she really wanted and expected, quite literally, a little doll or a pet. She wanted a pretty toy to dress up in lacy clothes and show off to her friends. That was the beginning and end of her interest in children. And to make matters worse, I did not remotely resemble that child. I was a tomboy from the word go. I hated dresses and dolls; I was athletic, active, and loved to play outdoors.

Surely, she had no interest in the basic drudgery of child care—the feeding, the cleaning-up-after, the noise, the clutter. But beyond that, she wasn't particularly curious about the development of a child's mind or personality. She never read to me, talked to me the way other mothers talk to their children, or took pleasure in childish games or pranks. "Children are to be seen and not heard" was the motto I heard from day one, and Mother took that expression to mean that I was, literally, to be as quiet as a mouse when I was inside our house.

Mary Lee remembers an incident one day shortly after I arrived. I was in my bedroom with my door closed playing my little guitar and singing. Mother walked by and said: "Listen to that little son-of-a-so-and-so tryin' to yodel." Knowing Mother, I'm sure she thought my singing was cute and funny, but she didn't have the inner resources to encourage me or even acknowledge appreciation.

Mother's background—her broken home, her own apparent lack of proper mothering, her deep-seated feelings of worthlessness because she could not bear a natural child—created the soil from which her sometimes cold and neglectful attitude grew. Beyond this, she was ill. She was an alcoholic and later addicted to prescriptive drugs, but like many addicts, she drank or took drugs to keep her far deeper emotional troubles in check.

For his part, I always felt that Daddy loved me, and when we were alone together, which was rare, I think he took pleasure in my company. But Daddy was also devoted to Mother. I think he loved her deeply, but because of that love—and her resulting jealousy—he was constricted in how much attention and affection he could lavish on me. As years passed, I came to believe that he catered to her only to keep her quiet—and she could curse like a sailor—and I think if circumstances had been different, he would have been a much more affectionate father. As it was, and true to Wayne Deupree, he provided me with every "thing" I ever wished for.

For my part, I was just a child. At the age of three, I just took life in, and, as yet, since I didn't have anything to compare it with, I just accepted it. We had no traditional family life— we never ate meals together, watched television together, or vacationed together when I was young. I can count on one hand the number of times Daddy and Mother attended a school function or involved themselves in any of my activities. In high school, I won lots of awards for various athletic pursuits, including the state volleyball championship, and they never came to a game. Indeed, they never even mentioned it.

If I needed to bring cookies to school, Mother would buy six dozen from the fanciest bakery in town. If I needed a new dress for a school dance, they would buy me the best. On birthdays or graduation, they always threw me an expensive party, like a roller-skating bash at an indoor rink or a blowout luncheon at an expensive club. As a matter of fact, some of my school friends thought I was a "rich kid," which really wasn't true. But my parents simply could not extend themselves to me personally or emotionally. Later, particularly in college, when I would describe my home life to friends, they would be appalled, but I didn't think of it as shocking as I lived it. That was just the way it was.

Although I didn't know it at the time and wouldn't discover the truth for years, during the first three years after I came to the Deuprees, I was living with them on a sort of probation. I was involved in a complicated lawsuit, which resulted in the two thousand dollars I received from Mrs. Stone when I turned twenty-one. Daddy and Mother were advised not to legally adopt me until this suit was settled because the adoption could have an impact on the suit. Surely, this "limbo" must have been exceedingly stressful for both of them; and given Mother's natural instability, the legal problems must only have added to the ambivalence she felt toward me.

At times during that period, Mother thought seriously about sending me back or giving me to Aunt Helen. But on this issue, Daddy put his foot down. He thought I had been bounced around enough, and no way would he allow me to leave.

Daddy and Mother evidently had been told the bare facts of my situation by the adoption agency—that my natural mother had given me to my grandmother, that my grandmother had died, and that I had been put into a foster home with a woman I called "Mama Cook." This was all they knew, and all they wanted to know. And, of course, they never told me any of this when I was young.

As a child, I had no memories at all of my natural mother or my grandmother, but early on I remembered quite a lot about Mama Cook, and would tell Mary Lee how Mama Cook cooked a certain dish or made things in a similar pot. Very quickly, however, I learned not to mention Mama Cook's name to Mother. She wanted me to forget Mama Cook—and any other tidbit that might be lurking in my memory—and so I did.

For all intents and purposes, Mary Lee Glover raised me; she was, in many—if not most—ways, my mother. Mary Lee says that shortly after the Deuprees got me, my Aunt Helen called her up and said: "You stay there now. That baby has a long, hard life ahead of her."

From the day I arrived at the Deupree home, Mary Lee completely took over my care. Aside from dressing me, fixing my meals, bathing me, putting me to bed, she taught me manners—how and when to say "Please" and "Thank you," as well as how to set a table, make a bed, and cook simple dishes—normal household matters.

Mary Lee never lived in with us, so she would get up early in the morning and take a bus from her house across town to ours. I would always be waiting for her out on the curb. She'd feed me breakfast, then she and Mother would make all sorts of convoluted plans for getting me to and from school, dancing class, or friends' homes. For example, I took dancing class two days a week, and Mary Lee would take me to class on the bus, and then when class was finished, I was told to wait on the stoop in front of the dancing school until my mother came to pick me up. Sometimes Mother would forget, or get caught up someplace, and I would sit there for hours. I was four years old at the time.

When I was alone with Mary Lee, I was allowed to behave like a normal child. Mary Lee had lived in Mobile all her life and she knew just about everybody in town, so when we would go off on the bus to run an errand or visit her family, she would permit me to walk up and down chatting with people she knew— and some she didn't. To friends and strangers alike I'd say, "Mary Lee lives at 751 Elmira Street. You come on over and visit with us sometime."

Mary Lee also provided constructive discipline. When I began school, Mary Lee always made me do my homework as soon as I got home. "I figured you should do your work right when you got home," Mary Lee says. "At night, you might do something wrong, and Mrs. Deupree might be in a bad mood and tell you to get the hell out of here."

Occasionally, when my parents would go out for the evening or be away on a trip, I'd go over to Mary Lee's for dinner. Mary Lee lived with her own mother and her daughter, Fanny, who was about four years older than I. We'd buy crabs and cook them up in a big pot, or we'd buy a chicken that Mary Lee would "fry up" and serve with her special homemade pork and beans. After dinner, I'd go out and play stickball in the street with other kids from her neighborhood.

Mary Lee provided me with a consistent sense of structure, security, and love. Without her, I would have been lost.

Several other people played important roles in my childhood— my upbringing, really—and in various ways became a sort of extended family for me: the Rogers family, the Gadel family, and, of course, Aunt Helen, my mother's sister.

Aunt Helen was four years older than Mother, and although she was not considered to be the beauty Mother was, she was a handsome woman. I am sure from the day Mother was born until the day she died, Aunt Helen felt responsible for her. Aunt Helen had had as difficult a life as Mother, but she handled it differently. She and her husband, Stanley, were never as afflu- ent as the Deuprees, and certainly Uncle Stanley never indulged Aunt Helen's every wish the way Daddy indulged Mother's. For many years, Aunt Helen worked as a beautician from a shop she installed in her home. Evidently Uncle Stanley was not able to be as generous with Aunt Helen as Daddy was with Mother— so Aunt Helen made her own money.

Aunt Helen was more stable emotionally than Mother, and as a result, exerted a great deal of influence over her. I don't know how many times I would have a conversation with Aunt Helen, go home, and hear exactly the same words come out of my mother's mouth. At the same time, the relationship between Aunt Helen and Mother was volatile. They would have feuds about the tiniest thing, and these fights might last for two or three years. Then they would make up, and the cycle would start all over again.

When I was small, Aunt Helen baby-sat for me frequently, and as I grew older, she served as a welcome sounding board for me. When I would have problems with Mother, I always felt I could confide in Aunt Helen. Because she was "family," she was aware of my mother's emotional problems, and she was always a source of support for me during those hard times.

Betty and Ed Rogers moved in across the street from us about three months after I arrived at the Deuprees. Betty and Ed (whom, not surprisingly, I called Aunt Betty and Uncle Ed) were several years younger than Mother and Daddy, but they already had three children—a boy, Cobb, then about eight; and two girls, Lee, age five, and Sally, age two. A few years later, they had a third daughter, Nell, whose birth was a major neighborhood event.

Lee and Sally instantly became my best friends—especially Sally. I would leave the house right after breakfast and go across the street to the Rogerses' and stay there—or play outdoors— all day. (My mother did not allow us to play in our house, not even in my bedroom. On Saturdays, when Mary Lee didn't come, she would lock the doors so that I couldn't get back into the house, and at lunch she would pass me a sandwich through the screen. If we wanted a drink of water, we'd have to get it from the outdoor faucet or the hose.)

If I know anything about normal family life, it is because of my relationship with the Rogers family. Fortunately, they treated me as though I was part of the family—I even had my own sign on their kitchen "dog house." To this day, Aunt Betty still says I am her "fifth child."

None of us girls were interested in dolls or girl-type games. Instead we played baseball (I don't think the Rogers family had a proper lawn until we were in high school) or war, where Cobb and some of the other neighborhood boys would tie us to stakes. My own personal favorite was lifeguard, in which we took turns sitting on a ladder turned backwards keeping watch over a wading pool. Aunt Betty still laughs over a game we concocted one day when we found a box of condoms on the street and blew up all the rubbers like circus balloons.

Aunt Betty and Uncle Ed didn't really socialize much with

Daddy and Mother. The Rogerses were a young couple with four small children and couldn't afford to go to Mardi Gras balls or country club dances, the kinds of activities Daddy and Mother relished. Nevertheless, because we were all basically neighborly, we sometimes had picnics together or Aunt Betty and Mother would chat over a cup of coffee.

Occasionally Mother would get it in her head to do something grand, and when I was ten, she decided that Aunt Betty and she should take Lee, Sally, and me for an overnight trip to New Orleans.

"Louise instigated this trip," Aunt Betty recalls. "Plus she told me that Wayne was going to pay for it. I wouldn't have gone otherwise. We couldn't afford it."

We got up at 4:00 A.M. and Mother drove us all to the train station, where we caught an early train to New Orleans. We spent the day walking around the French Quarter taking in the sights, then Mother and Aunt Betty took us for a fancy dinner at the Blue Room at the Roosevelt Hotel. Then Aunt Betty and Mother put us up in the hotel room and decided to go back down to Bourbon Street for a drink.

"I did not drink in those days," Betty remembers. "I drank Coca-Colas and that was it. I don't remember what Louise drank. How in the world we ever got separated, I don't know. Anyway, I finally went back to the hotel. She didn't come in all night."

"The next morning it was getting on time to catch the train to come home, and I still didn't know where Louise was," Betty goes on. "I finally went out on Bourbon Street, and I just went up and down, first one bar and then the other. I found her, sitting up on some bar stool with some man. I got her back to the hotel, and we got to the train by the skin of our teeth."

While we were in New Orleans, Daddy was up in Montgomery being initiated into the Shriners. He wasn't home when we got back, so Aunt Betty drove us back from the station because Mother was still pretty out of it. Aunt Betty must have known Mother was in trouble, because as soon as we got in the door, she called Mary Lee and asked her to come right over. After that, Mother just went downhill.

"She got so drunk in New Orleans, she was just goofy,"

Mary Lee remembers. "I couldn't get hold of Mr. Deupree, so I called Dr. Brown, and he said to sign her in at Emergency at the Mobile Infirmary, so I got her in the car and took her down there. The Sisters gave her a shot, and by the time we got her back into the car, she was just out. When I got back to the house, I couldn't get her out of the car, so Mr. Rogers came over and helped me."

This was not the first time Mary Lee had witnessed one of Mother's severe alcoholism attacks. A couple of years earlier, Mother and Daddy had gone to New Orleans—probably for a weekend holiday—and I was left at home in Mary Lee's care. Mother got "goofy drunk" and Daddy tried to put her in the hospital in New Orleans, and then ended up driving her home at two or three o'clock in the morning.

"That's the first time I'd ever seen anyone have a 'nervous breakdown,'" Mary Lee remembers. "She was shakin' all over. Her nerves—her flesh was like covered with worms—it was just crawling. All over her arms, all over her legs. Mr. Deupree told me to go in and shave her legs, because she wouldn't go to the hospital without shaving her legs, and he was afraid she would cut herself. So, I shaved her legs, but her flesh was just quivering the whole time."

After each of these incidents, Mother was hospitalized for about a month's time. Over the years, she was hospitalized four or five times for alcoholism, addiction to various prescription drugs, and psychiatric problems. Years later, I would learn that she received electroshock treatments several times. I have only vague memories of most of these hospitalizations. They began in 1959, when I was only six, tapered off during my adolescence, and then reoccurred frequently after I left for college.

One time, she was in the hospital over Christmas. On Christmas Eve, Daddy dropped me off over at Paul Brown's Department Store and told me to pick out anything I wanted. He went up to see Mother at the hospital, and when he got back he'd been drinking a little bit. By the time we got home and I had put all the Christmas stuff under the tree, he was drinking a lot. The next day, I didn't bother to get up early for Christmas because I had bought all my stuff already, and I knew there would be no surprises— at least none that I cared to investigate.

Although my friends Lee and Sally Rogers attended local public schools, Mother felt strongly that I should go to Holy Family, the parochial Catholic grammar school that was associated with our church. This school was run by the Sisters of Mercy, with the parish priest, Father Sullivan, as the director. (Later I would attend Bishop Toolen High School, the well-known Catholic girls' school.) It was at Holy Family, when I was in first grade, that I met Lenore Gadel, who would remain, like Sally, one of my life-long best friends.

Lenore and I looked very different— she was dark, and I was blond— but mostly we were soul mates. We were both tomboys, loved sports and competition, had a similar sense of humor. I also became as close to Lenore's family, her parents and her younger sister, Lisa, as I was to the Rogerses and, as I got older, lived at their house much the way I had lived at the Rogerses'.

Lenore's mother, Anita, turned out to be especially important to me. She was drafted by Father Sullivan to coach the volleyball and basketball teams for our grade. She also formed a Girl Scout troop for girls our age. Although Anita had a household to run, two children, and a full-time job as a nurse, she coached our volleyball teams for years and played a very active role in Scouting. During junior and senior high school, Scouting and sports were two of my passions.

Lenore and I shared a fascination for music as well. Mother wanted me to learn to play the violin or the piano, but I desperately wanted to play the guitar. When I was in sixth grade, Mother finally agreed to let me take lessons, but she didn't want to be bothered carting me to lessons or listening to me practice. As a result, she made a deal with Lenore's mother, Anita, to pay for part of Lenore's tuition if Anita would agree to drive us back and forth.

Interestingly enough, Mother and Anita became friendly as well— at least, they got as close as Mother could get with anyone. As a result, Anita and Lenore witnessed firsthand many of the problems I faced with Mother. Anita remembers a typical incident that reflected Mother's eternal ambivalence toward me.

"I had bought Lenore this dress and Louise liked it," Anita told me. "It was green plaid with a little white piqué inset that came up high at the neck. She wanted to have a portrait made of you. So, she asked me where I got the dress, and then she got you one just like it.

"You outgrew your dress right quick. It was like new—and Louise brought it over to us one Sunday in a paper bag. Mary Lee had washed, starched, and ironed it. Right there, in front of you—I'll never get over this—she gave me this dress, and said: 'I want you to give this to Lisa. It will look a whole lot better on Lisa than it ever did on Cathy.' "

As with Aunt Betty, Anita occasionally witnessed the extremes of Mother's addiction. She remembers clearly an incident that I only barely recall:

"I think you were in about fourth grade, and you called me up crying. You said: 'Mom's done something terrible, and I can't get her to get up—and she told me she's gonna die.'

"I didn't have a car and there was no bus service at the time, so I got on my child's bike and rode over. When I got there, I found a bottle of pills, and I realized that Louise had taken these pills and had been drinking. I could smell it. That's why she had more or less passed out."

"I fixed her up fine," Anita says. "I got a glass of water and filled it with Tide. I foamed it up and I made her drink it. It made her just deathly ill; she threw up all over everything. Everything was a mess—pills that had not dissolved, you know. She had taken whole bottles of whatever she could find. I made her a pot of coffee, then I stayed with her until I knew that she was all right."

Because Anita was trained as a practical nurse, Mother confided in her about her alcoholism, her electroshock treatments, her illnesses. Actually, one of Mother's most endearing and paradoxical qualities was her absolute openness. Sometimes she would shade the truth to make herself "look" better, but other times she would be breathtakingly frank about certain things that other people might have found shameful, like her drinking problems or her emotional difficulties.

All of these relationships ebbed and flowed over the years. My relationship with Sally and Lee faded some during high school, mostly because we attended different schools and had separate friends. During our junior year in high school, Lenore transferred from Bishop Toolen to Murphy, the largest public high school in Mobile. Beginning in seventh grade, I also went to camp for the entire summer, so I was not around during the summer months. Thus we began to drift apart.

Paradoxically, as I got older, my relationship with my parents got a little bit better. Unlike most kids who revolt against their parents during their teenage years, we grew closer together, partly because I accepted that in order to have a smooth relationship with Mother and appreciate her company, I had to function as "the mother," and I did.

In 1971, I went to college at the University of Alabama at Tuscaloosa. I joined Alpha Delta Pi Sorority, and lived at the sorority house most of the time I was in college. During summer vacations, I worked as a lifeguard or as a clerk at McDonald's, so I was out of the house most of the time. After my sophomore year, Daddy, Mother, and I took an extended trip to Europe together, which turned out to be great fun. They now considered me an adult, and I could enjoy them on their own terms.

During the Christmas vacation of my junior year in college, I met a wonderful guy named Michael Mayer. Michael had recently returned from Vietnam, and had come back to Mobile to start a career using his experience as a helicopter pilot. Like Daddy, he was one of seven children, and I liked his family very much.

We dated for a year and a half, and married in May 1975. I loved Michael—he was and is a wonderful man—but I was not in love with him. I think we married for the reason many kids marry right out of college—we didn't know what else to do.

Our wedding ended up being another of Mother's fiascos. She treated it as the social event of the season, so in effect, the wedding turned out to be more hers than mine. If she wasn't the bride, she was the star. When I went to try on my wedding dress— which Mother had picked out— the saleslady said: "Who's wedding are you gonna be in, honey?" because the dress looked more like a bridesmaid's dress than a bridal gown. Mother insisted that the ushers wear pink shirts to match her own pink dress.

But worse, in order to control things, she decided not to send out formal invitations, only announcements after the event. Michael was permitted to ask only his immediate family and one friend. My problems were more complex.

When we first began planning the wedding in the winter, I asked Sally Rogers to be one of my bridesmaids and her younger sister, Nell, to help serve. Then I went back to school and left the rest of the plans to Mother. As it turned out, Mother never contacted Aunt Betty, Sally, or Nell again, and during the few days preceding the wedding I was in tears most of the time because she refused to let me invite not only the Rogerses, but any other old friends, including the Gadels— and even Mary Lee. It was a small wedding— only about seventy-five people— but all the guests were social friends of Mother's, people I knew only casually.

On the day before the wedding, Mother finally let me call Sally and invite her. I'm sure she was very hurt, and she said no, she could not come. I was heartbroken. Right after the wedding— symbolically, it poured— Michael and I stopped over at the Rogerses' house. Needless to say, our meeting was tense, and more than seven years would pass before we patched up the wound. I left on my honeymoon devastated by the loss of my oldest friend, Sal.

After we were married, Michael and I moved to Montgomery, where Michael had found a good job as a pilot for a small corporation, flying corporate executives to conferences and meetings. I got a job as a director at a community center that offered everything from care for the elderly to programs for preschool children. We built a nice house in Deatsville, Alabama, a town just eight miles from Montgomery. I bought a horse, we got ourselves a wonderful Irish setter named Tooley, and we settled into a regular married life.

I hadn't forgotten about "maybe being Hank Williams' child," but it was a piece of information I put into a "box" in the back of my mind and rarely if ever spoke about to anyone, not even Michael. Because it was all conjecture, and because Mother had said "there is no proof" and "there is nothing you can do," I decided that I would just let it be, and go on living.

4
JUST WAITIN'

One afternoon in late 1980, my father called me at work with a fascinating piece of information. He told me that he had just seen a television interview with Hank Williams' son, who was by now thirty-one years old and a successful entertainer in his own right. Daddy was shocked because during the interview, Hank Jr. said something to the effect that he was enjoying an income of about $500,000 a year off the music of Hank Williams, Sr.

Daddy then repeated to me basically the same story Mother had told me on my twenty-first birthday: that in 1967, during some legal proceedings involving the Hank Williams estate, the possibility that Hank Williams, Sr., might have had another child, a daughter, had come up. Apparently, Mother and Daddy were contacted at this time and told that I might be that child. However, they were also informed that not only had the judge decided that I was unable to inherit, but no significant money was involved.

Over the years, even after I felt free to research my past, I never lost my intense fear of upsetting Daddy and Mother—particularly Mother—by discussing my natural parents with them. I never asked them precisely when or how they were informed that I might be Hank Williams' child. I also do not know who first told them, although I would later learn that, in 1967, they had discussions with a man named Drayton Hamilton, my guardian ad litem—the attorney charged with representing me during various proceedings—and Mr. Hamilton may well have been their source of information.

Hank Jr.'s revelation got Daddy to thinking, and the more he thought, the angrier and more frustrated he got. He said he felt he had made a mistake—perhaps a terrible mistake—by not pursuing the matter further in 1967. He also feared he had not been told the entire truth about my past. He said he was now prepared to help me any way he could, particularly to find out once and for all if Hank Williams really was my father. He didn't know quite how we should proceed, but he said he was going to start by sending me a packet of clippings and miscellaneous papers he had saved over the years.

For Wayne Deupree to bring up the subject of Hank Williams was absolutely astonishing. Even on my twenty-first birthday, when Mother had told me that Hank Williams might be my father and that I was to receive the two thousand dollars from Mrs. Stone's estate, Daddy had been noticeably quiet on the subject of my natural parents. He had not said a word about it that day, and he had not spoken to me about it for almost seven years. Mother was overtly the more emotional, the more easily upset, of my adoptive parents, but Daddy had strong feelings, too. I know he felt I was "his little girl," and he wasn't terribly interested in sharing that position. But his love for me included protecting me, and I had the sense, after his call, that he feared my interests had not been attended to properly. I imagine he felt a bit guilty, perhaps a little frightened, and—although he was going to sit on it awhile—I think he was angry.

A couple of days later, the packet Daddy mentioned arrived and I opened it with the same fascination and fear that always bubbled up when I was confronted with my past. In the packet were some scraps of paper with notes scribbled on them, some letters from the adoption agency, the photograph of "Jewel" I remembered finding in Mother's bureau drawer, and two or three yellowed newspaper clippings. The newspaper articles concerned the 1967 trial where "Hank Williams' daughter" had come up. The most interesting one from the *Montgomery Advertiser*, dated September 27, 1967, bore the headline: WILLIAMS MUSIC TRIAL TAKES TURN AS POSSIBLE DAUGHTER IS REPORTED. In part, it read:

> A complex trial involving copyrights of songs of the late Hank Williams became even more complicated Tuesday with mention that Williams possibly had a daughter.
>
> The child was mentioned several times . . .
>
> The question arose Tuesday when attorney Maury Smith representing Acuff-Rose Publishing Company told the court that Hank Williams had recognized "in a written contract" that a child had been born to a woman in Montgomery.

I really didn't understand quite what this all meant. The only thing I knew about "copyrights" were the little c's-in-a-circle printed in the fronts of books. I understood that writers secured copyrights so that no one could steal their work, so I deduced that songwriters must copyright their songs for the same reason. I couldn't understand what this would have to do with me. God knows, I hadn't stolen any of Ole Hank's songs— since my twenty-first birthday, I had been too frightened to even listen to his records. Just the sound of Hank Williams breathing made me feel strange. It would take years before I realized that "copyrights" also meant the rights to the income generated from a written work, and that, in the Hank Williams case specifically, it meant the rights of his potential heirs.

I also, of course, took note of the line "Hank Williams had recognized 'in a written contract' that a child had been born to a woman in Montgomery." What sort of a contract had he made? Whom had he made the agreement with? The newspaper didn't say he made the agreement with the "woman in Montgomery"; it said only that the child had been born to a woman in Montgomery. And even that line was confusing. I remembered that when I had glanced through *Sing a Sad Song* seven years before, the author had said the mother—my mother!—was a woman from Tennessee, not Montgomery, Alabama.

I recalled the photograph of Jewel and the loving inscription on the back of the picture. Mother had said she lived in the foster home, and I wondered how I would ever find her now. I didn't even know her last name. The photo looked like a high school graduation picture. Since twenty-five years had passed, I figured Jewel would now be a woman in her mid-forties, and I wondered if she would even remember me.

Finally, I picked up a scrap of paper with a note handwritten on it. It said:

Cathy is a sweet little girl. We have been boarding her since last March. I hope you will send us a picture of her at different times in life. I will be glad to send her a gift on her birthday and Christmas if you will let us know your address. Our's is: Mrs. J. H. Cook, Pine Level, Alabama. Cathy likes most anything to eat, especially meats with ketchup on it.

Mama Cook! The note was from Mama Cook! Just holding that note in my hand—and reading in her handwriting that she cared about me, that she wanted to know how I was doing, that she wanted to send me presents—made me want to cry. Learning that I liked ketchup on everything was one of the first concrete facts I had gleaned about my past. And inadvertently, Mama Cook had revealed something else. She said I had been with them since "last March." I knew I had gone with the Deuprees in February 1956; therefore "last March" must have been March 1955. This told me that I might well have lived with Mrs. Stone for over two years—unless, of course, I had stayed in yet another home that I did not remember.

How had Daddy and Mother received this note? It wasn't in an envelope, although perhaps the envelope had just been thrown out. I didn't recall receiving gifts from the Cooks, and I wondered what had happened. Knowing Mother, I assumed she had not responded to the note. I didn't know quite what I was going to do with this information, but before I had to figure it out Providence stepped in and took care of it for me.

Less than a week later, in early January 1981, a young woman named Elaine Henderson walked into the center where I worked. She was new in town, and she wanted to enroll her son in the preschool program at the Center. I noticed that she had just moved to Montgomery from Pine Level, Alabama, a town about twenty-five miles southeast of Montgomery, the community where the Cooks lived.

Before I could think twice, I said: "You don't happen to know someone named Cook, do you?"

"Why, yes," she said. "My husband's best friend is Jimmy Cook."

I was amazed, not so much because Elaine knew the Cook family, but because Elaine had walked in my door at the moment she did. I was certain that Pine Level was very small, so the neighbors would all be friendly. But if Elaine had arrived only a week before, I would have never noticed that she was from Pine Level. And when she mentioned Jimmy Cook, she triggered a dim memory of a big boy—a big boy I remembered liking very much. I took a deep breath.

"Would you do me a favor?" I asked. "The next time you see them, would you ask them if they remember anyone named Cathy."

"Cathy what?" she wanted to know.

"Just say 'Cathy,' " I answered.

Within days, Elaine was back at the center, and she seemed excited.

"My husband and I went down to Pine Level," she said. "We found Jimmy at his hunting cabin, and asked him if he knew a Cathy. He remembered you all right. You have the right Cooks. Jimmy says that they want you to come to Mr. and Mrs. Cook's fiftieth wedding anniversary on January twentieth."

I told Elaine that I wanted to see the Cooks very much, but I had mixed emotions about just dropping in on a fiftieth wedding anniversary celebration. Frankly, I was nervous—this was only a verbal invitation from a virtual stranger. A few days later Elaine came back and handed me an invitation.

At that point, I asked Elaine if she had ever heard of anyone named Jewel.

"Oh, yes,' she said. "Jewel is the Cooks' daughter."

On January 20, I drove down to Pine Level in a little brown Spitfire I owned at the time. Michael was working that weekend, but, in fact, I didn't mind going to the party alone. I was apprehensive, but somehow I felt that I wanted to explore my past by myself.

Pine Level is not even a town, really. It is a community of farms and its center consists of a general store, a gas station, and the Methodist church. The Cooks were holding their party in the auditorium of the Pine Level Methodist Church, and as I pulled up in front, I noticed two men sitting on the front steps.

I got out of my car and stood beside it for a second, gathering my courage, when suddenly one of the men came running toward me. He grabbed me, swung me up in the air, and hugged me.

"Cathy, nobody has to tell me who you are!" he said "This time we're not going to let you go."

I was flabbergasted. All these years I had wondered if anybody had ever even cared about me, and here was this big man squeezing me and telling me that "this time . . . this time" he wasn't "going to let me go." Of course, this was Jimmy Cook, the "big boy" I had remembered adoring when I was a toddler.

I didn't know what to say to Jimmy, so I just hugged him. He took me into the church, which was very crowded with the Cooks' friends and family. I wondered if I would recognize Mama Cook, but didn't have to wonder long. Mrs. Cook, who isn't quite as effervescent as Jimmy, walked up and embraced me, and as I looked into her warm, gentle eyes, twenty-five years dropped away. I knew her instantly.

"I always knew we'd meet again," she said.

Before I could even take in my memories of Mama Cook, I was embraced by another man, a man as warm and lovable as Jimmy. Daddy Cook! Of course, as soon as I saw him, I remembered how much I had loved him.

And, finally, there was Jewel. She had grown from a teenage girl into a warm, gentle woman. She and her husband, Tom, and their three children lived in Chicago, but they were at the Pine Level Methodist Church, celebrating her parents' fiftieth anniversary. Like her brother, Jimmy, and her parents, Jewel embraced me with tears in her eyes.

I also met the Cooks' two other daughters, Elaine and Eloise, and their families. I felt bad because I didn't remember Elaine and Eloise, but Mrs. Cook quickly explained that both "girls" had been married by the time I came to live with them.

Although they greeted me warmly, I still felt like I was imposing on their special day. I needn't have felt that way. Daddy Cook took me under his arm and walked with me out in the churchyard and showed me the cemetery where he wanted to be buried. At the end of the party, Mama and Daddy Cook insisted that I come back to their house. I wondered if perhaps this wasn't the right time for me to visit.

"Oh, no," Daddy Cook said. "Besides, I want a ride in that little car." He grabbed his hat and crawled into my little car with me. We drove back to their house, which, to my surprise, I did not recognize at all.

Their farm is located about two miles off the Troy highway, back up some winding roads. Their daughter Elaine lives in a pretty white house just down the road, and Jimmy, his wife, Joanne, and their children also live on the property. Mama Cook noticed my puzzled look when I entered their house.

"You don't remember this house, do you!" she said. "That's because it's not the same house. Our big old house burned several years ago and we built a new one. The old one had sixteen-foot ceilings and was made of beautiful old wood. I like this house, but it's not like our old one."

We had a wonderful time that evening. Because it was Mama and Daddy Cook's special evening, we didn't talk too much about their year with me, although Jimmy did tell me a few fascinating stories.

First, he said that he remembered that the first time he ever saw me, I was asleep in his bed. He was about fourteen at the time, and he had come home from school and gone into his room, and there I was. He went out to the kitchen to find his mother and said: "Mama, there's a baby in my bed and she doesn't have any lips and her hair doesn't have a wrinkle in it." According to all the Cooks, Jimmy and I formed a special relationship right away, and he had loved me so much that he had named his first daughter Cathy after me.

Jimmy also told me how Elaine Henderson and her husband, Danny, had told him about me. They had been out in a hunting cabin, and Jimmy was building a fire. Danny said: "Jimmy, do you know a girl named Cathy?"

"Yea, I know one," Jimmy said. "I have a daughter named Cathy." As Jimmy made this comment, he actually had a sense that Danny was talking about me.

"No, I mean someone else," Danny said. "We were enrolling the boy in this school, and we met someone named Cathy who knows you."

"Is she blond-headed and got a little round face?" Jimmy asked.

"Yep," Danny said.

Jimmy said that he immediately drove over to his mother's and told her that they had found "our pretty little Cathy."

As Jimmy was telling this story, Jewel cut in and said: "Why didn't you go sit outside the school and wait for her to come out?"

All the Cooks laughed, although I didn't catch on to the joke until Jewel explained.

"On the day you were taken away, Jimmy and I cut school— we went to Sidney Lanier High School in Montgomery," Jewel began. "We went down to the Department of Pensions and Security and hid in the bushes. We thought if we could get the license plate number of the family who was taking you, we could go get you back. We saw them bring you in, and we waited for hours. But we never saw you come out."

This story made me want to cry. The inscription on the back of Jewel's photograph had told me that someone had cared, but I had had no idea that an entire family had loved me so much.

After that first meeting, the Cook family became a second "home" to me. I'd drive down to Pine Level at least once a week to go fishing with Daddy Cook or visiting with Jimmy and his family. Shortly after the anniversary celebration, Mrs. Cook fell and broke her hip and was in the hospital in Montgomery for a couple of weeks. Joanne Cook called me and told me about it, and I went over almost every day with a sandwich in a paper sack and had lunch with Mrs. Cook. I was afraid she would get sick of me or annoyed that I was interrupting her favorite soap opera, but she seemed to genuinely enjoy my visits, and she slowly filled me in on the details of my year with them.

As I had surmised, I arrived at their home in March 1955. Mrs. Cook told me that when I came, I was a very frightened little girl. Later she told me that it was her understanding that my grandmother had died, and for a few weeks I had been moved from home to home, and she wasn't sure what was going to happen next. She said that I cried for days after I arrived, and it got to the point where Mrs. Cook thought seriously about calling the welfare department because she didn't think she could handle me. Apparently, Jimmy was the only family member who could reach me at first. After two or three days, Jimmy got me to sit in a little toy car I had brought with me, and riding in that car apparently settled me down. In fact, Mrs. Cook said I was pretty rambunctious in that car, and at some point drove it right off their porch. Ironically, that little toy car was baby blue, the same color as the car Hank Williams died in.

Mrs. Cook also told me that whoever had cared for me before obviously loved me very much. When I arrived, I came with piles of adorable clothes—socks trimmed with lace, patent leather shoes, lots of dresses, and a red leather cowgirl outfit with a white fringe. In addition to the baby blue car, I came with a crate full of toys, including a little guitar.

"I had an aunt in Montgomery," Mrs. Cook confided one day years later, "and she was keeping children, too. Word gets around, you know, and she came down one day and said: 'Do you know whose child that is? That's Hank Williams' daughter. She was living with her grandmother and her grandmother died.' "

That was the extent of Mrs. Cook's knowledge about my past. She did say that I would sit on the piano bench and point to sheet music Jewel had bought—songs by Hank Williams that bore his picture on the front—and say, "That's Hank."

Although I gradually became very close to the Cook family, I never lost my fear of strangers during the months I lived with them. When a stranger came to visit, I would cling to Mama Cook. When we went to church, I would hang on Daddy Cook's legs. Once when Mama and Daddy Cook were going into Montgomery for a family celebration, they took me along, but didn't take Jimmy or Jewel. Apparently, I refused to leave unless all of the family was in the car. As Mrs. Cook said, I was clearly afraid that I would be sent away again.

When it came time for me to be "placed" with the Deuprees, we were all very upset. By then I was just three years old, and according to Mrs. Cook, the welfare worker had told me that I would be leaving. On the morning of my departure, Mrs. Cook was giving me a bath. We were both crying our hearts out, but I understood the situation completely.

"Why are you cryin', Mama?" I had said. "You ain't goin' nowhere."

Mrs. Cook said this made her cry all the more. She had tucked the note about my penchant for ketchup in the sleeve of my little leather cowgirl jacket. She knew I loved that jacket, and I would find it—or my new mother would find it.

Daddy Cook was equally upset about my departure. He was on jury duty that day, and he left, drove about ten miles, and then turned around and came back. Supposedly, he had forgotten his glasses, but Mama Cook said he had tears streaming down his face when he drove back in the yard for one more hug.

And, of course, Jimmy and Jewel had their own plan. They cut school and waited in the bushes, hoping to catch a glimpse of my new adoptive parents.

Mrs. Cook also told me something else that astonished me. The first Christmas I spent with the Deuprees, Mother sent the Cooks a Christmas card telling them that she and Daddy would be happy to have them come down and see me any time, and a couple of weeks later Mama and Daddy Cook, together with their daughter Eloise and her family, drove down to Mobile. They checked into a hotel and called the Deuprees. Apparently Daddy and I drove over to the hotel and brought the Cooks back to our house.

Mrs. Cook said that they stayed for several hours and had a pleasant time. I gave her a tour of my bedroom and showed her all my toys—including a new bicycle and my own television set. The Cooks got the impression that I was happy and loved by the Deuprees. The next day they drove home, but they made a very important decision.

They realized that maybe it would be best if they did not remain a part of my life. As Mrs. Cook put it, "We didn't want to upset you anymore. We thought we should just let you be with that family and love them instead of going back up here and loving us—and wanting to stay with us and maybe not wanting to go back." I recognized that Mama and Daddy Cook made this decision out of love for me.

For me, finding the Cooks was a turning point in my life. I had grown up thinking that nobody ever wanted me, and to go back and discover that these people loved me, cared about me, and tried to do what was best for me gave me the courage to go on. Also, if it had not been for the Cooks, I don't know whether or not I would have made it, mentally or emotionally. Had I not had that year of their love—especially given what I would later learn about the events that preceded my months with the Cooks— I suspect I would have had a host of additional problems. I have no doubt that the Cooks played a major role in the development of my character.

Because the Cooks had not been a secret in our house and because Daddy had sent me the papers that included Mrs. Cook's message, I was open—for the first time in my life—with my parents about my desires to search for my roots. I downplayed the significance of these events, but I did tell them about finding the Cooks, and I also shared with them the news about the Cooks' anniversary party.

One week after the Cooks' party, Mother was admitted to the hospital suffering from a severe depression. She remained in the hospital for a month, came out in late February, and then, in early March, tried to commit suicide by taking an overdose of alcohol and pills. Again she was hospitalized for a couple of weeks.

At the time, I didn't know whether or not my reunion with the Cooks had anything to do with Mother's depression, but I suspected that it did—and I was certain that my enthusiasm did not help her in any way. Over the next few years, I came to believe that any efforts I made to discover my past triggered a depressive "episode" in Mother. Years later, when I put together a complete history of my mother's health, I would learn that the events and relationships of my past had been disturbing her since the day I came into their lives. I decided that I had to be far more discreet about my "search." I also noted that if the Cooks' love for me had molded one aspect of my character, Mother's problems and fears had shaped another.

5
SWEET YVONE COMES HOME

Once my father offered to help me and I had reestablished a relationship with the Cooks, my emotional floodgates opened. It quickly became clear to me that I had suppressed a well of feeling for years. Because my father sanctioned it, I now felt free to pursue my roots. I firmly believed that I couldn't get on with my life until I was absolutely certain that Hank Williams was—or was not—my father. (Or, at least, I wanted to know that it could never be proven, one way or the other.) I also realized that I now had the courage to face the truth about my natural mother—of whom I knew virtually nothing—and when I looked closely at my feelings, I saw that I desperately wanted to find her.

In a way, I felt like a private detective, looking for clues wherever I could find them. I started with the Alabama Department of Pensions and Security, the adoption agency in Montgomery. Actually, I had gone to Pensions and Security once before, in October 1979, and had met with a social worker named Emogene Austin, who was a comforting woman in her late fifties. At that time, my curiosity about my natural parents was simmering just under the surface, but I still felt very concerned about hurting my adoptive parents by searching for the truth. I justified the visit under the guise that I was considering the notion of one day having a child and I wanted to know more about health-related matters.

At that time, I explained to Miss Austin that I did not wish to hurt my adoptive parents, but I wanted to know something about my family history. I said I understood all about the Hank Williams "thing," although I was stretching the truth. I pretended to know more, hoping that Miss Austin would inadvertently reveal some information.

Although Miss Austin refused to provide the names of my natural parents, she read descriptions of them from my files. She described my mother as an "attractive blond woman" about five-one in height, who had held some responsible jobs, and had had a difficult time when I was born. She referred to my "alleged father" as a man about six feet two inches tall with a very slender build, dark hair, brown eyes, and an olive complexion. She said that he was musical, and that his work made it necessary for him to travel quite a bit. She also said that he died suddenly from a heart attack. That was the extent of the information she gave me.

In late 1980, at the same time as he sent me the news articles and other papers, Daddy also gave me the name of the lawyer for the Department of Pensions and Security, a woman named Mary Lee Stapp. I called her, and she referred me to Louise Pittman, the director of the Bureau of Child Welfare, who had been with the department for over thirty years. I would learn much later that, as a result of her long tenure, Miss Pittman had been familiar with my case from the moment I entered the welfare system in 1955. Miss Pittman had also supervised the social worker who had worked with me during the months I lived with Mama Cook.

Miss Pittman was somewhat more informative than Miss Austin had been. For example, she told me that my natural mother had named me Antha Belle. I asked Miss Pittman if she would give me the name of my biological mother, but she refused, saying that she could not give out this information without my mother's consent. Nevertheless, she told me that I could view my original birth certificate at the Department of Vital Statistics, which was her way of "giving" me the information, I'm sure. The next day, I went over to Vital Statistics, and they showed me my birth certificate, dated January 6, 1953, for Antha Belle Jett. The place where the father's name should have been listed was left blank, but the mother's name was clear: Bobbie Webb Jett. I also learned from this certificate that Bobbie Webb Jett was born in the state of Tennessee, was thirty years old at the time of my birth, and to my amazement and distress, had one other living child.

During the next few months, I met with Miss Pittman two or three more times. I told her that I wanted to contact my mother, and we talked at length about the pros and cons of such a meeting. She suggested that my mother's lifestyle might well be very different from mine. She also said that my mother might have married and might have had other children. She pointed out that I should consider all these issues very carefully before I made an attempt to find her. What's more, I should be absolutely positive that I wanted to make contact, since if they called her, and then I decided I did not wish to meet her, I could be upsetting her and her family unnecessarily.

Obviously, I was very eager to learn anything I could about both my natural parents. However, I also realized that Miss Pittman was sympathetic and her advice made sense, so I told her I would like to think about the issue of actually "making contact" a bit longer.

During the spring of 1981, I also arranged a meeting with Drayton Hamilton, the man who had been mentioned in the old news articles as my court-appointed lawyer or "guardian ad litem." Initially, I went to see him with the hope that he might be able to answer my questions about my natural parents.

By 1981, he was man in his late fifties or early sixties, tall, slender, and rather courtly in the old Southern manner. He was extremely polite to me and seemed to have no doubt that I was who I said I was, although he insisted that I provide identification. But then, to my amazement, he refused to tell me anything. I told him that I knew about the 1967 trials—which was a white lie because I didn't understand about them at all—but still he was mute.

I tried to press him to tell me about the "written contract" mentioned in the 1967 newspaper articles. He assured me that the contract contained no important information—it had something to do with medical expenses—and would be of no help to me. What's more, he wasn't sure if it still existed, and doubted that I could get it even if it did.

Despite his resistance, I continued to ask him various questions, and finally he responded by saying that he wasn't certain that he should be speaking to me at all, that talking to me was somehow "unethical." I was shocked and hurt by this, and told him so. "Ethics," I said. "I thought I was your client. Surely you can tell your client what you know." Still he revealed very little.

He did attempt to fill me in on the situation that resulted in the two-thousand-dollar check I had received from Mrs. Stone's estate. He told me that in the mid-1950s he had represented me as my guardian ad litem in a case between me and Irene Williams Smith, Hank Williams' sister. Although I had been adopted by Mrs. Stone, I had not been mentioned in her will, which had been made before she adopted me. Apparently, there was a question regarding whether or not an adopted child could inherit in this situation, and the Supreme Court of Alabama had decided that I could not. As a result, I received only a token piece of the estate, the two thousand dollars. Nevertheless, although I had lost my case, Mr. Hamilton's plea had worked somehow to change the law so that adopted children left out of a will could inherit the same as a natural child. He proudly showed me the decision in one of his law books. I didn't understand exactly what he was talking about, and was mildly annoyed that he referred to my situation as a "landmark case," although I personally had lost.

I left my meeting with Mr. Hamilton feeling very frustrated and angry. All I wanted to know was if Hank Williams was really my father and how I could find my natural mother. These seemed like fairly straightforward questions to me, and although I understood Miss Pittman's concerns about upsetting Bobbie Jett,

I still felt it was my problem, not the state of Alabama's. Yet when I asked these questions, I always received answers that were vague and confusing.

During this period, I came across the name Charles Carr, the young man who had been the driver of the car Hank died in. He supposedly had lived in Montgomery at one time, so one day I decided to look up his name in the Montgomery telephone book. Although almost thirty years had passed, I found Charles Carr listed.

I could feel my adrenaline running full tilt, but I didn't let my terror stand in my way. I picked up the phone, dialed his number, and within seconds he answered. I asked him, flat out, if he was the same Charles Carr who had been with Hank Williams on the night he died. He said yes, so I told him that I had reason to believe I might be Hank Williams' daughter, and I wanted to know more about Hank and his family.

To my amazement, he knew exactly who I was; he was even well aware that my name was Cathy. He didn't think it odd that a young woman would claim to be Hank Williams' daughter; in fact, unlike my guardian ad litem, he didn't even ask me to prove my identity. He just said, "Oh, yea," and then proceeded to talk to me for a few minutes.

Early on in our conversation, he made a very interesting comment; he said, "I know it's okay for me to talk to you since the estate has been settled." Here it was again— a vague reference to a "settlement" of an "estate." Once again, I felt this confirmation— this assurance, really— that as far as any legal matters were concerned, my fate had been decided. At the same time, I was confused by this remark.

Charles was less than open when I questioned him about Hank's death. I asked him if Hank had died of a heart attack or of a drug overdose, which was a rumor I had heard many times. He said "heart attack," but then refused to give me any details about the events of the hours he had spent with Hank. He told me only that he had worshiped Hank, and certainly felt honored to have been asked to drive him to Canton, Ohio.

I had expected Charles Carr to have information only regarding Hank. But curiously, he told me that he had met my natural mother, although, again, he gave me few details—except that he had run into Bobbie at Mrs. Stone's boardinghouse. He also mentioned a woman named Marie who had lived at Mrs. Stone's house. He believed that if Marie was still alive, she could, most likely, tell me everything I needed to know. He described her as a woman who would now be in her late fifties or early sixties, and that she had a distinctive birthmark on her face.

By the time I hung up the phone, I was shaking all over. For the first time, someone connected with Hank Williams seemed to know about me. He had not appeared uncertain that Hank had a daughter or that I might be that daughter. By mentioning Marie, he indicated to me that others in Montgomery might well have relevant information about me.

Now, of course, I knew I had to find Marie, but I didn't know where to begin. As it turned out, the reality of finding Marie was as coincidental and bizarre as relocating Mama Cook and her family had been. Within days of my telephone conversation with Charles Carr, an interview with a woman who was Hank Williams' cousin ran in the *Montgomery Advertiser*, the local newspaper. The woman's name was Marie Harvell. As fortune would have it, the paper also ran a photograph of Marie, and, sure enough, she was an older woman with a noticeable birthmark on her face.

I was certain this was the same "Marie" that Charles Carr had referred to, but this time, I was not so lucky with the Montgomery telephone book. No one named Harvell was listed there, so I drove over to the public library, and checked the City Directory, a reference book that lists the names, addresses, phone numbers, and occupations of everybody in town. I discovered that Marie Harvell and her husband, Edward, lived on Pickett Street, which was near the center where I worked.

At lunchtime that same day, I drove over to Pickett Street, which was in an older section of town. Again, I felt a tight, jumbled fear in my stomach as I walked up the steps, but it was fast becoming a rather familiar feeling. I knocked on the door, and before I had a moment to catch my breath, Marie herself appeared behind the screen. This time, especially since it was a face-to-face encounter, I moved slowly into the situation.

"Excuse me," I said. "I'm a journalist, and I'd like to talk with you about Hank Williams."

"What newspaper are you from?" Marie asked. She apparently had been interviewed enough times to know to ask a few questions.

"Actually, I'm not with a particular newspaper," I answered. "But I saw the article in the *Advertiser*, and I'm a big fan of Hank's."

"I can't talk to you now, honey," she said. "I'm going out to the grocery store. But you come back at five o'clock, and I'll talk with you. By the way, what is your name?"

"Cathy," I said, deliberately not giving her my last name. I wondered if the name Cathy would set her to thinking, although it didn't seem to register.

At five on the dot, I was back on Marie's doorstep. This time she opened the screen and I saw her clearly. Not only did she have a disfiguring birthmark on her face, but her left arm was withered. She also wore the thickest glasses I'd ever seen— I was sure she must be legally blind. Nevertheless, as she ushered me into her kitchen, I noticed that she seemed to be looking at me in a questioning way.

"Do you know who I am?" I asked.

"I think I do," she said. "Let me see your arm."

I knew exactly what she meant, and my heart started pounding. She knew about the scar! I knew that she wanted to see the scar on my right arm, but to test her, I held out my left arm. Without blinking, she said, "No, the other arm."

She pulled me toward the window so she could get a good look at the scar in the light. She focused on the scar for only a second or two, and then she grabbed my shoulders, embraced me, and started wailing, "My baby's come home. My baby's come home! My baby."

I began to have the feeling that this woman who was holding me and weeping might well be my mother. I feared that all the talk about Bobbie Webb Jett from the state of Tennessee was just that—talk. Maybe Marie was my mother. Maybe that was why Charles Carr thought that Marie could tell me anything I wanted to know.

"I'm not your mother," she said flatly, as though she both read my mind and hated admitting the truth. "I'm Lillie's niece, Hank's first cousin. Bobbie Jett is your mother. But I raised you, I did. You . . . you were my baby."

She answered one question, but by answering it she raised scores of others. How did she know Bobbie Jett? What did she mean when she said she "raised" me? But I realized that this was not the moment to ask her these questions. Marie was visibly shaken. She called out for her husband, who was in the back of the house, and for her son, Louis, who lived next door. Louis, a man in his late thirties, came running over and, like Jimmy Cook had done, grabbed me and hugged me.

"My little sister's come home," Louis kept saying. "My little sister's come home."

For the next hour or so, Marie went on and on about how she had prayed for me every night of her life. She had worried and prayed for almost thirty years, yet she never thought she'd see me again. Now her little "Cathy baby" had come home.

Finally, Marie and Louis collected themselves, and she began to explain the part she had played in my life. I knew that I had lived with Mrs. Stone until I was two years old, and that I had been adopted by her shortly before her death. It turned out that Marie had lived with "Aunt Lillie," as she called her, at the boardinghouse for seventeen years, since the late 1930s. She'd come up to Montgomery from somewhere down in south Alabama —I forget which town—and helped out with the cooking and cleaning at the house. After I was born, Marie became, in a sense, my nursemaid, hence the reason she felt that she "raised" me.

For the first time, all the people I had heard or read about— especially Lillian Williams and Hank—were starting to become real to me. What's more, they might be my relatives. As with Charles Carr, I was surprised Marie had no doubt about who I was—no doubt at all. In a certain way, she seemed to know more about me—at least about the first two years of my life— than I knew about myself. I had no memory of Marie, but clearly she remembered me. I felt very detached, and, at certain moments, I found it hard to believe she was talking about my past, talking about me.

On that first day, Marie presented me with various things that were startling. She brought out a pair of little baby shoes that she said I had worn home from the hospital. She showed me a picture of myself when I was just a couple of weeks old, lying on a blanket on the grass. My "First Day Home" image had always been the one of a little girl, age three, sitting on an ottoman. As amazing as it must sound, I had never seen a photograph of myself as a newborn, and seeing it for the first time at age twenty-eight was incredibly disconcerting.

She also explained to me about the scar on my arm. She said I had been running in the yard with a glass in one hand and a photograph of Louis in the other. I fell and cut myself badly. Lillie had taken me to the hospital in a Yellow Cab, yet even after I had hurt myself, I refused to let go of the picture of "Bubber," which was what I called Louis. I had stayed in the hospital for a few days, and then had worn a cast on my arm for a few weeks.

Although I could not remember Marie herself, or recall some of the stories she told me, I could feel a few of the gaps in my consciousness filling up. My mother had told me that when I was very small I would point to a passing Yellow Cab and announce I had ridden in "that car." Apparently, I assumed that all Yellow Cabs were the same automobile, although Mother could never quite figure out what I was talking about. In a vague, hazy way, I had always remembered being held by my grandmother in that taxicab. She was the large, comforting woman with no waist.

Having Marie relate these stories to me was like looking through a lens of a camera, seeing a blurred image, and then, after a bit of fiddling, finally forcing the picture to come into focus. I had had memories of various incidents, thoughts that I had presumed were just dreams, and now I had a witness. Many of my memories were facts, but I had been too young to remember them clearly. What's more, having been adopted, I had never had anyone close to me who could confirm them.

Over the next several months, I met with Marie many times. She related several anecdotes about me as a baby, the sorts of stories most people hear from their parents or relations from birth.

Clearly, Marie had adored me, even though now, at times, she seemed a little standoffish to me.

She told me that when I was a toddler, my hair had been very straight and thin. Of course, this was hardly news to me, since Mother had always considered my "mousy blond" hair a cross to bear, Aunt Helen had tried to give me a number of unsuccessful home permanents, and even Jimmy Cook noticed that my hair didn't have "a wrinkle in it." Someone had suggested to Marie that if she cut off all my hair it would grow in thicker. So apparently, Marie had sat me down on a washtub and shaved my head. This story made me laugh—I could almost chronicle my life history based on various attempts people had made to do something creative with my hair.

At first, Marie spoke mainly about me as a baby and about her life in the boardinghouse with Aunt Lillie, but before long she began to talk about Hank. Clearly, she had been devoted to him, but her stories, for the most part, were detached and anecdotal. She never revealed anything intimate or personal. Hank, of course, was Montgomery's biggest celebrity, and because Marie was his cousin, she had been able to bask in some of the reflected glory. Yet, for me, her talk was exciting, and she made Hank come alive—walk off his legendary stage and into reality.

For example, Marie told a story about how one day Hank had wanted to walk downtown, but he didn't want to be recognized. He put on an overcoat, a regular man's hat, and dress shoes—no cowboy garb—and to make sure he was completely disguised, he slipped on a pair of sunglasses. He didn't get half a block down the street when the first person he passed said, "Hi, Hank, how ya' doin'."

Marie also told me that the name Yvonne, mentioned in lines from Hank's song "Jambalaya," was Hank's favorite female name, and that Lillie had called me Catherine Yvone because of Hank's affection for that name. (According to Marie, the name Catherine came from the main character in Emily Brontë's *Wuthering Heights*, which was Lillie's favorite book.) But Marie would reveal nothing more than that I was named for the "Sweet Yvonne" in Hank's famous song, and she refused to connect me directly with Hank Williams in any way.

Curiously, although she refused to tie me to Hank, she was able to tell me much about my mother, Bobbie Jett. Marie explained to me that Bobbie had come down to Montgomery from Nashville during the summer of 1952, to live with Lillian until I was born in January 1953. At that time, Lillie's boardinghouse was at 318 McDonough Street, and Mrs. Williams also owned the house next door at 320 McDonough. It was there, in one room, that Bobbie stayed until I was born.

Marie also confirmed the fact I had already discovered from my birth certificate—that Bobbie had another child. Apparently this child was a girl named Jo (according to Marie, little Jo was the person mentioned in the first line of the song "Jambalaya") and all of the family members and even the tenants took quite a shine to Jo, who was about three at the time of my birth.

Again, as with Hank, Marie was full of little anecdotes about Bobbie and Jo. She told me about taking Jo to a café to eat, where Jo insisted on playing "Hey, Good Lookin' " on the jukebox. Marie recalled that Jo always called Hank "Daddy Hank." Marie also described a trip that she, Bobbie, Jo, and Hank had taken to Nashville in the fall of 1952, and the fun they had all had in a hotel. According to Marie, there was no love lost between Hank and Bobbie—they enjoyed each other's company and they ran around together—but they weren't in love and never intended to marry.

Marie also told me that on the December morning Hank left on his trip to Canton, Ohio, he came into her room and gave her forty dollars. Marie said Hank told her that he feared the baby would be born before he returned, and he wanted Marie to keep an eye on Bobbie. The money was for Marie's taxicab fare to and from the hospital.

But then Hank died, and five days later I was born. According to Marie, Bobbie stayed in the hospital for a week, then early one morning returned to the boardinghouse, picked up Jo, and left town. Shortly after Bobbie left Montgomery, Lillian collected me from the hospital, brought me to 318 McDonough Street, and there I stayed until Lillie died two years later.

I took in all of Marie's stories, and I didn't doubt that she was telling the truth. The problem was I couldn't seem to find the connecting thread—it was as though she was telling me the truth, but not the "whole truth." On a few occasions I got up the nerve to ask Marie the hard question, that doubtful issue that clung in my craw, the question that had haunted me for years and would trouble me for years to come:

"So am I Hank Williams' child?" I asked once after she had wondered why I didn't refer to Hank as "Daddy Hank" as Jo had done.

"Honey, I wasn't at the havin' and I wasn't at the gettin'," she answered. "So, I just can't say."

But I couldn't help wondering why Bobbie, a woman who just "enjoyed somebody's company," would come and stay with Hank's mother during her pregnancy. Or more startling, why, after giving birth, she would leave her baby with her "friend's" mother. But Marie dodged the issue completely.

Marie was much more direct about her own personal feelings toward me. She told me how painful it had been for her when I was taken away shortly after Lillie's death in 1955. I could see that it must have been traumatic for her—first she lost Lillie, with whom she had lived for seventeen years, and then she lost me.

She said that a few days after Lillian died, Irene Williams Smith, Hank's sister, came to Montgomery and quickly made arrangements to turn me over to the welfare department to be adopted out again. When the woman from the welfare department came to take me away, Marie said I screamed hysterically. I knew this was true because Mama Cook had said that I cried for two or three days after I arrived in Pine Level.

After I had known Marie for several months, she also told me one last fact that I found difficult to bear. She said that shortly after I was taken away, she managed to track down Bobbie Jett in California. She called Bobbie and told her that Lillie had died and that I had been taken away, but, according to Marie, Bobbie said that she was married again, that her husband knew nothing about me, and that she could do nothing.

———

Despite Marie's joy at seeing me and her cries that I was her "baby," somehow, I felt as though she didn't trust me completely, and I didn't understand quite why. We would have pleasant visits, and she would begin to tell me tales about the Williamses—or even about the Jetts—and then suddenly she would clam up. On one hand, she was acting the way I had always dreamed a Williams would behave—as though I was wanted and loved—yet, on the other hand, just below the surface, I sensed an icy chill.

I felt her coldness most when she mentioned Audrey Williams, Hank's first wife, and her son, Hank Jr. Marie had liked Audrey and she swore that Audrey and Hank Jr. had always treated her well. But I wondered about this. I figured Hank Jr. couldn't be too happy to know his daddy might well have had another child. I reasoned that Marie must have told him that I'd been around to visit, and I could see how a long-lost little sister just might "set him off." Also I wondered just how Audrey and Hank Jr. had treated Marie well. I didn't see a big house, a swimming pool, or a couple of color television sets over there on Pickett Street.

Marie was confusing to me. She hedged her bets with regard to me from the moment I walked into her kitchen. In some ways she clarified many questions I had, yet in other ways she muddied the waters. And I didn't know why.

6
BOBBIE

After making contact with Marie Harvell, I realized that although I was collecting many pieces of my life's puzzle, I obviously had many more pieces to find. My discussions with Miss Pittman and Miss Austin at Pensions and Security had been basically unproductive, and as the months passed, I began to get angry and impatient. I thought, I'm a grown woman, twenty-eight years old. I want to find out once and for all who in God's name my father really was. I want to make contact with my mother, and I am ready to accept the consequences.

I told Miss Pittman and Miss Austin how I felt, and they eventually came to realize how desperately I wanted to find Bobbie Jett. Only Bobbie could answer my questions, starting with confirming whether or not Hank Williams really was my father. Of course, I also wanted to know why she had abandoned me. When I had first heard about Bobbie, I was unable to cope with her rejection of me; I couldn't even think about it. Now I realized I could take her explanation—and even her rejection—if only she would tell me the truth.

Finally, Miss Pittman and the Department of Pensions and Security agreed to try to contact someone in the Jett family. They told me they would write some letters to the Tennessee authorities. If they could locate my natural mother and she agreed, they would set up a meeting. Miss Pittman refused to tell me precisely how they were going to find Bobbie—she would not even confirm that Bobbie originally came from Nashville, a fact I had culled from Marie Harvell. She felt strongly that they had to follow official policy and procedures.

Actually, Marie had been able to tell me quite a lot about Bobbie. She had told me that Bobbie sometimes went by the name of Bobbie Hale. Marie also said that my sister's name was Jo Hale, and that she suspected that both Bobbie and Jo still lived in California, where she had last found them. One day late in the summer of 1981, when I was visiting Marie, she mentioned the name Willard Jett, who, she explained, was Bobbie's uncle and lived in Nashville. She told me that when she had tried to find Bobbie in 1955 after I had been turned over to the welfare department, she had started her search by telephoning Willard. I asked her if she had his number, but, of course, more than twenty-five years had passed, and Marie did not know whether or not Willard was even alive, let alone have his number.

I spent the evening with my friend Gene Westbrook. By now, I also felt freer about discussing my potential "natural parents" with friends, and I told her about Jo Hale and Willard Jett. We decided it might be interesting to try to track down my sister, so we started making calls. We called every major city in California and asked for the number of anyone named Jo Hale, Josephine Hale, or J. Hale. At one point, we found somebody who had a sister named Jo Hale, but after another call, we discovered this was not the right Jo Hale.

We also tried calling Nashville information to see if they had a listing for a Willard Jett, but the closest name they could find was Richard W. Jett. So we tried this number, but got no answer.

About eleven o'clock, I went home, but I was so wired up I couldn't sleep. Michael was off on a trip, so I sat alone for a while and had a couple of stiff drinks. The liquor didn't make me sleepy, but it loosened me up a little bit and I decided to try calling Richard W. Jett one more time.

By now I was pretty loaded, but despite my inebriated state, I remembered my game plan. I had concluded that I couldn't just state, flat out, that I was Bobbie Jett's daughter. The Jetts might not even know Bobbie had had another child—and, in any case, they might not be too thrilled to hear from me after almost thirty years.

The phone rang a couple of times and then, to my surprise, a man answered, a sort of gruff-sounding old fellow. Part of my game plan was to give him a fake name, but I can't even remember what I said at first, except that I tried to sound casual and friendly.

"I'm an old friend of Bobbie's," I said, "and I haven't heard from her in a couple of years and I just wondered if you could tell me how I could get in touch with her?"

There was a long silence on the other end of the phone, and I heard what sounded like someone picking up an extension.

"Who is this?" Willard finally said.

"Well, like I told you, I'm an old friend of Bobbie's."

He didn't buy my story for a second. Moreover, I could tell he was angry. Again, there was a long silence. Then he said, still in that gruff voice, "Listen, girl, I know who you are. You're Cathy from Alabama, and you can stop lookin' for your mother right now. She's dead."

I couldn't believe it.

"You're lying!" I yelled at him. "I don't believe you. I know you're lying. She just told you to tell me she's dead if I ever came looking. I know what you're doing."

"Listen, I'm not lying!" he said. "Hell, I know she's dead. I paid for her goddamn funeral."

I was in shock and only half listening. The woman on the extension identified herself as Willard's wife, Patsy. She mentioned something about California and other children. Bobbie was dead! She had given me away and had kept her other children! I couldn't handle it.

I couldn't believe how cruel they sounded, and I became

absolutely hysterical. I slammed the phone down and lay on the floor crying so hard that I was sick. I was in a state of complete emotional collapse.

It had never crossed my mind that Bobbie might be dead. I had fantasized about our meeting over and over in my mind a million times. I had created and discarded a number of scenarios: from pretending that my car had broken down in front of her house and asking her for help to showing up at her door selling Hank Williams albums and shocking her into a response. In any case, most of my fantasies ended with a warm, loving reunion.

Now I would never know the truth. My father was dead, and as fate would have it, so was my mother. Nobody else was "at the havin' and the gettin'," as Marie had put it, and I had never felt so alone.

By the next morning, I began to feel guilty for upsetting those two elderly people up in Nashville. They must have thought I was crazy to have called in the middle of the night—I realized in the morning that I had placed the call well after midnight— and then to have gotten so hysterical that I hung up on them. I decided the decent thing to do was to call back and apologize.

Willard was almost as gruff as he had been the night before, but I could tell this time he was trying to be a bit more gentle with me, and that, at some level, he understood my position. He also told me that my call hadn't been quite as shocking as I had thought. I wondered whether or not he had received a letter from Miss Pittman or a call from the Tennessee Pensions and Security office, but when I asked him, he said no.

His wife, Patsy Jett, also got on the phone again, and she was particularly understanding. She told me that she was coming down to Montgomery in a couple of weeks to visit some friends of hers, and she wanted us to meet. Patsy's warmth made me feel a whole lot better, and, what's more, I had the sense that maybe she could tell me something about my natural parents.

A couple of days after I talked to Willard and Patsy Jett, I stopped over at Pensions and Security to tell Miss Pittman and Miss Austin what I had discovered. The moment I sat down in the office, I could tell they were getting a bit impatient with me.

They said, "Cathy, as we've told you, we've written to the Tennessee authorities on your behalf."

By now, of course, I was feeling proud of myself, and I knew they were going to be amazed that I'd tracked the Jetts down on my own.

"Do you mean, you wrote to Richard W. Jett in Nashville, Tennessee?" I asked, watching the surprised look cross their faces. "Well I've talked to him myself," I went on. "So I doubt if he'll be calling back." Then I explained to them all about my midnight call.

I told them how upset I was to learn that Bobbie Jett had died. Miss Pittman, as usual, sympathized with my frustration. She seemed glad that I'd made the contact with Willard and Patsy, and asked me to keep them informed about my progress with them.

We also discussed my fears about hurting my parents by telling them that I was searching for my natural relations. After Mother's response to my telling her about Mama Cook, I had stopped confiding in both my parents. I knew Mother couldn't handle it at all, and I didn't want to put Daddy in an untenable position. I had not told them about finding Marie Harvell, and I didn't plan on telling them anything about the Jett family either. Miss Pittman and Miss Austin agreed that this was the best route to follow — at least for the moment.

After I made the contact with the Jetts in August 1981, I needed to sit back and think about all the connections I had made in the past nine months. I had reestablished a relationship with Mama Cook and her family, I had met Marie and believed that we had a sort of friendship, and now I had found an important member of the Jett family and learned that my natural mother was dead. It was my understanding that most adoptees, when they are given an address or number of a natural family member, often become reluctant to make that first important call. However, once I was somewhat liberated by my adoptive father's interest and support, I just pushed ahead as fast as I could. I realized that my passion to find my roots must have been burning for years, but, particularly because of my adoptive mother's problems, I had just not felt free to even examine my feelings.

Now that I had uncovered some information about both the Williamses and the Jetts, I was intrigued. What I found most interesting was that when I would say, "I think I might be Hank Williams' child," nobody ever said, "What the hell are you talkin' about, girl?" Instead, they would say, "Oh yea . . . Cathy," as Charles Carr had done, or embrace me and say, "My baby's come home," like Marie. I had not even had to introduce myself to Willard Jett—I didn't even have to state, "I think Bobbie Jett might be my mother"—he just blurted out what was clearly the truth: "I know who you are. You're Cathy from Alabama."

At the same time, I was beginning to realize that the puzzle of my life was perhaps much larger and more complicated than I had imagined. Every heartfelt or honest response to me was accompanied by an evasion of some sort. Everyone who had known of me would dodge my deepest questions with simple evasions, like Marie's "I wasn't at the havin'," or with rage like Willard, or even with some sort of legal mumbo jumbo like Drayton Hamilton, who suggested that a conversation with me might, in fact, be unethical.

They had all taken one look at me—at that gash on my arm or the blue in my eye—and none of them said, "Prove it, girl. Show me you're Cathy." They all knew who "Cathy" was; they all accepted that I was that self-same Cathy. Over the last few months, I had gathered more pieces to my life's puzzle, but I was beginning to think it was rather ironic that although they all knew who Cathy was, I still did not.

Patsy Jett came to Montgomery the following Friday, and as she had promised, she called me and asked me to meet her at her friend Barbara Meyer's house. I was very nervous. Even though Patsy wasn't a blood relative, she was the closest I had come to my mother and her family, and perhaps the closest I would ever get. I desperately wanted to make a good impression, and hoped that our meeting would lead to others.

I knew that Willard was Bobbie's uncle and therefore prob-

My father:
Hank Williams

My mother:
Bobbie Jett

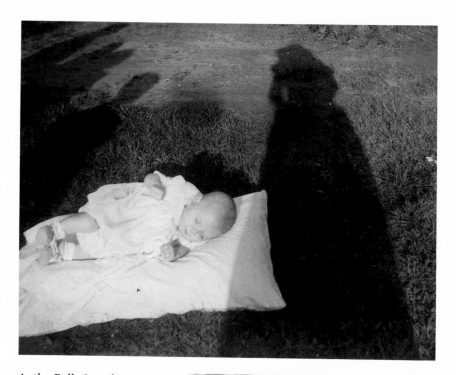

Antha Belle Jett, three months old, in a photograph I didn't see until I was twenty-eight. I've always wondered who cast those looming shadows.

Louis Harvell (center) and me, one year old, playing in the backyard of my grandmother's boardinghouse in Montgomery.

Here I am, about two years old, sitting on the stoop of my grandmother's boardinghouse wearing a cowboy hat and strummin' my guitar.

I look very contented in the arms of my grandmother, Lillian Williams Stone, and, apparently, I was.

Marie Harvell and me in early 1955, shortly before my grandmother's death and my removal by the welfare department.

A photograph that Mama Cook had taken of me during the year I lived with them, 1955–56.

The "First Nite Home" photograph, taken the evening I came home with the Deuprees, February 21, 1956.

The first "formal" portrait Mother had taken of me, spring 1956, shortly after I arrived. Apparently, Aunt Helen had already taken a pass at my hair.

*My cousin
Stanley Foun-
tain and me on
my new bike,
summer 1956.
I loved that
cowgirl outfit.*

*Mother and me on our
front steps in Mobile in
late 1956. I always
thought she was more
glamorous than Elizabeth
Taylor, while I was a
more casual type.*

Aunt Helen, Mother, me, and Stanley Boy at the Roosevelt Hotel in New Orleans, 1958.

Here I am, circa 1961, at the Mobile State Fair, in yet another cowgirl outfit. The mink-collared sweater, coupled with the cowboy hat and holster, is vintage Louise Deupree.

Sally Rogers, me, Mother, Aunt Betty Rogers, and Lee Rogers at the Roosevelt
Hotel in New Orleans, summer 1961. Later that evening, Mother "lost"
Aunt Betty on Bourbon Street.

Wayne Deupree,
circa 1980. This is
the only photograph
I have of Daddy.

ably a man in his late sixties. I was expecting Patsy to be a woman about the same age, and was surprised to discover, when I arrived at Mrs. Meyer's home, that Patsy Jett was an energetic woman in her mid-fifties. It turned out that not only was she eighteen years younger than Willard, but she was six years younger than Bobbie. We had a friendly drink at Mrs. Meyer's house, and by the time Patsy and I left for dinner at a new Chinese restaurant in south Montgomery, I was feeling much more comfortable.

We talked for several hours over dinner, and Patsy filled me in on the "family" in Nashville. She told me that her own family ran a well-known restaurant in Nashville called Kelly's and, like the Jetts, had been Nashville natives for many years. She and Willard had gone out together for years before she married him in 1954, and during that time—especially in the late forties and early fifties—she had gotten to know Bobbie fairly well.

She described Bobbie as a beautiful blond woman about five feet two inches tall, and built very much like me—which was also something Marie had said. I asked Patsy to explain all the Jett family relationships, and as it turned out, they were fairly complicated. Bobbie's mother's name was Antha Pauline Jett, one of five children of Ocie Belle Jett. Antha Pauline's brother, Willard, was born in 1910, and thus he was only twelve years older than Bobbie, who was born on October 5, 1922. Willard was the acknowledged patriarch of the family.

Patsy also explained that Bobbie's upbringing had been rather unusual. Antha Pauline, Bobbie's mother, had married a man known as "Miller" sometime in the early 1920s. In the mid-twenties, shortly after Bobbie was born (and Antha's marriage had fallen apart), Antha went to nursing school in Cincinnati, Ohio, then joined the army and moved to California, leaving Bobbie with her grandmother, Ocie Belle. Ocie had then adopted Bobbie and changed her name from Miller to Jett. Thus Willard became Bobbie's older brother as well as her uncle, and since he was living at home throughout Bobbie's childhood, he functioned much like a father.

This story had an astonishing déjà vu aspect to it. Bobbie's mother had run off to California, leaving her baby to be brought up by her grandmother, precisely as Bobbie had done with me. I, too, had been adopted by my grandmother.

Patsy said that during World War II, Bobbie had worked as a secretary at the Selective Service Agency in Nashville, and then shortly after the war, she had gone out to California to live with her mother, Antha Pauline. While she was in California, she supposedly had married an actor who was Jo's father, but the marriage had been a bust. Bobbie came back to Nashville in 1949 with Jo. In the late 1940s, Ocie Belle had a stroke, and Willard thought Bobbie would be useful at home. So Bobbie and "Jo-Jo" moved in with Willard and Ocie, Bobbie took care of Ocie, little Jo, and the house, and Willard took care of the whole passel of them.

According to Patsy, things didn't work out quite as smoothly as Willard might have liked. Bobbie was still young, beautiful, and star-struck. She began dating a bit, often guys from the Grand Ole Opry, which was, of course, the biggest show in town. She liked to party, and at times Willard became very upset because of the late hours she sometimes kept. Nevertheless, over the next two or three years, they created a fairly normal family life. Patsy glossed right over my birth, but explained that in 1953, Bobbie went back out to California and married again.

By the time we finished dinner, Patsy had filled me in with more information than I had hoped for. Toward the end of dinner, she passed me a photograph. I was afraid to look at it because I feared it was a picture of Bobbie, and the idea of finally looking into the face of my mother was almost more than I could bear right then. But I looked down at the photo and saw that it was a picture of Bobbie's gravestone. On it was engraved: "Bobbie Jett Tippins; Born: October 5, 1922; Died: April 17, 1974.

"Go ahead and cry if you want to, honey," Patsy said after she handed me the picture. She knew I would be upset, but she and Willard felt it was important for me to see that Bobbie had truly died. I was afraid that if I started to cry, I would break down completely, so I held back my tears. I still did not want to accept that fact that my mother was dead.

After Patsy showed me the photograph of Bobbie's grave,

she expanded on the one other thing that had troubled me, a fact that she had alluded to on the first night I had telephoned. Shortly after Bobbie returned to California, she began living with a guy named John Tippins. With John Tippins, she had had six other children— three girls; Linda, Melissa, and a baby girl who died at birth; and three boys; John, Richard, and Ronnie.

This information was incredibly painful to me. I simply could not understand or accept why Bobbie had kept Jo and all these other children—and not kept me. More than anything I was being forced to accept—even Bobbie's death—this fact was the most difficult. At the same time, after having been an "only child" all my life, I was intrigued with the idea that I was actually one of eight! In fact, I was one of nine if you counted Hank Williams, Jr.

All of this information made me wonder about Bobbie. Apparently she had been a fun-loving, good-looking young woman who liked to have a good time. But it seemed to me that she had not been too lucky with her men. I didn't know—and I didn't ask—what happened between her and Jo's father, except that she was left with a child and not the father. If she had been stranded or rejected by Jo's father—and then by Hank—I wanted to believe that she might have had a good reason for wanting to give me away. But she had had six more children by a man named Tippins. She seemed to have been trying to make it right— whatever "it" was. I wondered if she ever succeeded.

After dinner, Patsy asked me to come back to her friend Barbara's house. She wanted to call Jo, who, as it turned out, did live in southern California. Patsy filled me in a bit on Jo's life as well. Jo had gotten married when she was sixteen and had a child, a daughter named Michelle. After Bobbie died, when Jo was about twenty-six, Jo had taken over the rearing of all her younger siblings, the youngest, Melissa, being only about twelve or thirteen years old at the time. A few years later, Jo divorced her first husband and married a man named Bob Tanguay.

Patsy and I returned to Barbara's house, and Patsy placed a call to Jo. The moment I heard Jo's voice—she has a deep, friendly way of speaking—I just shook my head in disbelief. Only a few months before, I hadn't known I had a sister, and now I was talking to her on the phone. Apparently, Willard and Patsy had told Jo about me, because she didn't seem upset or disturbed. She welcomed me like a long-lost sister—which, of course, is precisely what I was. Patsy got on the extension, and I found it difficult to ask Jo questions about our mother in this situation. I asked her to give me her number and told her I would call her back. I left Patsy and the Meyers soon after we got off the phone, and when I got back to my own house, I called Jo.

Jo told me many of the same facts about Bobbie and the Jett family that Patsy had just finished relating over dinner. Patsy, however, had colored her story in a slightly different way. Patsy had remembered Bobbie as being basically irresponsible, especially during her years in Nashville in the early fifties. Patsy believed that Bobbie had frequently neglected Jo. But Jo, on the other hand, raved about what a warm and wonderful person our mother had been. She believed Bobbie had been a marvelous mother. I found these varied viewpoints a bit disconcerting. I didn't know who to believe, so I decided I would simply take in all the information and try to figure it all out later when I had more facts. When Jo and I concluded our phone call that night we decided that I would come out to California as soon as possible and meet all my brothers and sisters.

I must have passed muster with Patsy, too, because she called me the next morning and we got together again on Sunday for brunch before she returned to Nashville. She also invited me to come up to visit in Nashville soon. She had made it clear that Willard was a central figure in the Jett family, and he thought it was important for us to meet.

But for me, California came first. I now knew for certain that I would never know my mother, but I'd discovered the next best thing—my sisters and brothers—and I wanted to meet them immediately—face-to-face.

I was well aware that meeting my natural siblings could be traumatic for me, and I needed to know what to do—not only about the Jetts, but about my adoptive family. I did have a "support system." Of course, my husband, Michael, knew all about my search, my acquaintance with Marie, and now my emerging relationship with the Jetts. He was behind me 100-percent but, in fairness to Michael, I think I was hell-bent on exploring my roots by myself and he respected my feelings. I also had confided in my Aunt Helen. I had told her everything and I relied on her to provide me with an honest appraisal of my mother's physical and emotional health. She supported my plans for meeting the Jetts, but she believed that Mother would not take the news well.

I had not told my parents about Marie Harvell, nor had I told them about finding Willard and Patsy Jett. Now that I had decided to go to California, I had to think seriously about their feelings in this regard. I would have welcomed their support— it would have made what I suspected might be an emotionally difficult encounter much easier—but if Mother fell apart after my reunion with the Cook family, she could disintegrate completely if she knew I was becoming friendly with the Jetts.

Both Miss Pittman and Miss Austin at Pensions and Security agreed with me. They recommended that I not tell either Daddy or Mother about my trip—at least at this time. Miss Pittman not only agreed that Mother would have great difficulty accepting my relationship with my natural family, but she confirmed that my decision to meet my natural family should be my own decision, and no one else's.

I decided that I wanted to take advantage of the trip to spend some time with Jewel Cook, who lived in Chicago. Of course, I had seen her the previous January at her parents' fiftieth wedding anniversary, but I had not been able to talk to her at length. Over the past nine months, the Cooks had become like a second family to me, and I longed to feel as close to Jewel as I did to her parents and her brother, Jimmy. As it turned out, I was able to schedule a flight that connected through Chicago. In retrospect, I believe I considered Jewel to be as much a "sister" to me as Jo. Since I felt secure in the Cooks' love, I suspect I needed a good dose of surefire "sisterly" affection from Jewel before I faced the Tippins kids, who might not feel quite so warmhearted toward me.

I spent four days with Jewel and her family, and they were wonderful. In addition to Jewel, I had also met her husband,

Tom, at the anniversary party in Pine Level. Now we had our own little reunion, and, as I had hoped, they welcomed me as part of their family. I had never been to Chicago, so they showed me the sights—the Sears Tower, where Tom worked; Michigan Avenue; and a number of their favorite restaurants. We even took a short day trip to a historic village in Wisconsin.

The days sped by, and although I was still nervous about meeting the Tippins kids, I felt more secure and confident, thanks to the affection Jewel and her family showed me. As Jewel was driving me to the airport for the flight to California, I mentioned the photograph of her that Mother had kept, and I reminded her of the loving inscription she had written on the back. I thanked her for it, and told her how important it had been to me, even as a child, to know that somebody "out there" had loved me.

She said that of course she had loved me. What's more, she had also kept something for me for twenty-five years, and she wanted to give it back to me now. She pulled out a little garnet baby ring in a sterling silver setting. She said that I had been wearing the ring when I came to live with them, and when I left, she had taken it off my finger. At that time, she had feared that she would never see me again, and had wanted to have a token to remember me by. Since we were now reunited, she wanted to give it back.

I was incredibly touched. I was also fascinated by the ring itself. Mama Cook had mentioned many times that she had been impressed by the numbers of little outfits and toys I had arrived with, and she felt certain that I had been loved very much. This ring was concrete proof and probably the only memento of my grandmother—aside from the two thousand dollars—I would ever have.

After the warm reception I'd received from Jewel's family—and particularly after Jewel gave me the ring—I got on the plane to Los Angeles feeling comfortable and excited. Finally I was going to see my family—my real brothers and sisters. But as the miles and the hours passed, and we got closer and closer to L.A., my nervousness returned. The man sitting next to me asked me if I wanted a beer, and I said "Sure," thinking a drink would calm me down. The stewardess brought it quickly but told me that since we were due to land soon, this was the only drink I could have.

I downed that beer pretty fast, and realized that I needed another drink to fortify me for this meeting. I walked back to the bay and asked the stewardesses if I could possibly get another, but they insisted that they were not serving anymore.

"Listen," I said, "if you all knew what I was getting ready to go through, you might relax that rule a bit." Then I explained that I was adopted, and although my natural mother had died, I was about to meet my half sisters and half brothers, whom I had never met before in my life.

Without another word, they started pouring me drinks. I had been too nervous to eat, so I drank a tall Jack Daniels straight on an empty stomach.

As we were getting off the plane, all of the stewardesses wished me luck. One handed me a bottle of champagne, compliments of American Airlines. Another stewardess asked me if she could walk with me and witness the reunion. By the time we entered the terminal, the entire crew was walking behind me, and I felt like an actress or politician forging through with my entire entourage. By now, I was flying high—both on adrenaline and alcohol. I started waving the bottle of champagne around yelling, "Fly American."

Patsy had shown me pictures of my sisters Jo, Linda, and Melissa, and when we got inside, I looked over and immediately recognized them. Jo, particularly, is a very striking-looking woman with bright blond hair and very dramatic makeup. Apparently, they recognized me, too, because they immediately came over and put their arms around me and laughed at all the fuss.

This meeting was decidedly different from my first encounter with Marie Harvell. Unlike Marie, none of my sisters had known anything about me. I had played no part in their lives. Out of the corner of my eye, I could see them sort of scrutinizing me, and later they would tell me that they recognized me because I looked so much like Bobbie. But they were as unnerved and disoriented by this reunion as I was, so we just all played it by ear.

Norwalk, California, the suburb where Jo lived, was about an hour's drive from the airport, so by the time we got to Jo's house, I was in bad shape, in part due to the liquor, but more because of this bizarre and unnerving situation. Although I wasn't aware of it at the time—nor could I have begun to define my feelings—in retrospect, I believe I felt incredibly lonely and frightened. Despite the girls' friendliness, for some inexplicable reason, I sensed a certain kind of odd rejection. And by the end of the evening, I was outraged.

When we got to Jo's place, which was a trim little house in a middle-class neighborhood, a huge party was going on. Jo and her husband had invited scores of their friends over to meet their new sister. I realized that they wanted me to feel welcome, but I just couldn't handle greeting all these strangers. I walked on through the crowd, trying to smile, and went into a bedroom and closed the door.

There were bunk beds in the room, so I lay on the bottom bunk and kind of passed out from physical and emotional exhaustion. I just had to shut down. Every now and then I would open my eyes to find somebody was looking at me, or sitting on the floor waiting for me to wake up. Finally, I began to get a grip on myself—or, at least, I realized that I was not going to be able to rest unless I made some sort of friendly gesture.

By this time, Jo was standing in the room. She started to talk about "our mother," and the fact that she wanted me to meet a woman named Janis who was "our mother's" best friend.

"Janis wrote this letter for you telling you all about our mother," Jo said. "She wrote it first for Michelle, my daughter, because she was never going to know her grandmother, but Janis transcribed it over to you."

I sat on the edge of the bed in my rumpled clothes, feeling exhausted and unnerved. Jo was holding Janis's letter in her hand, and once again, as she had done to me on the telephone, she went into raptures about what a wonderful mother Bobbie had been. I looked at Jo, and then at each of the others, all of whom were by then standing there, looking at me, and beaming with pride.

Suddenly, all the rage I had built up toward Bobbie Jett just overpowered me. I had pined for her, I had searched for her, I had traveled all this way to find her. In part, I guess I had not totally accepted that she was dead; as irrational as it sounds, I expected Bobbie to be waiting there for me. And, by God, she wasn't there. She had rejected me at birth, and I felt she was refusing me—even now. The smiles on the faces of her other children made me furious. Rationally, I knew they were trying to be kind, but I experienced their smiles as taunts. Bobbie had kept them—but she had not kept me.

I grabbed Janis's letter out of Jo's hands, ripped it into pieces, and threw it in her face.

Of course, this made Jo steaming mad.

"Who in the hell are you to come to California and put my mother down after she raised all these kids," she yelled. "You just can't do that!"

The next thing I knew, she hauled me up off the bed and shoved me into a nearby bathroom. She was screaming at me, and pushing me so hard that my head banged against the wall. In self-defense, I began pushing her back, and before I knew what was happening, we were in a knock-down-drag-out fight. At one point, I even tried to climb out the bathroom window to escape, but she yanked me back inside.

Suddenly, the door burst open and Jo's husband, Bob, came in and tried to pull us apart. He dragged us back into the bedroom and pushed Jo down on the bed and sat on top of her. For a moment, I calmed down and told him he could let her get up, but the minute he let go of Jo, I jumped on her again and resumed fighting. Bob tried to separate us again, but finally we both gave up and just stood in the middle of the room trembling.

For years, I had fantasized about meeting my mother face-to-face. I'd dreamed about a calm talk, warm hugs, and tears of reconciliation. I had mentally written scores of scripts, and had wondered exactly how such a meeting would have gone. But now I knew exactly what would have happened: I would have beaten her half to death.

By now, Jo's friends had decided that this wasn't quite the homecoming everybody had expected it to be, and most of them had gone home. I had a splitting headache; but more, I felt like

AIN'T NOTHIN' AS SWEET AS MY BABY

I was falling apart, physically and emotionally. I told Jo that I needed to go for a walk, so I just walked out the door and circled around the block for an hour or so.

So many thoughts were streaming through my head. I could see that my natural siblings and I came from two different walks of life. With my adoptive parents, although we weren't rich or socially prominent, I had enjoyed a much more privileged life than the Tippins kids had known. I'd had a college education, trips to Europe, and all sorts of material things that I could see they had not been able to afford. I was a part of their mother, but I had been raised in a very different way.

I wondered whether or not Jo and the other girls—and probably the boys, too, although I had barely spoken to them— didn't observe these differences and harbor some hurt feelings too. I could see that they had gone to great trouble to make me feel welcome, but they were as confused as I was about what we should do. I could see that my arrival was almost as difficult for them as it was for me. Still, I couldn't get over my jealousy and hurt. They had known Bobbie. She had loved them. She had kept them. And she had left me behind.

When I got back from my walk, they had all gone to bed, so I just sat down in a chair and fell asleep. When I woke up in the morning, I noticed instantly that someone had put a blanket over me. This was such a small gesture, but I recognized the kindness. Then I noticed that the little ring that Jewel had given to me was gone, and once again I felt distraught.

I got up and knocked on Jo's bedroom door. When she opened it I said, "I'm going to go back to Alabama now. I just want you to know that I'm packing."

"No you're not!" Jo said, with great force. "You've come this far, and we're going to give this thing a chance."

I was too worn out to argue with her, so I went back to the room with the bunk beds and fell asleep for a couple more hours. It was close to noon by the time I got up again. I went out to the kitchen and found Linda and Melissa sitting at the kitchen table trying to tape the letter I'd torn up back together again. I thought of Jo's words: "We're going to give this thing a chance," and I knew she was right. I asked the girls if I could see the letter.

As Jo had said, it had originally been written to Jo's daughter, Michelle, but Janis had rewritten it, addressing it to me. She talked about how much Bobbie loved her children, her husband, and her friends, and how generous she was with everyone. I was struck by a sentence she wrote concerning Bobbie's relationship with John Tippins. She said: "Sometimes they had funny ways of showing their love for each other." I wondered if in some sort of mystical way, this might express Bobbie's feelings toward me—God knows, she had "funny ways of showing her love" for me, too. Janis ended that part by saying: ". . . but it [the love] was always there and everyone knew it." Perhaps that was true for Bobbie and me, too.

Janis ended her letter by saying: "She may not be there with you, but she's watching over you from heaven—that's the kind of person she was. Her love will follow you all the days of your life and she will touch your life from God's heaven."

I desperately wanted to believe that Bobbie was watching over me and that her love would touch me, but as I stood in the kitchen reading this letter, I didn't feel much love coming my way. Suddenly the telephone rang. It was my Aunt Helen, calling from Mobile. (Michael had telephoned the night before, but I was incoherent. He had then called Aunt Helen and she was checking up on me.) I told her everything was fine, and I asked her to call Michael and assure him that I'd arrived safely and would call him myself soon. I think it helped that the girls heard me talking in a loving way to Aunt Helen. So far, they'd only seen me high on Jack Daniels and in a screaming rage with Jo. God, I thought, no wonder they are a little cool.

When I hung up the telephone, I thanked them for letting me read the letter, especially after the fight. I told them how difficult coming to see them was for me. At that point they opened up and began telling me how much I looked like Bobbie, and that my appearance had been disturbing to them. As we were talking, Jo came in, and the four of us spent the rest of the day talking in that kitchen.

Oddly enough, Bobbie had mentioned me obliquely to both Linda and Melissa. Linda remembered that Bobbie had told her that she had wanted to name her Cathy, but that John Tippins, her father, had said, "No, let's call her Linda." Linda had never forgotten this remark, and was surprised when she found out that Bobbie already had a daughter named Cathy.

Melissa had a very touching memory, one that meant a great deal to me. When she was about six years old, she had walked into the kitchen one day and found Bobbie crying. Of course, she asked why, and Bobbie had said: "We have to sing 'Happy Birthday.' There's a girl named Cathy in Alabama and she is sweet sixteen today." Then the two of them stood in the kitchen and sang to me.

Bobbie's behavior made no sense to Melissa, who, at age six, naturally thought birthdays were supposed to be happy events. Bobbie never mentioned anyone named Cathy again, and Melissa forgot about the incident until I showed up. Like most adopted children, I would always wonder on my birthday if my mother was thinking of me. Now I knew that she had been.

Like the girls, the boys knew nothing about me, and I found it more difficult to relate to them. In 1981, Richard was in the Navy, and was not home at the time I came to visit. Only John and Ronnie were in California, and although I saw them a couple of times during my stay and liked them very much, I didn't connect as emotionally with them as I had with the three girls.

By the end of the day, Jo, Linda, Melissa, and I were hugging and laughing—and crying—and starting to make friends. Meeting them that first night had been one of the most emotionally upsetting experiences in my life, but after just a few hours, we were getting closer. Late that afternoon, somebody found my baby ring, and I thought that was a positive sign. Maybe Bobbie was watching from God's heaven.

I ended up staying at Jo's house for ten days. Over that week and a half, I met several of Bobbie's friends, including Janis, who had written the letter. Like Janis, all of Bobbie's friends thought the world of her—that she was a sunny, warm person and a special friend. One woman gave me a drinking mug that Bobbie always used. Several of her friends told me that when she was a little tipsy, she'd start talking about Hank Williams and how she had known him years ago in Nashville. They had always thought that maybe she was just talking in her beer, and never really questioned her closely about it. And Bobbie, apparently, never elaborated on her friendship with Hank.

Shortly after I'd arrived, Jo asked me if I wanted to visit Bobbie's mother, our grandmother Antha Pauline, who now lived in a nursing home nearby. I told Jo I absolutely had to see her, even if she didn't know who I was. Not only was I her granddaughter, I was her namesake: Bobbie had named me Antha.

Linda and Melissa drove me over to the nursing home, and when we got to Antha Pauline's room, we found her sitting on the edge of her bed, staring straight ahead with a fixed gaze, smoking a cigarette. I explained to her that I was one of Bobbie's girls, and that although my name was now Cathy, I had originally been named—by Bobbie—for her. Still, she didn't say anything; in fact, she would not even look at me. Finally I said, "Why do you think Bobbie named me Antha?"; she answered simply: "Well, I guess she wanted to." I suspected—especially since I knew that Antha had left Bobbie to be raised and adopted by her mother, Ocie—that Antha had a story to tell, but clearly she was not going to tell me now.

We sat with her quietly for a few minutes. Linda and Melissa made small talk—and she was quite responsive toward them—but I couldn't think of anything else to say. As we got up to leave, I kissed her on the cheek and told her how happy I was to finally meet her. Still, she refused to look at me.

As we walked through the parking lot to our car, I turned to take one last look at her window. I could see that she'd gotten up and was pulling the curtains open. I waved, and although she stared right at me, she did not wave back or smile. She just closed the curtain.

Later that day, Linda and Melissa took me out to Bobbie's grave. As I laid flowers on her gravestone, I felt like crying. Many times over the past ten days I had experienced a host of feelings toward Bobbie: rejection, rage, disappointment, and even love. As I prepared to leave, I realized that I, quite literally, missed her terribly. The feeling was similar to grieving for someone after they have died—but it went beyond grief. I had missed her completely—"missed her" in the sense of arriving at her home too late. She was my mother, and yet we had bypassed each other completely. And there was something terrible about that loss. Now that I was acquainted with her other daughters, and saw what nice women they were, I yearned for Bobbie, too. It would take years before I began to reconcile all these feelings; in fact, sometimes I wonder if I ever will.

A couple of weeks after I returned from California, I decided to accept Patsy's invitation and visit with her and Willard in Nashville. Now that I had met Bobbie's children, I realized that it was imperative that I get to know Willard. All of the Jetts agreed that Willard was the family patriarch, and I figured if I was ever going to understand Bobbie at all, I had to know Willard.

As with my visit to the Tippins kids, I needed to make this trip by myself. Michael, of course, was aware that my trip to California had been emotionally draining, but he accepted my decision to drive up to Nashville alone, and didn't push me one way or the other.

Patsy and Willard lived in a relatively new, luxurious highrise apartment building in a dignified western suburb of the city, not far from the famous Nashville Parthenon. As I pulled into the driveway of their building, an older man with steel-gray hair and a rather officious manner waved me over. I knew right away that this must be Willard, and I suspected that he'd been waiting in the lobby for me to arrive, although he pretended that he was on his way to the store.

"Saw your Alabama plates," he said. "You're Cathy. You park over there, then go on upstairs. I'll be right back."

Willard was just as curmudgeonly as he'd sounded on the telephone, but he reminded me a little bit of Wayne Deupree—I learned later that they were exactly the same age—and, as a result, I liked him immediately. When I got upstairs, Patsy greeted me like an old friend—or rather, like a daughter. When Willard got back from his "errand," he sat down beside me and he began talking. I got the feeling that he wanted to tell me about the Jett family—and he wanted me to know his own version of the family history.

First of all, he told me all about himself. He'd been a Colonel in the U.S. Army (in fact, many family members referred to him as "the Colonel"), and later chief of detectives for the Nashville police force. He was very proud of his army experience, especially his involvement during the Nuremburg trials, when he supervised the inmates at the prison in Germany. He had had a distinguished career with the Nashville police, and I could see that, as a result, he knew every important person in the city.

He was equally proud of the Jett family history. He told me that the Jetts had played a role in the development of the state of Tennessee and the city of Nashville. He spoke lovingly of Bobbie, and told me what a beautiful, lively girl she had been. But he would not confirm that Hank Williams and Bobbie had even known each other. When I asked him about Hank and Bobbie, he said: "That was a long time ago, and I don't remember." I pushed him a bit, but then I backed down. At this point, I was glad that he and Patsy accepted me at all, and suspected that his decision to acknowledge me had not been easy.

The following evening, Willard and Patsy hosted a little dinner party for all the Jett relatives in Nashville. Willard's brother Leslie and his wife, Marie, came over, and everyone was friendly and gracious. I left Nashville and the Jetts feeling that, at last, I had uncovered my roots, at least as far as my mother was concerned. One of the ironies—of which there were many—was that no one, including Willard and the Tippins family, had a photograph of Bobbie. I mentioned to Virginia Jett Harpst, Willard's sister, how disappointed I felt not to be able to see Bobbie's face.

A week or so after I returned from Nashville, I was entertaining a few friends one evening when the doorbell rang. It was my neighbor, and she handed me a large brown envelope that had been delivered to her home by mistake. It had Virginia Harpst's return address on it, and I could tell that it contained a photograph. Without telling my friends, I took the envelope into the bathroom and sat on the floor staring at it for several minutes. The same fear that had gripped me when Patsy had handed me the photo of Bobbie's grave grabbed me again—only this time I felt certain that when I opened the envelope I would see Bobbie's face. Finally, I took a deep breath, broke the seal, and pulled out the picture.

Immediately, all my fears melted away. Meeting Bobbie Jett—my mother—was not frightening at all. What I saw was a fashionable-looking woman about my own age, with an absolutely beautiful face, clear light-colored eyes, and a warm half-smile. As I looked at the picture, I didn't cry or wail or get angry, as I had done with Jo. Instead, I felt an emotion I'm sure Willard Jett would have appreciated: I felt very proud.

7
KEITH

In the spring of 1982, Patsy Jett threw a big family reunion as a surprise for Willard. Jo and Linda, at Patsy's expense, came to Nashville, and Patsy invited me as well. I guess they felt that I was as much a link to their past as they were to mine. We three "girls" stayed with Willard and Patsy for several days, and then Patsy drove us down through Alabama and Florida so that Jo and Linda could get a little taste of the South and we could spend more time together. I was beginning to feel a part of this family.

I found this process of getting to know the Jetts extremely intriguing. I very much wanted to explore my roots—not as a substitute for my adoptive family, but as a complement and a completion to my life. Although Jo and Linda had not known the material advantages I had known, they seemed to have enjoyed a close family life, and I envied them that security—especially, of course, their intimacy with Bobbie.

By mid-1982, Michael and I had been married for seven years. Our marriage was a comfortable one. We were both kind and good to each other; we gave each other lots of space. I thought I loved him, and I know he loved me. We shared certain interests—like waterskiing, camping, and entertaining friends. In retrospect, I don't think we communicated very deeply, but our marriage seemed satisfactory to both of us.

In June, Michael's employer sold his Lear jet to a private corporation in Mobile, and Michael decided to go along as part of the package. He moved down to Mobile while I stayed behind to sell our house. This was an uncertain time for us financially, and we thought it would be better if I kept my secure job at the center in order to make mortgage payments. After Michael moved, we began a period of weekend commuting. One weekend I would drive down to Mobile; the next he would drive up to Montgomery, unless, of course, he was working.

One weekend shortly after Michael moved, when I was in Mobile, I stopped over to see my parents. We sat around for a few minutes talking, when suddenly, out of the blue, Mother grabbed me by the hands and led me into the bathroom and closed the door.

"If you want to know who your natural mother is, I'll help," she said.

I was shocked that she was saying this at all—let alone with such sincerity—but it took maybe a second and a half for me to realize that Aunt Helen had probably already told her the truth. I felt relieved that she knew, and she was, in effect, telling me that it was all right with her.

"I already have found out!" I "confessed" naturally and unguardedly.

"Oh, I'm so happy," she said, although she didn't ask me for very many details about the Jetts. I told her that Bobbie was dead, and I could tell she was relieved.

But later that evening, Mother called me at home and managed to turn everything around—as she had done so many times in the past.

"Cathy, I told your father that you had seen your natural mother's family," she began, "and he said it was enough to make him puke. You've really betrayed us, Cathy."

"That's not true!" I said, starting to cry. I tried to explain to her that I had not meant to hurt them. In fact, I'd done everything I could not to cause them pain.

"Say what you want," she said. "But your actions speak for themselves. We both feel the same way." Then she hung up the phone.

Daddy phoned me later and said Mother had "suckered" me with her sweet talk in the bathroom. She had wanted to know the truth about what I had been up to, and that was her way of pulling the information out of me. As far as Daddy was concerned, he told me that he supported me totally—as he had promised two years earlier. He even said that he wanted to reimburse me for my airfare to California.

Now that Mother knew I'd made some headway in my search for my roots, I feared she would never leave me in peace again. She believed I had betrayed her, and I feared she was going to make me pay for it.

In the early winter of 1983, Daddy was diagnosed as having lung cancer. He called me on my birthday, January 6, and told me that he had, at best, six months to live. During the months of his illness, I traveled to Mobile every weekend to visit with him and, of course, to see Michael. It turned out to be a very important time for Daddy and me, and we became very close.

I was surprised that during Daddy's illness Mother remained relatively strong and realistic. She knew he was dying, and she seemed to be accepting it and planning for the future. At times, though, I became distressed by what appeared to be her callousness. She once told me, while Daddy sat within earshot in the next room watching television, that she had already made his funeral arrangements. True to form, about six weeks before he died, she had a face-lift. Although she, of course, would never have said so out loud, I knew she wanted to look her best at his funeral. As with my wedding, Louise had to be the center of attention.

Daddy died on August 4, 1983. Aunt Helen called me in Montgomery and without any preliminary conversation to prepare me, she just blurted out: "Your father's dead." I was very upset and wanted to drive down to Mobile immediately, but she insisted that I wait until the next morning. To make matters worse, Michael was out of town, so I had to endure this alone.

I got to my parents' house about 9:00 A.M. that Friday morning and found Mother crying with some friends who had dropped by. I wanted to go to the funeral home to see Daddy, and I expected Mother to go with me. I was shocked and disturbed when she announced that she had decided that no one was going to view the body. She also said the obituary would not appear until after Daddy was buried.

That afternoon, I told her I was going to go to the funeral home whether she wanted me to go or not. At first she refused to go with me, but then asked my cousin, Stanley, to drive both of us over. I thought Stanley's presence was strange, but when Mother and I went into the room with the casket, Stanley stayed in the lobby smoking cigarettes.

Mother went over to the casket and patted Daddy's head.

"You look real good, hon," she said to Daddy, as though he could hear her. She had come this far, but she just wouldn't stay.

"I'm leaving," she said instantly, "but you stay as long as you want, Cathy."

I stood looking at Daddy for several minutes. I felt incredibly sad and began to realize how much I would miss him. The room was so empty, and the emptiness only increased my sadness. Wayne Deupree had lived in Mobile most of his life. There should have been a steady stream of his many good friends there paying their respects, but most of them didn't even know he had died and wouldn't find out until after he was buried.

Mother was in great form on the day of the funeral. Her new face-lift made her look younger, and instead of a black dress, she insisted on wearing a white one, which she knew looked terrific on her with her olive complexion. She also was adamant about driving herself to the funeral. Aunt Helen was very distressed about this.

"Louise," she yelled out to Mother in the den as we were leaving, "a widow doesn't drive herself to her own husband's funeral."

"Well, God damn it, I do!" Louise yelled back. None of us bothered to argue with her.

Even though Daddy's death had not been reported in the paper yet, news got around and a number of people came to the cemetery for the burial. I was touched because Aunt Betty and Lee came by, although I knew this reunion was hard for them. We had not been in touch for the past seven years, since my wedding. I knew Betty had felt devastated at her daughter Sally's being left out of my wedding party, but she knew Mother, and decided comforting me was more important than nursing an old—and major—slight. When Aunt Betty and Lee walked into the funeral home, Mother looked at them as though she'd never seen them before in her life.

"Mother, it's Aunt Betty and Lee," I said, thinking that perhaps she was grieving more than I realized and couldn't recognize old friends.

"Yes, I know," she said, and turned away.

I was embarrassed by Mother's behavior, but thank goodness Aunt Betty understood, as she always had. I knew then that I would never let Aunt Betty, Lee, or Sally out of my life again.

The one person I felt I could turn to for support was Aunt Helen. She had always been a source of strength for me, but after Daddy died, she became my anchor. She was the only member of my adoptive family to whom I felt comfortable revealing all my feelings, as well as the truth about my search for my roots.

Uncle Stanley had died in 1979, but Aunt Helen supported herself with her widow's pension and her beauty shop. Stanley, now in his mid-thirties, lived in Gulf Shores, but was still very close to his mother. He'd gotten into the real estate business, and seemed to be doing well. From the beginning of my search in 1981, I kept Aunt Helen posted every step of the way. I trusted her completely for advice, counsel, and a current assessment of Mother's emotional condition.

After my father's death, I found that two or three weeks would go by between visits to Mobile—and to Michael. Without quite realizing it, we began living separate lives, although we never really discussed it. This transient lifestyle lasted for a year.

In August 1984, I was finally able to sell our house in Montgomery and move down to Mobile. In September 1984, before I was even settled in, Aunt Helen told me about an investigative attorney she had heard about through a friend. His name was Keith Adkinson, and he had worked for the Senate Rackets Committee in Washington, D.C. She thought he might be able to assist me in my search for the truth about Hank Williams.

She showed me Adkinson's curriculum vitae, and I was impressed. He'd gone to the University of Virginia and the University of Virginia Law School. He'd worked for a few years for a law firm in Beverly Hills, California, and then as their East Coast representative, taking cases for well-known Hollywood entertainers. Now he lived in Washington, D.C., and I was particularly intrigued with the "investigative" experience he'd had on the Senate Rackets Committee. I had done everything I could to run down a cold, thirty-one-year-old trail, and I didn't know what to do next. My hope was that Mr. Adkinson could tell me if there was a next step—and, if so, what it was.

I told Aunt Helen, without hesitation, that I wanted to meet Keith Adkinson, so long as it did not take him away from her friend's case.

"I'll see what I can do," she said.

About seven that evening the phone rang. Aunt Helen's friend introduced us over the phone, and put Keith Adkinson on the line. He was courteous, professional, and agreed to meet with me in Gulf Shores the next morning at his client's home.

The morning I drove down to Gulf Shores was typical of the Alabama Gulf Coast in late September; it was the kind of morning that Southerners wait for, full of sunshine that would burn away the early chill long before noon. At the same time, there was a promise of autumn in the air.

I tried to imagine how Mr. Adkinson would behave. I figured he would either think I was crazy or he would just sit there, smile politely, and listen to me tell my story while his mind drifted off to other business. My greatest fear was that he would confirm what others had said—that there was nothing I could do. Given his background, I decided that if he felt that way, I would seriously consider giving up. Then again, perhaps he might know what I should do. Perhaps he could get some answers.

I turned my brown Spitfire onto Interstate 10 along the Alabama coast and sped along the shoreline of Mobile Bay. By the time I reached the far side of Mobile Bay, much of my anxiety about the meeting had faded. It was a warm, beautiful day, and I felt alive and optimistic.

The road to Gulf Shores was familiar and comforting to me. I had driven it many times back when I was in high school, my car packed with friends and beer, headed to the beaches whose sand, some swore, looked like spun sugar. Old, formidable Fort Morgan sat perched at the end of Gulf Shores. Its symbolism wasn't lost on me. During the War Between the States, Admiral Farragut's attack on the fort had been delayed because Confederate mines had been scattered across the bay. The admiral was undaunted. "Damn the torpedoes, full speed ahead," he'd ordered. Well, by God, I was beginning to feel like "damn the torpedoes" myself. And I hoped Mr. Adkinson agreed.

I wasn't quite sure why I felt this way. I knew, of course, that I was frustrated and angry. My fistfight with Jo, who had pain of her own, certainly proved that to me. But it was more than that. Although I had no idea what it might be, I suspected that I was missing a very important piece to this jigsaw puzzle that was my life. My suspicion grew from those averted eyes of Drayton Hamilton, Marie Harvell, the ladies at Pensions and Security, and even Uncle Willard, as much as I loved him. They knew something—or knew there was something to know—and they just weren't telling me.

Later Keith would tell me that, as I suspected, if there was one thing he did not feel like doing that morning, it was talking to some friend of his client's. All he wanted to do was get moving on the fraud case he was currently working on. He'd been in Gulf Shores for days working out the case's details. Although he liked Gulf Shores, this was a place to come to for relaxation, not eighteen hours a day of work.

Nevertheless, he said, he'd been intrigued by my story. Just a few weeks before we met, he'd gone on a dove hunt with a

113

group of his buddies—ex-cops, ex-spooks, and gun enthusiasts—in east Texas. On the ten-hour ride to and from the Dallas airport to Uvalde, Texas, where these guys met up, Keith's friend had played hours and hours of old Hank Williams songs, including Luke the Drifter songs and hymns. Keith said it was the first time he had listened to Hank Williams in years, and the only time he had heard so many of Hank's songs. To his amazement, he loved them.

Then he'd just been taking it easy, looking out the window of the pickup truck, sipping a beer, and listening to Hank's sorrowful voice. He thought it was mighty interesting that only a couple of weeks later he was about to meet a woman who thought she might be Hank's lost daughter.

Keith Adkinson did not look at all like the man I'd been expecting. Even though I'd seen from his vitae that he'd graduated from law school in the late 1960s, I somehow had formulated this picture of a much older man, pompous and surly, a little plump around the midsection, and unctuous as hell. Instead, he looked like he had just walked off the pages of GQ wearing a brown, three-piece suit that looked as though it had been tailored exclusively for him. I was impressed that he'd gotten so formally dressed for a meeting at the beach. His smile was friendly, and I hoped he was as sincere as he seemed to be.

We sat down at the kitchen table and he poured me a cup of coffee. Although he was extremely professional, Mr. Adkinson, who insisted that I call him Keith, made me feel at ease, and he didn't seem to be in a hurry for me to leave.

He patiently sat and listened as I gave him a detailed account of my entire quest, from the moment my mother told me about Lillian Williams Stone's two-thousand-dollar check, through my meeting with Marie, Hank's cousin, to my reunion with my natural mother's family. I had brought the few papers I'd collected over the years, including the newspaper clippings from the 1967 trial, and the little note from Mama Cook describing my love for ketchup. I was sort of embarrassed sharing the sentimental stuff and my feelings with him. But he seemed as sincerely interested in what I felt as what I had done. I liked that.

He was courteous, polite, and attentive. He focused in on me and what I was saying as if I was the most important client in the world. While I expect that's how any good lawyer should make a potential client feel, it made him much easier to talk to. He would alternate between looking deep into my eyes and making notes. But not once did I feel I was boring him or inconveniencing him. I liked that, too.

Finally, I told him about my frustrating visits to Pensions and Security, and my confusing discussion with Drayton Hamilton. I tried to keep my rage in check and sound very understanding of Mr. Hamilton's reluctance to tell me anything. I didn't want to offend Keith Adkinson, but I quickly realized I needn't have been so polite.

"I hate that more than anything," Keith blurted out.

"What?"

"The good-old-boy network," he said. "It sounds to me like there have been a lot of people in Montgomery, especially in the legal profession, trying to keep you in the dark."

I laughed, and sighed with relief. He understood.

"Does that mean I've been screwed?" I asked.

"Very possibly. And probably with malice aforethought," he said. "I've seen it happen far too many times."

I watched him frown as he shuffled through the few scraps of paper I had brought him. I could tell he was sympathetic, but I still felt uneasy.

"There's not really enough here to hang much of a case on," Keith said. "Paternity is never easy to prove, even when both parents are alive and willing to testify. I don't even know if there is a mechanism in Alabama to prove paternity at this stage."

I didn't know what a "mechanism" was, but I couldn't mistake the general tenor of his comments. I smiled a resigned, disappointed smile.

At the same time, he didn't seem to be giving up quite yet. He began reading the wrinkled, yellowed newspaper article from the *Montgomery Advertiser* dated September 27, 1967, the one that mentioned the remote possibility that Hank Williams might have fathered an illegitimate daughter during the final months of his life.

"Well," Keith said, "it looks like a number of Montgomery's finest lawyers were talking a hell of a lot about you in 1967. You seem to have been right in the middle of a legal feud between Hank's ex-wife and son against his sister and publisher."

"Yes, I know," I said, although the details of the actual legal case in which my existence had been mentioned never interested me too much, probably because it seemed incomprehensible and because I feared Mother was right and my fate had been sealed at that time.

Keith smiled, leaned back, and drained his coffee mug.

"An amazing thing occurs when greed takes hold of families—when ex-wives and sons and sisters all get mad and start fighting over a dead man's money," Keith began. "They generally leave a long paper trail scattered behind them, and most times, that paper trail reveals secrets that were never meant to see the light of day."

He stood up, stretched a bit, and poured each of us another cup of coffee. I could see something had clicked in his brain, and the fresh coffee proved, at the very least, that he was going to pursue this a little further.

"That paper trail is your one chance, Cathy," Keith said. "And it's the best chance you've got. Now, I can get damned excited about the prospect of following a paper trail somewhere. I love paper. Over the years, many a crook has been wrapped in his own paper and shipped off to a federal pen."

The headline on the article was intriguing: WILLIAMS MUSIC TRIAL TAKES TURN AS POSSIBLE DAUGHTER IS REPORTED. Keith read on further: "The question arose Tuesday when attorney Maury Smith, representing Acuff-Rose Publishing Company, told the court that Hank Williams had recognized 'in a written contract' that a child had been born to a woman in Montgomery."

He repeated that phrase "in a written contract."

"And you believe that you're that child," Keith said.

"I sure do."

In silence, he studied me intently for a long time, as though he was trying to read something in my eyes. I thought he was still thinking about the newspaper articles, but suddenly he smiled and said something utterly unexpected.

"I don't suppose there's a bat's chance in hell that you play the guitar."

I shrugged. "Well, I took lessons for years, and I've been picking a guitar for as long as I can remember."

"Can you sing?"

"I like to sing. When I was in high school and college, I sang with my friends all the time."

"Have you written any songs?"

"I've got a whole folder full of songs at home, but I doubt if they're any good. I only write when I'm sad or lonesome. It's how I express what I'm feeling."

Keith laughed, but not in a mocking sort of way. "Now you're even sounding like Hank Williams," he said.

"All I want to know is if he's my father," I said.

"I want you to know up front that it'll be damn hard to prove that you're Hank Williams' daughter," Keith said. "The only two people who can verify your claim have been dead for a long time. And if you are, there's no telling what that will mean."

Keith wasn't telling me anything I didn't already know. Of course, he hadn't seen me crying my heart out after my first telephone conversation with Willard Jett.

"So, what are my chances?" I asked, ready to hear the truth.

"About ninety-nine to one."

"Against?" I asked, knowing the answer, but hoping still.

Keith nodded. "Any success you might have in proving your identity could depend on getting your hands on that document Hank allegedly signed regarding you," he said. "That might be a good lead—depending on what's in it, of course."

"But it didn't make any difference in 1967—why should it help now? They had it then and they decided everything against me," I said.

"I don't know," Keith answered. "The court certainly seemed to know about it at the time, and you're right, it doesn't seem to have made any difference then. But you just don't know."

"Well, I talked to Drayton Hamilton about it, and he said it only had to do with medical bills and it wasn't important. He also said that I couldn't have a copy of it, and he didn't even know if a copy still existed."

"He may be right—it may not be important. And it may not exist. But if it's out there, it can be gotten," he answered wryly. "Unless of course, somebody has destroyed it."

"Why would anybody do that?" I asked.

"Money and self-protection are generally the two main reasons," he said.

Maybe Daddy had been onto something, I thought. Maybe money did have something to do with this. Surely, Randall had to be interested in the money. That's what got Daddy thinking. And if what Daddy had heard Randall bragging about on TV was true, he was enjoying about half a million dollars a year.

Suddenly, Keith looked at me with great intensity. "Cathy, my experience suggests that there is either going to be a lot of paper buried somewhere, or no paper at all. If the documents are inadequate or have vanished—if somebody did destroy them— you will at least know once and for all that you'll never be able to know for sure. That's the worst-case scenario."

We were quiet again for a moment. Then Keith added: "Then again, you never know just what'll fall out of a tree until you shake it. And just watch what happens when you take a chain-saw to it."

I liked his attitude. He had been honest and fair with me. He had told me the truth as he saw it. He had not made any promises that he could not keep. In fact, he had not made any promises at all.

Suddenly, he asked me to stand up, walk out into the middle of the room and slowly turn around, once, then twice.

"Why are you asking me to do this?" I asked.

"Because if you really are a living part of the Hank Williams legacy, then the whole world will be looking at you. I want to see what the whole world is going to be looking at."

Keith was quiet for a moment, then he said, "If you are Hank's daughter—and we can prove it—your life will never be the same. The avenues that will open for you could change your life forever. It could put a terrible strain on your marriage. Are you prepared for that?"

"Yes," I said without hesitation. "We are very independent." My relationship with Michael would not be a problem.

Michael never made demands on me. He had never been able to say no to me, and if he had, I doubt that it would have made any difference. It had been that way for our entire relationship. We were better friends than we were lovers. Not just friends, best friends.

"And another thing," Keith went on. "The truth isn't always pretty. Sure, we might find out the truth about Hank Williams, but it might include some things we haven't even thought of. The truth can be cruel and hurtful. It usually destroys all our grand illusions. If you come face-to-face with your past, you may not like what you see."

"I can take it," I said. In fact, I must have said it with a certain force, because Keith didn't press the point further. I had told him lots of facts, but I hadn't told him much about the feelings behind the facts. And I had mentioned very little about my adoptive parents.

"Go home and think about it," Keith said as he walked me to my car. "Make sure you're doing what you want to do."

"I don't need to think about it," I answered. "I've made up my mind. I don't want to spend the rest of my life wondering 'What if . . .'"

"Think about it anyway," Keith said. Then he added something real strange. "I'd like to hear you sing," he said. "Strum a little on your guitar and sing. I'm taking a flight tonight from Mobile. I can stop by your house, and you can give me a little concert. Well, just a song or two. Would that be okay?"

I had no idea what he was thinking. He had not told me whether or not he would be willing to help me, and I had been afraid to ask him point-blank. I was afraid he would say no, and I didn't want to hear no.

"All right," I said.

Early that evening, Keith arrived. He only had an hour or so before he had to leave for the airport, but I'd practiced a couple of my favorite Hank Williams songs during the day and gave him, as he'd put it, "a little concert." I felt like I was auditioning—and, in fact, I was.

I started to sing "Jambalaya." After the first verse, Keith

asked if I would mind if he recorded it. I said no, then I asked why. He said he knew someone he thought ought to hear it. His request did not lessen my anxiety.

I sang "Jambalaya," and to add to my growing embarrassment, my cockatiel joined in, making this a truly unique rendition of what is already a pretty interesting song. I told Keith that "Jambalaya" was one of my favorite Hank Williams songs, and that learning from Marie Harvell that I was "Yvonne" only made it more special.

I then sang "Your Cheatin' Heart." Keith said he was really impressed with the quality of my voice, which I thought was nice of him to say whether he meant it or not.

"Well, what do you think?" I finally asked, meaning what did he think about becoming my lawyer.

"I think you're a helluva singer."

"You do?" I said.

"In my opinion, you've got what it takes to be a singer whether you're Hank Williams' daughter or not," Keith said. "But I'm not a music producer. I only know what I like, and I like what I hear."

I was beginning to trust Keith; I felt his sincerity. He may have met with me earlier that day as a favor to a client, but he sure hadn't driven over to my house to hear me sing as a favor to anybody. Although he didn't say much, I could almost see the wheels turning in his head. Something was happening.

"Well, I've thought about what you said this morning," I finally said. "I'm where I was then. Have you thought any more about the possibility of us jumping into this thing together and finding out once and for all who I am?"

Keith smiled. "I find your story fascinating," he said. "And I find you fascinating."

"What are you saying?" I asked.

"I think I'm going to look into it," he said.

8
THE PAPER CHASE

I knew Keith had lots of responsibilities back in Washington, so I had no idea whether or not he would help me, or how long it would take for him to decide. But the next evening the telephone rang, and I recognized Keith's voice immediately.

"If you still want me to help you," he said, "I'm ready."

His words thrilled me. I'd been so close to giving up, and now this lawyer was saying he'd help.

"I've got some other good news, too," Keith went on. "I just finished having a drink with a friend of mine—Jim Morris—and he thinks you're terrific. And by the way, he's the Director of Performing Arts for the Smithsonian Institution."

I was floored. Less than thirty-six hours before, I'd been driving down to Gulf Shores, wondering whether this man would even consider me seriously, and now he was telling me that not only would he look into my situation from a legal point of view but he had played the tape of my singing for the Director of Performing Arts at the Smithsonian. It seemed inconceivable to me.

Keith went on to explain that Jim Morris was a professional musicologist and had himself been a professional singer—opera was his specialty. For eighteen years, he had worked at the Smithsonian. As Director of Performing Arts, he had produced many of the Smithsonian's highly regarded albums, which included the country music collection.

The evening before, as Keith had been waiting for his plane out of Mobile, he had called Jim and asked him to come over the next evening and listen to the tape he had made. On the plane, Keith had played the tape over and over, and by the time Jim got there on Friday evening, he was convinced Jim would be impressed. According to Keith, Jim had not only been affected, especially by the timbre of my voice, but he believed I had a real shot as a professional singer.

"Does she have talent?" Keith said he had asked.

"Good God, yes," Mr. Morris had answered. "She's loaded with it."

"Does she have a shot at a singing career?" Keith asked.

"With a little work—no doubt about it," Jim answered.

When Keith told him that I might be Hank Williams' daughter, Mr. Morris was surprised, of course. But I was blown away when Keith said that Mr. Morris thought I had enough talent to pursue a career regardless of whether or not I was Hank Williams' daughter. Just as I was starting to react to the implications of what it meant to have a respected professional in the music business listen to my singing—and like it!—Keith brought me back to our business at hand.

"I'm going down to Montgomery first thing Monday morning," he said.

"On my case?"

"Absolutely," he said. "I want to rummage around in the courthouse for a few days. Like I told you yesterday, when a family starts fighting over money, they can generate a whole lot of paper. I noticed the name of a friend of mine on one of the papers you gave me—a man I met during the 1980 presidential campaign. He's a lawyer in Montgomery, and he just might remember something about this case. I also thought I might pay a visit to your buddy, Drayton Hamilton," he continued.

"Mr. Hamilton is not my buddy," I snapped. "He couldn't tell me anything—or didn't tell me anything."

"I'm kidding. Look, I'll try to call you by Wednesday night and give you an update."

I didn't sleep very much that night. In fact, I didn't sleep much for the next several days. I had a strong sense that all of this was going to lead someplace, but I couldn't quite imagine where. Many times over the years while I was chasing down this ghost of Hank Williams, I had felt like I was walking through someone else's life, and yet, paradoxically, it all seemed so right. I'm not normally one who is mystical or who believes that your life is driven by fate. On the other hand, I do think that sometimes inexplicable things happen that have real meaning.

For example, during the past summer, I had had a strange experience. I was getting ready to move from Montgomery to Mobile, and I had emptied our house, sent our furniture down to Mobile with the movers, and was packing the last few things into my car. It was late afternoon and it had been raining most of the day. In front of our house was a wide flat field, and I stood there for a moment, by myself, just looking across the field and thinking about the years Michael and I had spent living in this house. I was feeling sort of sentimental and sad, and I was a little worried about what would be in store for me now that I was leaving Montgomery.

Suddenly, as if by magic, a double rainbow appeared in the sky stretching across the field. The sky was steel-gray, and the two arches of sparkling color stood out vividly against it. I had a feeling that God was trying to tell me that my life was going to change radically. And this change was good.

I had forgotten about that double rainbow until Keith called me back to tell me he was taking on my case. In the month since I'd been back living in Mobile, nothing had quite come together. I hadn't started job hunting, and nothing interested me. Michael and I had rented a house, but my heart wasn't in it. Our house was just a five-minute walk from my old friend Lenore's home, so I was seeing Lenore, her husband, Butch, and their kids, Lisa and Gaines, frequently. At the same time, Michael was on the road almost constantly. So although I was integrating my old life with my new one, I felt lonely and at odds with my-self.

I thought about these things in the days following Keith's call. I felt confident he was going to find something. I recognized the prospect that Keith had so carefully explained—the possibility that any trace of my relationship to Hank Williams might have been carefully obliterated, but somehow I sensed that my quest was just beginning, not coming to an end. And Keith's enthusiasm about my singing thrilled me. I kept thinking of that double rainbow, and suspected that its meaning was close to coming clear.

On Wednesday night about nine o'clock, the telephone rang. I knew it was Keith, and I grabbed the telephone on the first ring.

"Well, I've just spent three days in the basement of the Montgomery courthouse," Keith began. "I caught up with my friend, Perry Hooper, and he graciously took me to the court-house basement. There is an acre of material down there on the Williams estate—and no telling what else."

"Did you learn anything?" I asked.

"Yes, ma'am. I learned quite a lot," Keith said almost sar-castically. "For one thing, I learned that lawyers in this town can remove papers from these files without making any record of their withdrawals."

"Oh, I knew that!" I said. "Mr. Hamilton took a whole box of stuff from the courthouse. I was with him. Is that unusual?"

"Unusual?" Keith said angrily. "It seems that these guys can walk out with original records. If the clerk knows him, that is. If this really is standard practice, it means anybody can make anything just disappear and nobody knows who took it, when it left, or where it has gone. I suspect that is a little more than 'unusual.' "

This revelation made me very uneasy—and I could tell it made Keith furious.

"By the way, I dropped in on Drayton Hamilton," Keith went on.

"And . . ."

"He was about as helpful to me as he had been with you,"

Keith said. "I asked him about the 'contract' between Hank Williams and Bobbie Jett mentioned in that newspaper article, and he told me that it would be of no use to me. He said it wasn't anything—it had to do with medical expenses, and I probably couldn't get it anyway."

"Do you think that's right?" I asked.

"Damned if I know," Keith said. "But I'll tell you this, the moment somebody tells me that I don't want something, I suspect that little item is the very thing I'm looking for."

I sighed. I'd been in his place before. For me, this was the brick wall, and I was fearful that Keith would find that wall just as tough to scale as I had. Fortunately, he was not intimidated.

He could see things in all those papers that I could not begin to understand. After just a couple of days of digging up to his elbows, he was able to make some sense out of much of the "paper." Better yet, he was able to explain to me—in plain English—the two cases that had involved me and the Williams family. Nobody—not my parents, not Drayton Hamilton, not the ladies at Pensions and Security, nobody—had been able to tell me straight out what these two suits meant.

First of all, he was finally able to fill in all the holes relating to the mysterious two thousand dollars I had received in 1974 from the estate of Mrs. Lillian Williams Stone. According to various documents Keith found in the Montgomery courthouse, on the day of my birth, January 6, 1953, Robert Stewart, Mrs. Stone's lawyer, had appeared at Mrs. Stone's door with two documents for her to sign. One was her application to become the administratrix of Hank's estate. The other document was a draft of a new will. As Keith put it, it was a "one-page, throwaway little will— a ridiculous will." But the pivotal point here was that this will left everything to Irene Williams Smith and didn't mention me, even though, by the time it was executed, I had already been born.

Two years later, Mrs. Stone died with that will, dated January 13, 1953, in effect. By this time, Hank's mother had adopted me, and therefore she had two daughters, one by adoption and one naturally, Irene. It seemed odd that someone as shrewd and responsible as Mrs. Stone didn't execute another will after I was adopted to provide for my care in case of her death. But somehow, she had not.

In any case, once I was adopted by Mrs. Stone, I should have become what is known as a "pretermitted heir." In other words, if a child is "born" after a will is executed, by law he can sometimes inherit whether or not he is mentioned in the will. Irene's attorney, Robert Stewart, argued that Mrs. Stone's will would stand, while my guardian ad litem, Drayton Hamilton, to his credit, dragged the case through the lower courts and ultimately to the Supreme Court of Alabama, arguing that I should share in Mrs. Stone's estate. But in Alabama, at that time, no law existed that would permit an adopted child to become a pretermitted heir. Therefore, I lost, in an argument that to me sounded like a double negative: Since no law existed with regard to adopted children, the answer must be no.

This was the case that Drayton Hamilton had shown me in the law book in 1981. It seems that after he argued my case in the Supreme Court of Alabama—and lost—they changed the law. Today, adopted children in the state of Alabama can qualify as pretermitted heirs.

The final irony to all of this was the two thousand dollars. As Keith explained to me, somebody apparently had a guilty conscience. It seemed to me that if no law existed to define the rights of an adopted pretermitted heir, clearly no law existed for making any sort of recompense. But somebody came up with a convoluted formula based on homestead rights. A little bit of money was set aside for me—a sum based on "living expenses" until I "turned twenty-one." This, of course, was the two thousand dollars I picked up at the Montgomery courthouse in 1974.

Keith was also starting to uncover records that looked like they would explain the details of the 1967–68 proceedings and my part in that lawsuit. This was the suit that Mother had mentioned to me when she first told me that Hank Williams might be my father.

Keith said it appeared that in the mid-sixties, Hank's exwife, Audrey, and her son, Randall, had sued Hank's sister, Irene Williams Smith, and Acuff-Rose, Hank Williams' publishers, in the Circuit Court of Montgomery, Alabama. A few years earlier, in 1963, Irene (acting in her capacity as administratrix of Hank Williams' estate) had sold the renewal rights to Hank's copyrights to Acuff-Rose for twenty-five thousand dollars. Evidently, Audrey Williams took the position that the renewal rights were worth much more, and in the trial she must have brought in witnesses who testified that those rights were indeed worth substantially more.

"This is when you surfaced," Keith said.

To demonstrate that the royalties really were less valuable, Maury Smith, the lawyer for Acuff-Rose, mentioned that there might be another child. That's what made the press. Keith said he found references to "closed hearings" and "sealed files," but it was clear that these public records had holes in them.

"It's unbelievable," Keith said. "Not only can you walk off with files without logging them in and out—the files themselves are a mess. I find papers torn in half, logs with references obviously inked in after the fact—all sorts of strange stuff. Of course, most of them are twenty or thirty years old."

I sighed again. I'd always thought this whole thing was indecipherable to me because I wasn't a lawyer. Now I was beginning to feel like: "Well, damn it! No wonder I can't figure this out. If it's tough for a guy who's been a lawyer for almost twenty years to figure out—why should I have been able to?" I still felt frustrated, but I also felt a whole lot better.

"I can stay until Friday," Keith said. "I'll give you a call then. Maybe this jigsaw puzzle will start to make sense."

When Keith called on Friday night he was already back in Washington. It had taken some doing—and he would never admit how he did it—but he had struck gold. He got his hands on a copy of the elusive agreement. The contents of the agreement were startling—so provocative that Keith had gotten back on the plane and gone home to Washington, in order to give himself time to think about it a bit. He was worried as to how I would take it.

"Are you ready to find out who your father was and if he wanted you or not?" Keith said.

I thought how badly I wanted to hear the truth, even if it hurt.

"Yes, I want to know," I said.

"Well, I've found something that will be very interesting to you. The document Drayton Hamilton said would be of no use to us," Keith said.

"Read it." I don't remember breathing while Keith read the contents of the contract, word for word.

Here is what it said:

STATE OF ALABAMA
MONTGOMERY COUNTY

This agreement made this 15th day of October, 1952, by and between Hank Williams of Montgomery, Alabama, and Bobbie W. Jett of Nashville, Tennessee,

WITNESSETH

WHEREAS, the said Bobbie W. Jett is at the present time pregnant and expects to be delivered of a child on or about the 1st day of January, 1953, and the said Hank Williams may be the father of said child, and,

WHEREAS, it is the mutual desire of both parties to provide for the necessary expenses of the said Bobbie W. Jett and of the child to be born, and,

WHEREAS, both parties have reached a mutual agreement and understanding in regard to all matters involved.

IT IS NOW, THEREFORE, mutually agreed by and between the said Bobbie W. Jett and the said Hank Williams as follows:

1. That the said Hank Williams will provide room and board for the said Bobbie W. Jett in Montgomery, Alabama, from October 15th until the date said child is born, and has paid to Mrs. W. W. Stone the sum of $172.00 as room and board through January 15, 1953.

2. That the said Hank Williams will pay for the necessary expenses over and above room and board the sum of $100.00 per month from October 15, 1952, until the said child is born and the further sum of $200.00 in cash for the payment of immediate and necessary expenses, said sum having been paid this day to Mrs. W. W. Stone and to be paid out by her. The monthly payments herein provided for shall be due and payable on the 15th

day of each month beginning with the 15th day of November and ending with the 15th day of the month preceding the birth of said child.

3. The said Hank Williams shall pay all doctors and hospital bills in connection with the confinement of the mother and birth of the child, and it is mutually agreed that Dr. W. M. Stokes of Montgomery shall be the attending physician and that the doctor and the mother shall jointly select the hospital.

4. Beginning with the 15th day of the month following the birth of said child, the said Hank Williams shall pay to the said Bobbie W. Jett the sum of $100.00 per month on the 15th day of each succeeding month thereafter provided said child is born and lives, but in the event said child does not live after birth then there shall be due only a lump sum of $200.00.

5. Within 30 days after the birth of said child, the said Hank Williams shall provide a one-way plane ticket to the said Bobbie W. Jett from Montgomery to any place in California which she may designate, but the plane ticket or the money therefor shall be available only for a period of 45 days, being 75 days after birth, and if not used at the end of such time, he shall not be further liable for said transportation expenses.

6. The said child shall bear the name of the mother upon the birth certificate and in connection with any and all papers or documents required in connection with the birth of said child.

7. After the birth of said child, both parties agree that it shall be placed with Mrs. W. W. Stone of Montgomery, and that she shall have full custody and control of said child for a period of two years after its birth and that during said time the said Hank Williams will provide and pay for a nurse and will pay all necessary expenses for clothing, food, medical care, and other attention which is required by the child during said two-year period. During said two-year period that the child is in the custody of Mrs. Stone, both the father, Hank Williams, and the said Bobbie W. Jett shall have the right to visit said child at convenient and reasonable hours. Beginning at the third birthday of said child, its custody and control shall vest in the said Hank Williams and the child shall live with him continuously and be wholly and completely supported for by him, and cared for by him until it reaches its fifth birthday at which time the custody of the child shall be divided between both parties; that is, during the winter months or school months the child shall remain with Hank

Williams and during the summer months or school vacation months the custody shall be in the mother. The responsibility for the support of said child shall be in Hank Williams both during the times when he has custody of the child and when it is visiting with the mother. During the time that the child is in the custody of the father, Hank Williams, the mother shall have the right to visit it at reasonable times and at reasonable hours, and during the time it is in the custody of the mother during the summer months the father shall have the same privilege of visitation.

9. [sic] In view of the fact that the paternity of said child is in doubt and is not to be in any way construed as admitted by this agreement which is made solely because of the possibility of paternity, the said Bobbie W. Jett does hereby release the said Hank Williams from any and all further claims arising out of her condition or the birth of said child.

IN WITNESS WHEREOF, the parties have hereunto set their hands and seals on the day and date first above written.
Bobbie W. Jett
Hank Williams

STATE OF ALABAMA
MONTGOMERY COUNTY

I, Robert B. Stewart, a Notary Public, in and for said County in said State, hereby certify that Hank Williams and Bobbie W. Jett, whose names are signed to the foregoing instrument, and who are known to me, acknowledged before me on this day that, being informed of the contents of the instrument, they executed the same voluntarily on the day the same bears date.

Given under my hand this 15th day of October, 1952.
Robert B. Stewart
Notary Public

By the time Keith got finished reading, I was crying. I could think of only one thing to say.

"Read it again."

Without missing a beat, Keith launched right in and read it all the way through one more time. Before we said another word to each other, I made him read it, front to back, three times.

"Father." Hank Williams was referred to as my "father"

throughout the contract. The third time Keith read it all, I counted the word "father" three times.

Proof at last. A written piece of paper, signed by Hank Williams and Bobbie Jett, saying he was my father. Not only did it say he was my father, it said that he had wanted me. He was going to keep me. I was his.

"Wait a minute," I said. "Read me the part where it says paternity is in doubt and not admitted by this agreement—that part."

"That's the lawyer talking," Keith said. "It's boilerplate language to try to protect his client—Hank—from a future claim by your mother. It doesn't mean a thing."

"But—" I started to interrupt.

"Look, Cathy, this document refers to Hank Williams unequivocally as the father; he was taking custody of you; he was taking you to raise. This is proof positive that Hank Williams is your father and it is proof positive that he wanted you and was going to raise you."

"Period . . ." I chuckled.

"Period . . ." Keith said.

And yet it wasn't quite so simple.

"This wasn't the only thing I found," Keith said. "As I told you on Wednesday, there are piles of papers down there, Cathy, but it all says the same thing to me: There is something mighty wrong with the way this whole thing was handled. There are a lot of people who are still probably making a lot of money off Hank's music. I don't know who did what to whom yet, or exactly how they did it. But, one thing seems certain, a number of people went to a lot of trouble to keep you their secret. They had a reason and that reason must be money. Do you hear me?"

My mind was in a whirl, but, of course, I knew what he was saying. On one hand, I didn't understand it; on the other hand, it made perfect sense.

"I hear you," I said.

"This little document is not the end. In fact it could be the key to unlocking the secrets." Keith went on. "We have no idea what's there. But I want to take a hard look—it's going to be tough, real tough, but I'm willing to give it a try. If you want us to try, that is."

"Give it a try, hell," I told him. "Let's *do* it."

As Keith suspected, the contract between Bobbie and Hank was a "smoking gun"—or, to use another well-worn cliché, it turned out to be the tip of the iceberg. And this wasn't just a little frozen country lake, this was the Arctic Circle.

A few weeks after finding the contract, Keith made another trip down to Montgomery to chase more paper. Keith was certain we had a legal "problem" here, and before long it looked to him like there was a good chance that there might have been a deliberate effort to prevent me from ever knowing who I was. But at this point in time, he was only in the data-collecting stage. Each piece of paper was another colorful piece to the puzzle, but it would take many months before all the pieces were collected, and even more time before we were able to put the pieces together and figure out what had happened.

The estate of Hank Williams had generated hundreds of pounds of paper. In one box, Keith found an undated petition with half a page missing, filed by Drayton Hamilton, my guardian ad litem, wherein Audrey Williams, Hank's ex-wife, is quoted as saying that "certain other persons may claim to have an interest in said estate." In the same petition, Irene Williams Smith is quoted as saying that she had in her possession "certain documents which may give rise to or affect the right of another minor to share in said estate." In another petition, Drayton Hamilton asked for a court order for "all correspondence with Dr. W. M. Stokes . . . relating to the delivery of the baby of Bobbie W. Jett, written or received on behalf of Hiriam 'Hank' Williams."

The meaning of all these petitions and orders (I was quickly becoming used to Keith's legalese) was that Audrey Williams and Irene Williams Smith, although they were on opposing sides of the 1967 suit, both seemed to know of my existence—and that Irene Smith's lawyer, Robert Stewart, was involved.

In fact, it soon became clear that Mr. Stewart was involved in all phases of the Williams legal affairs. To Keith, this was bothersome—if not downright suspicious. Stewart had drafted Hank and Bobbie's agreement; he represented Hank's mother as adminstratrix of Hank's estate and in all other matters, including my adoption by her; he represented Hank's sister, Irene Williams Smith, both in her suit involving Audrey and in the suit involving me and Mrs. Stone's estate; and ultimately, he emerged as administrator of Hank Williams' estate itself. (In 1969, Irene Williams Smith was convicted of cocaine smuggling and ended up being sentenced to seven years in jail. Her tenure as adminstratrix of Hank's estate ended with her conviction.)

Keith didn't like the sight or sound of this situation, but he was reluctant to go talk to Mr. Stewart until he had the answers to some more questions. Finally, however, Keith thought he had begun to piece together what had happened with regard to me in the 1967 suit between Audrey and Irene. Once the contract between Bobbie and Hank surfaced, it was obvious that there might be another child, but, of course, it was equally clear that the child was, at best, illegitimate. But the judge, Richard P. Emmet, did not concern himself with paternity. Instead he decided not to rule on the issue of whether or not I was the child of Hank Williams, because he said it didn't make any difference anyway. First of all, I had been adopted, and according to Alabama law, an adopted child could not make a claim against its natural father. Moreover, I was also illegitimate, and according to Alabama law in 1967, an illegitimate child could not inherit from the estate of a natural intestate father, only from the natural mother; and Judge Emmet ruled that he was going to abide by this law.

My guardian ad litem, Drayton Hamilton, apparently argued that the law was unconstitutional and the U.S. Supreme Court, in reference to an unrelated case, was expected to declare it so within a few months. Nevertheless, Judge Emmet ruled that possible future changes in the law did not alter the present situation. By law, on that day, it was legally irrelevant whether or not I was Hank's child, and Randall Hank Williams was declared the sole heir of Hank Williams, Sr.

To me, it looked like Drayton Hamilton had played an active role in this whole thing, and, as I said to Keith, I was confused by this because Mr. Hamilton had always been so elusive during our meetings during the early years of my quest. But Keith knew enough to ask a stunningly obvious question. Why hadn't Drayton Hamilton appealed this decision to the Alabama Supreme Court? After all, he had aggressively pushed my cause through the courts in the suit with Irene Williams Smith a decade earlier.

"You know that answer," Keith said to me on the telephone one evening. "At least, in part you know."

Evidently, at this juncture during the 1967 trial my adoptive parents were contacted about my existence being brought up in a case. Somewhere it was suggested that they felt strongly that they didn't want me to be upset or embarrassed. I was only fourteen years old at the time, and I guess they felt that any public acknowledgment of my natural parentage would be hurtful to me—especially for the few thousand dollars Daddy had been told was involved. And, as he also said, they also told him I didn't have much of a chance to win anyway.

"Based on what they must have been told, I can appreciate their position," Keith said. "What didn't make sense was Drayton Hamilton's response to the Deuprees' request. Obviously, many of these proceedings must have been closed from the start, so your name would never have been made public anyway. What's more, the reason the court appoints a guardian ad litem for a minor is to insure that everything that should be done is, in fact, done. He should have appealed Judge Emmet's decision."

In fact, Keith later stumbled on an odd twist that confirmed his opinion. One of the infinite papers he found was an interlineated entry in a clerk's logbook indicating that Mr. Hamilton had gotten a court order directing him not to appeal. The entry was suspicious; the order was, according to Keith, extraordinarily unusual. But it accomplished one thing. It insulated Hamilton from a later malpractice suit.

After Keith's first trips to Montgomery, he believed the questions he was unearthing were almost as fascinating as their ultimate answers would be. Certainly this list of questions was far longer than the answers he'd been able to find so far. He was also convinced that many answers—and probably more questions—lay in my adoption files.

Getting those files was not going to be easy. During one of his early trips to Montgomery, he called Pensions and Security and they stonewalled him as strongly as they had barred me. Keith knew the law was notoriously rigid with regard to adoption files, but he was determined to get them. And I was beginning to see that when Keith was determined, things got done.

9
CROONIN' IN THE
DISTRICT

Based on the information Keith was beginning to find in the dusty bowels of the Montgomery courthouse, he was beginning to weave together all the strands that made up the "Hank Williams Project," as he called it. He now believed that I was not just a secret side story in Hank's life, but an important thread. Already Keith had broken the problems down into three broad sections.

First he wanted to explore the Williams estate—not just Hank's legacy, but Mrs. Stone's estate. Clearly, Hank had intended to care for me; we knew that from the contract. We also knew that Mrs. Stone had adopted me, a fact I had known for years, but I had been left out of her will. This seemed odd to both Keith and me, and he wanted to know why.

Keith also wanted to find out who, exactly, shared in Hank's inheritance, how much his estate was actually worth, and if, in fact, I should have been part of it. The same was true of all of the income generated from Hank Williams' recordings and songs; in other words, all the works that were copyrighted. Keith assumed that Hank's estate had been closed for decades, but when it was open, the estate must have received a percentage of royalties and his publishers, Acuff-Rose, must have received a portion, which was standard procedure. But Keith had discovered that others must have shared in it too, and he needed to find out who all these people were, how much they received, whether or not I should have been part of this, and finally, whether there was anything I could do about it now.

Although during his first foray into the Montgomery courthouse Keith found only disjointed pieces, it was obvious to him that something was amiss. My existence was mentioned—and then suppressed—in the 1967 court case. In part, this was done at the request of the Deuprees, but Keith strongly suspected there was more to the story.

Finally, Keith told me that he had been doing a lot of thinking about my singing and the possibilities and avenues for launching a career. He had had years of experience working in the entertainment world, and he wanted to see if he could explore some avenues toward a career for me in singing.

We decided to make two agreements. First, he would work on exploring the legal situation surrounding my paternity and the Williams estate. He suspected that it wouldn't take long for him to uncover strong reasons for me to consider suing, for my adoption records, if nothing else. We also decided to form a professional relationship, with Keith as my manager.

Keith invited me to come up to Washington on October 15, 1984, to discuss how we were going to proceed with my legal situation. He also told me that he had been discussing my "career" with Jim Morris, and together they decided that I should make a demo tape.

I felt as if I was walking in a fog. A career as a singer had long been a secret fantasy of mine, but one that I never told anyone. Now here was Keith—and Mr. Morris—telling me that perhaps the impossible was possible. It was as though they had read my mind. When I told Michael about the plans, he was almost as excited as I was and encouraged me to "go for it."

I had visited Washington, D.C., only once, years before, when I had brought a group of senior citizens from the center I worked at in Montgomery on a tour. I had thought it was one of the most beautiful cities in the world. The stately monuments, the gracious parks, the wide streets, and the undercurrent of strength and power all moved me.

During the years I had been married to Michael, I had made many trips by myself—including, of course, the memorable trip to California to meet Jo and my other Jett siblings. But despite my independence, I was particularly nervous about this trip. The idea of singing in front of strangers was unnerving to me, and I couldn't imagine what I was supposed to do. I was worried about all the other things Keith might have uncovered in Montgomery. And then, there was an indefinable "something" lurking in the back of my mind; a sense that my life was about to change radically stayed with me, and I felt both fearful and excited.

Keith had told me that he would send someone to pick me up at the D.C. airport, but I was flabbergasted when, as I stood in front of the National Airport terminal, a beautiful black antique Rolls-Royce pulled up and a chauffeur got out and took my bags. He "escorted" me to the back seat of the car, like I was the Queen of England or something, and we started out for Keith's office.

We crossed the stately Memorial Bridge and then drove up to Keith's office, which was in the Barr Building on 17th Street, across from Farragut Square. The driver opened the car door for me, then squired me up to Keith's office. The building was one of those wonderful old edifices, built in the twenties or thirties and Keith's office had a frosted glass door with "Law Offices of F. Keith Adkinson" printed on it. It looked like a scene right out of a Raymond Chandler novel. Keith was there to greet me with all his Virginia gentlemanliness. His secretary, Angie, was cordial as well, which was a relief to me since I knew I would be staying at her apartment for the next four days.

Keith took me into his office and before I could sit down, he handed me a three-page document. My hands trembled as I started to read it, but by now I knew the words almost by heart. There it was, three times: "the father, Hank Williams." On the third page were three signatures: On the left was a name I would come to know well, Robert Stewart; on the right, in a big generous scrawl, was the name Hank Williams, and under it, Bobbie W. Jett. I couldn't speak and my eyes filled with tears. There, in my hands, was my parents' agreement. Suddenly the date registered in my mind and I realized that the contract was dated October 15, 1952, and today was October 15, 1984— thirty-two years to the day since Bobbie and Hank had made their arrangement. A double rainbow.

Everybody else in that office—Angie and Keith's friend Clifton Dinneen, who had an adjoining office—seemed as moved and happy as I did at the sight of the agreement. What might have been a sort of awkward, emotional moment felt so comfortable—and comforting—to me. I felt like I was with family, a warm and supportive family.

Finally, I sat down and Keith filled me in on all the other information he had uncovered in Montgomery during his five-day sojourn. We had talked on the telephone several times while he had been in Montgomery, but Keith now explained in greater detail the meaning behind the documents he had uncovered— although, as yet, the implications of those papers were not clear.

"Enough of all this legal mumbo jumbo," Keith said. "Let's get movin', B.J."

"Get movin'?" I said. "But I just got here." Then it struck me.

"Why did you call me B.J.?" I asked.

"That's my nickname for you," Keith said, laughing. "All these documents I've found in Montgomery on you are titled "In Re: The Matter of Baby Jett." So, in my mind, I've been calling you B.J."

Just what I need, I thought. Another name.

I was beginning to see that Keith Adkinson was not a man who could sit idle, and I liked that quality. When necessary, Keith could and would sit for hours and listen or explain complicated information—as he had done on that day when we first met at Gulf Shores. But when something needed to get done, Keith got it done. And now he wanted to make a recording.

"I want you to meet Jim Morris," he said. "Then we can get started on this demo."

We descended back down the elevator and out to that big black Rolls.

"By the way," I said, "Is this your car?"

"Yes," Keith said matter-of-factly. Then he sort of laughed. "I love cars—all kinds. I have an old Bentley, and a couple of Jaguars, too. I just tinker around with them. It's fun. I thought you'd get a kick out of it."

I just sort of looked at him. Strangely enough, I'd always loved cars, too. When I was a teenager, Daddy had once bought me an old stripped-down police car—the kind with no handles inside so the convicts couldn't escape—and I had taught myself how to keep it running and I loved playing around with it. Later on, I'd bought myself that brown Spitfire. Cars are kind of an odd hobby for a girl, particularly a Southern girl, so, like my singing dreams, I didn't talk about this little passion either.

I was starting to like this man, so much so that I was beginning to wonder if maybe we didn't have more things in common than just my legal problems and my singing. For a brief second I wondered if maybe I was liking him a little bit more than I should have.

Keith took me to lunch at a place called Charlie's Crab, and there I met his friend Jim Morris for the first time. I liked Mr. Morris immediately. He is a handsome man—kind, generous, and very knowledgeable about music. Although he was trained as an opera singer, he loved country music, had long been a devoted Hank Williams fan, and had some creative ideas about how to present my singing on the demo tape.

First of all, he thought that, of course, I should sing a few Hank Williams songs, and we decided on "Your Cheatin' Heart," "Hey, Good Lookin'," "Jambalaya," and "Move It On Over." Mr. Morris believed that if Hank had lived, he would have crossed over into the realm of rock and roll, so he wanted me to sing a lively rock tune in a style that Hank might have developed. For that, he chose "Splish Splash," which had been a big Bobby Darin hit in the fifties. Finally, he chose the wonderful Irving Berlin song "What'll I Do," which he said he had arranged with a bit of a country lilt to it.

I was excited by these choices, although I was a little nervous about doing "Splish Splash." I'd never sung rock and roll before, and although "Splish Splash" is considered by some to be a throwaway, gimmicky song, it is tricky to put across effectively. Nevertheless, I was game.

Mr. Morris and Keith had decided that I would work with Mr. Morris for the next few days, practicing the songs, then we'd go to a studio and make the demo tape on Friday.

By the end of lunch, I was feeling thoroughly and completely overwhelmed. Keith drove me over to northwest Washington, where I would be staying with Angie and her roommate, Susan. Angie had worked as Keith's assistant for several years, and functioned as his right arm. Angie was about my age, dark and attractive, and both she and her roommate were very hospitable. I felt like I was in good hands.

That night as I went to sleep, I couldn't help thinking that, for the first time—possibly ever—I was on the "right track." For years, I frequently expressed the notion that my life had been running along two tracks—one that I knew about, and one that I didn't. All my adult life, I had felt that I had something special to do, but as much as I enjoyed my job in Montgomery, I knew that community work was not the answer for me. Now, I realized that finally these two tracks had met, and we—Keith and I—were going to steam ahead full force.

For the next four days, I worked constantly with Mr. Morris or with Mike Aldridge and Pete Kennedy, two of the men Keith had hired to back me up. Mike played steel for a renowned bluegrass troupe called the Seldom Scene, and Pete was a well-known local guitarist. I had never had any formal voice training, so Mr. Morris explained the rudiments of technique like breathing and phrasing. Other times, Mike, Pete, and I would practice singing the tunes I would be recording.

On Friday, October 19, Mr. Morris picked me up and we drove through the wide, busy streets of Washington. Within about twenty minutes we pulled up to a recording studio in Silver Spring, Maryland. Both Mr. Morris and Keith had mentioned the ragtag appearance of the building—the studio was situated upstairs over a retail store, and did look a little dingy—but it certainly impressed me, especially since I'd never been in a recording studio in my life.

When we walked in the door, Mike, Pete, and three other musicians Keith had hired were waiting. In addition to Mike on steel and Pete on guitar, we had a piano player, a bass player, and a drummer. Keith arrived about fifteen minutes after we did, and we all dove in and started working.

I felt a mixture of anxiety and exhilaration about this session. But after a few minutes, I became fascinated with all the goings-on, and I just sang out. We worked hard for the next eight hours. When the engineer announced that he was going to play back the tape over the speakers, Mr. Morris said he wanted to stand behind me to catch me. He was convinced I would fall over the first time I heard my own voice. It's a good thing he did. When my voice blasted out of those speakers, I couldn't believe it! Was that me? But neither Keith nor Mr. Morris was surprised. They told me I sounded great, and the musicians and the engineer agreed.

By late evening, only Keith, the engineer, and I were left. Keith had brought me one red rose—for luck—and I sat in that chair, twiddling that rose around, simply baffled at where I was and what I had done.

Finally, at about midnight, we walked out of the studio with the finished demo tape. We went over to Angie's apartment and played it over and over again. Initially I'd been awed at the sound of my own voice coming off a recording, but now I was feeling kind of critical. I could see where I should have sung this one a little higher or that one a little faster. Nevertheless, both Keith and I loved my rendition of Irving Berlin's "What'll I Do." I felt a little guilty, because of all the songs I sang that day, "What'll I Do," in all honesty, was my favorite. I was sort of sorry—and wondered if maybe it wasn't kind of odd—that it wasn't one of Hank's songs that moved me so that night.

Keith and I sat up until 5:00 A.M. and played the tape over and over again, particularly "What'll I Do." I was feeling the strangest things, confusing things, things I had never felt before.

Much later, Keith would tell me that that was the night he fell in love.

For me, at this time, the notion of "falling in love" was unthinkable. For starters, I was a married woman. But more, I didn't know what "falling in love" was—mostly because I'd never "fallen in love" before in my life. Of course I loved Michael, but our relationship had always been a steady one. I had never experienced a deep passion for anyone. I know now, though, that I fell in love with Keith that night too.

There was one last curious little twist to the tale of my recording debut. Many months later, a wonderful man named Owen Bradley told me that another remarkable guy—a singer and songwriter named Hank Williams—had a weakness for popular American songs written in the early twenties. Honest, heartfelt love songs. Songs like "What'll I Do."

Once I heard that, I knew my real daddy would understand. He would understand it all.

After a sleepless night in Washington, I boarded the plane for Mobile. I carried home my copy of the demo tape and played it for Michael, my mother, Aunt Helen, and friends like Lenore and Sally. They were all interested and supportive, but I could tell they felt somewhat uneasy—perhaps they feared I might be off on some wild goose chase. They were complimentary to me about my singing, and seemed as happy as I was about the impressive results on the demo tape. But none of them seemed to be able to imagine that this whole adventure would go much further.

Not me. I knew I wanted to be a professional singer; it just felt right. What's more, I believed it was meant to be. Perhaps because of Keith's support and drive, I now finally felt comfortable enough to let my dreams be known—and my own enthusiasm show. That old double rainbow glowed in my mind's eye, and I was ready to go with it.

Meanwhile, Keith had some special plans of his own. On Monday morning, Keith started making a few calls to executives in the record business, people he had worked with over the years.

He, of course, thought our demo was good, but he wanted that opinion confirmed by a couple of professionals.

After only two or three phone calls, he'd managed to hook up with a man who was the head of talent development for a major record label in New York that had a successful stable of country-western recording artists. Late that week, Keith and Jim Morris hopped on an early-morning train to New York and spent a couple of hours chatting with this recording executive. In many ways, the meeting went much the same way Keith's initial meeting with Mr. Morris had gone. Without telling the recording executive who I was, Keith played the demo tape, telling the man that he very much wanted an honest opinion. In fact, the executive's response was very positive. When Keith told the man that I was Hank Williams' lost daughter, the man immediately began talking about a potential record contract.

Keith was thrilled with this response, and when he telephoned me that night with the news, I was ecstatic. But although, as Keith put it, he wanted to "test-market" my demo in New York, he felt strongly that the place to start exploring the possibility of a record contract was Nashville.

Nashville was, of course, where Hank Williams had burst onto the national scene; but more to the point, Nashville was Music City, U.S.A., the center for country music. Not only was I country by "blood," both Mr. Morris and the New York recording executive had said that my voice and style were naturally "country." Keith also suspected that if the professionals in Nashville accepted me as Hank Williams' daughter, my quest for a career in music would be easier. Conversely, if certain high rollers in the country music business resisted me because of my relationship to Hank Williams, Keith wanted to know about it sooner rather than later.

By now, Keith and I were talking on the telephone almost daily, and he was carefully keeping me informed about everything he was thinking and doing on both fronts—the legal issues and the singing career issues. And Keith decided, after one more trip to Montgomery to chase paper, he wanted to check out Music City, U.S.A.

10
NASHVILLE

Nashville, Tennessee, a city of some 500,000 people, sits nestled in one of the curvy loops of the Cumberland river smack-dab in the middle of the American South. Nashvillians share an old Southern graciousness with their Virginia and Carolina neighbors. They take great pride in their sixteen fine colleges and universities, especially Vanderbilt; their fascinating "native son," Andrew Jackson; and particularly their unquestioned status as "The Athens of the South," replete with a remarkable replica of the Greek Parthenon. Nashvillians tend to divide themselves into two distinct groups. There are the old-guard folks, sure of their roots, proud of their heritage, respected and respectable. These are the people who belong to the Daughters of the Confederacy or hold their wedding receptions at the Parthenon.

And then there are those music people.

Nashville came to be called Music City, U.S.A., as a direct result of the influence of the Grand Ole Opry, and the Opry, itself, possesses one of the most colorful histories in American music—as important as jazz, Tin Pan Alley, and Broadway.

In the early 1920s, radio stations grew like weeds across America, and radio's influence was felt in all aspects of American life—political, economic, social, and certainly in the field of entertainment. The first radio program—the airing of the returns of the Harding/Cox campaign—was broadcast in 1920. At that time, less than five thousand "receiving sets" existed in the United States. By 1925, when radio station WSM began broadcasting, more than two and a half million homes had radios.

Radio station WSM, owned by the National Life and Accident Insurance Company, began broadcasting on October 5, 1925, and chose the call letters "WSM" as an acronym for their advertising slogan, "We Shield Millions." Less than two months later, on November 28, 1925, WSM launched a program called "The WSM Barn Dance," featuring a popular young announcer named George D. Hay.

George Hay started his career as a newspaperman for the *Memphis Commercial Appeal*, originated the WLS National Barn Dance in Chicago in 1924, and moved to Nashville in 1925 to work on the WSM Barn Dance. Calling himself "The Solemn Old Judge," although he was only thirty years old at the time, the flamboyant Hay brought an entertaining assortment of "hillbilly" musicians to the airwaves, including such colorful groups as the Gully Jumpers, the Fruit Jar Drinkers, the Binkley Brothers and their Clod Hoppers, and Dr. Humphrey Bate and the Possum Hunters. One of the early performers was Uncle Dave Macon, known as the Dixie Dewdrop, who became one of the Opry's top stars for many years. "The WSM Barn Dance" became an overnight sensation.

WSM also featured a program called "The Music Appreciation Hour," which came on the air just before "The WSM Barn Dance" each Saturday night. Of course "The Music Appreciation Hour" specialized in so-called classical music—symphonies, concertos, and opera. One night, as the Solemn Old Judge introduced the evening's entertainment, he said, "For the past hour we have been listening to music taken largely from Grand Opera, but from now on we will present 'The Grand Ole Opry.'" And thus the Opry was christened.

The Opry was first broadcast from a studio in the National Life and Accident Insurance Company Building in downtown Nashville. From the beginning, fans crowded the corridors of the studio hoping to catch a glimpse of some of the performers. This popularity led to the decision to build Studio C, an auditorium capable of holding five hundred fans as well as broadcasting the program. Thus, from the beginning, part of the appeal of the Grand Ole Opry was that it was performed before a live audience. Within months, it was clear that Studio C could not accommodate all the fans, and the Opry moved to a former movie house. Over the next several years, the Opry moved two or three more times, always in an effort to accommodate the ever-increasing studio audience. Finally, in 1943, the program moved to the Ryman Auditorium in central Nashville, where it would remain for over thirty years.

In the late thirties, the Opry began to introduce more singers into its repertoire, the first and most instantly famous was a young man named Roy Acuff. He and his Smokey Mountain Boys became one of the highlights of the Grand Ole Opry, and their records, including "Big Speckled Bird" and "Wabash Cannonball," became blockbusters. Acuff was quickly followed by several other remarkable male singers, like Eddy Arnold, Red Foley, Ernest Tubb, and then, of course, Hank Williams.

Hundreds of stars have crossed the stage and the air waves of the Grand Ole Opry—many of whom are synonymous with American country music: Minnie Pearl, Johnny and Jack, Ray Price, Hank Snow, Mother Maybelle Carter, Ferlin Husky, Little Jimmy Dickens, Kitty Wells, Faron Young, Jim Reeves, Johnny Cash, the Everly Brothers, Patsy Cline, Cowboy Copas, Porter Wagoner, Skeeter Davis, Tex Ritter, Loretta Lynn, Dolly Parton, Mel Tillis, Barbara Mandrell, George Jones, Larry Gatlin, Ricky Skaggs, and Ronnie Milsap. Many of these performers have performed at the Opry for many years—some, like Roy Acuff, for as long as half a century.

Each year almost a million fans from literally around the

world travel to see the performances at the Opry. In 1972, Opryland U.S.A., "The Home of American Music," opened. Once again, fans had "forced " the Opryland executives to build new facilities to accommodate the throngs, and instead of just one new auditorium, they conceived an incredible four-hundred-acre complex. Opryland is to American music what Disneyland is to fantasy—a theme park divided into musical areas that present live musical shows together with animal habitats, rides, restaurants, gift shops. The new Opry House, which seats 4,400, opened in 1974, and a couple of years later the Opryland Hotel, Tennessee's largest hotel and convention center, opened. In 1983, WSM/Opryland—now a huge, sophisticated business—was purchased by Gaylord Broadcasting.

Some people feel that the soul of the Opry died when it grew out of the Ryman and into a major theme park and recreational complex. But in fact, it has never completely lost its homespun appeal.

Once Keith had researched the Williams estate as far as he could for the moment, he decided to go to Nashville and see what kind of reception Hank Williams' long-lost daughter might hope to receive there. A few days before Thanksgiving 1984, Keith flew into Nashville and checked into the Opryland Hotel. Through his research and discussions with his acquaintances in New York, and his political contacts in Washington, Keith had secured introductions to several people he wanted very much to meet, including Wesley Rose, head of Acuff-Rose Publishers, and another man who was the head of a major record company.

Keith was not at all sure what either one of these men would think about Hank Williams' daughter coming onto the scene. He could not anticipate Wesley Rose's response at all, since Wesley Rose had spent years defending the "myth" of Hank Williams, playing down his drinking and other less savory aspects of his life. Surely he knew about me; his lawyer had been the first to bring up my existence in the 1967 trials. Keith knew, therefore, that Mr. Rose would not be shocked, although he very possibly might not warm to the idea. Keith was absolutely positive that the recording executive was just being polite to even agree to see him. As it turned out, both Mr. Rose and the recording executive greeted Keith with tremendous grace.

Wesley Rose was the son of Fred Rose, the man who had been so important in shaping the career of Hank Williams. (Wesley had been his father's table tennis partner on the September 1946 day when Audrey and Hank ventured into the Acuff-Rose offices.) He listened to our demo tape, and assured Keith that he very much wanted to meet me. Keith was amused but understanding when Mr. Rose pressed him on the issue of whether or not I had written any songs. The Hank Williams catalog was one of the most valuable properties Acuff-Rose owned, and Wesley Rose was, of course, very curious about the possibility of some more long-term best-sellers to add to their list.

The recording executive's response to Keith and to my existence was even more surprising. Keith suspected that he would be lukewarm at best, but this man's enthusiasm astonished Keith. He was intrigued with my life story and, like others, thought my demo tape showed great promise. He was concerned about my commitment to a career as a singer, but implied that once we met, and this fear was put to rest, he might be prepared to discuss a recording contract.

Keith quickly discerned that the success of a record depended not only on the artist but also on the person producing the record. In the recording business, the producer holds the same position as the director of a movie or the editor of a book. The artist brings the talent, but the producer (or director or editor) shapes the material. It didn't take Keith long to discover that one of the best producers in Nashville was a man named Owen Bradley.

Owen Bradley, perhaps best known for his work as artistic director of Decca Records and later MCA, can be summed up in one phrase: He is the architect of the "Nashville sound," the style of music made famous by such stars as Kitty Wells, Brenda Lee, Conway Twitty, Patsy Cline, and Loretta Lynn. (Mr. Bradley, a disarmingly humble man, would be quick to say that he shares this honor with Chet Atkins, who in addition to his career as a guitarist held a comparable position at RCA.) In fact, Mr. Bradley was the producer of the sound tracks to the movies about the lives of Patsy Cline and Loretta Lynn: Patsy's *Sweet Dreams* and Loretta's *Coal Miner's Daughter.*

Owen Bradley was brought up in Westmoreland, Tennessee, about fifty miles north of Nashville. During his boyhood, he suffered an eye injury that kept him out of school for several months, and during that time he became obsessed with music and learned to play the piano, guitar, harmonica, fiddle. By the age of fifteen, he started playing in local bands and clubs.

In the mid-1930s, when he was in his early twenties, Owen began working at station WSM in Nashville as what was called a "spot worker," or someone who filled in by singing or playing an instrument during a lull in a program. (He shared the honor with a young student from Vanderbilt University named Dinah Shore.) Within a few years he had worked himself up to the role of musical director at WSM.

In the late forties, he began working as an unofficial assistant to Paul Cohen, another well-known artistic director at Decca Records, and it was under Paul Cohen that he learned and perfected the art of record production. Perhaps because of his easy, professional manner, Mr. Bradley was often given what were perceived as problematic assignments.

For example, in about 1950, Decca was having great success with a singing duo, Johnny and Jack, and Johnny asked Decca to pay some attention to his wife, a young unknown singer named Kitty Wells. Dealing with the spouses of "stars" is considered by some to be an unpleasant task, but Kitty and Owen put together "It Wasn't God Who Made Honky Tonk Angels" and turned Kitty Wells into one of the great female country stars of all time.

Several years later, Paul Cohen gave Owen yet another difficult assignment: a young female artist who was under contract with Coral Records, a subsidiary of Decca. Her name was Patsy Cline. At the time Patsy met Owen, she had recorded one hit, "Walkin' After Midnight," but due to a wrinkle in her contract, she was somewhat restricted in what she was able to record, and therefore had trouble finding appropriate songs. However, when her Coral contract ran out, she decided to stay with Decca (and Owen), and together they chose "I Fall to Pieces" and turned

Patsy into a meteoric star. As Owen says, "Patsy was known to be difficult to work with—but I never found that to be true. We'd disagree, but we'd come to a compromise." Obviously, those compromises were productive.

Although Fred Rose produced all of Hank Williams' records, Owen Bradley had played a part in Hank's success as well. In the late forties, Owen was still artistic director at WSM, but he also worked as a backup musician on many of Hank's records and wrote many of the lead sheets. When we met in December of 1984, Mr. Bradley was finishing up work on the music for *Sweet Dreams*, the movie depicting Patsy Cline's life story.

Owen's son, Jerry Bradley, was also a major force in the music business in Nashville, having been, after Chet Atkins, head of RCA, and later an independent producer for, among others, Charlie Pride. Keith was able to set up a meeting with Jerry Bradley, but for a short while after their interview began, feared that our good luck had run out. They chatted briefly, and then Keith played the demo tape, but Jerry appeared uninterested. Then Keith explained my "bloodline," and although Keith spotted a glimmer of interest, he thought Jerry still wasn't sold. Nevertheless, he kept right on pitching.

Keith explained that a New York label had expressed interest; and that even a Nashville recording executive had shown enthusiasm, but we were looking for something more personal.

"Do you have any suggestions as to who might produce this little girl?" Keith asked. As Keith told me later, this question was followed by an interminable pause.

"Well, there's only one person in Nashville who should produce this girl," Jerry said.

"Who's that?" Keith asked.

"My father," Jerry answered.

Keith then understood that Jerry Bradley was never one to play his hand too quickly. However, after making the hoped-for statement, Jerry launched into a litany of reasons why his father probably could not take me on: Mr. Bradley was getting older, the work on *Sweet Dreams* had been demanding, and it had been a long time since his father had taken on the development of a new artist. But Keith sensed that Jerry Bradley was interested.

Sure enough, by the end of their meeting, despite his reserve, Jerry had promised to talk to his father about me, and arranged an interview with Mr. Bradley the moment I could get to Nashville.

"It doesn't get any better than this!" Keith told me later, laughing. "I've told all of these men that you'll be coming down to meet them," Keith went on. "I can make arrangements for the week of December seventh. How's that with you?"

"I'll be there," I said without hesitating a moment.

As the weeks went by, I began to allow myself to finally accept that the mythical Hank Williams was my flesh-and-blood father. Until Keith found the contract between Bobbie and Hank, I feared allowing myself to face this fact. I thought, because I couldn't prove it, others would think I was out of my mind. Now, of course, we had a contract with Hank's signature on it, and I could prove my bloodline without a doubt.

Nevertheless, as Keith told me of his meetings with these doyens of Music City, I marveled at how quickly they accepted me. I had never once come up against somebody who said: "This can't be true." Wesley Rose, who had known Hank Williams well, accepted my existence without question. Owen Bradley seemed eager to meet me. And even the recording executive, who had never known Hank Sr., didn't seem a bit skeptical.

During his talks with various people in Nashville, Keith had run up against another curious phenomenon. It seemed that many people in the Nashville music establishment were not too crazy about Hank Jr. Nevertheless, I also knew that, by 1984, at age thirty-five, Hank Jr. was one of the most successful stars in country music, and we doubted that he wanted to share any honors with his little sister.

In many ways, Hank Jr. has been as haunted by our father's ghost as I have been, and I sympathized with him on that issue. Randall was only three and a half years old when Hank died, and by then Audrey and Hank had been living apart for a year. I suspected that Randall didn't remember much, if anything, about our father, at least firsthand. His mother had put him on stage, singing Hank Williams songs in the Hank Williams style, at the age of eight, and very soon thereafter he was appearing at the Grand Ole Opry. Fortunately, he exhibited talent, and even sang on the sound track to *Your Cheatin' Heart* when he was only fifteen.

By the time he was eighteen, he had broken with his mother, who up until then had managed his career, and begun to go off on his own. In the mid-1970s he suffered a near-fatal accident when he fell off a mountain in Montana and injured his head so severely that his face had to be totally reconstructed. He was laid up in bed for almost a year.

In the late seventies and early eighties, Hank Jr. aligned himself with the "outlaws" of country music, including such singers as Waylon Jennings, Kris Kristofferson, and Willie Nelson. In other words, he didn't consider himself part of the Nashville establishment at all. He no longer worked at the Opry. The music he wrote and his performances were characterized by a certain wildness or rowdiness, and his personal life fit right in with this image. He often put down the old style of country music, and he added harsh, hard-rock overtones to much of his work. Nevertheless, his rowdy style seemed to account for his vast appeal.

As Keith discovered, much of the Nashville music establishment objected to Junior's manner of pretending to run from the ghost of Hank Williams, yet, at the same time, using our daddy's fame to the hilt. On one hand, he expressed boredom with "classical" country music, but, on the other hand, he didn't hesitate to bring up the fact that he was "Little Bocephus," his father's pride and joy, or to announce that certain of his songs—despite their harsher feel—were just like our daddy's.

Personally, I thought he had every right to take advantage of his ties to Hank Sr., but it had not escaped me that he seemed ambivalent about it. I recognized that being Hank Williams, Jr., helped launch his career, but he had built an awesome audience of his own—one that had little in common with Hank Williams, Sr., or his music.

Although Hank Jr. has never really crossed over into the pop market as Hank Sr. did—or as many contemporary artists like Dolly Parton, Kenny Rogers, and even fellow "outlaw" Willie Nelson have done—he is one of the great lights in the country field, not to mention one of the biggest money earners. As a result, although Hank Jr. is apparently not personally popular in Nashville, he wields plenty of power.

And Keith wondered how that power was going to affect me once Nashville got wind of the fact that I was going to launch a career of my own. I, on the other hand, was concerned with his personal reaction to me. Keith had established proof positive that he must have known about me at least since the late 1960s, when I had been an obstacle to him and his mother in their suit over the copyrights. I couldn't help but believe that he would not be thrilled by my appearance in Nashville.

On December 7, 1984, the day I arrived, it was frigid in Nashville, the kind of dry, stinging cold that sometimes descends on this normally temperate Southern city. It had snowed an inch or two, and it was extremely windy and icy—so much so that they closed the airport shortly after my plane landed. Keith, who had flown up from Gulf Shores, where he had been working, greeted me at the gate with one red rose—for luck—since he and I both hoped this would be a very memorable visit.

Keith had set up a replay of all the appointments he had made during the trip he made to Nashville before Thanksgiving. The moment we arrived he drove me over to meet with Wesley Rose at the Acuff-Rose offices, which were in a modern building in downtown Nashville. Keith was far more businesslike than I, and had come up with a number of questions Mr. Rose might ask me. He tried to prepare me in the car for this meeting, but I was much too wired up to concentrate. I told him that I would absorb what I could, but I just had to be myself—that was the best I could do.

Mr. Rose's office was large, with mementos of his forty years in the recording business lining the walls. Mr. Rose was then in his mid-sixties, about the same age Hank Sr. would have been, and was still running the business side of the Acuff-Rose Publishing Company, as he had almost since its inception. The company was formed in 1942 by Fred Rose, Wesley's father, and

Roy Acuff. In 1945, Fred Rose turned the business side of it over to Wesley so that he could focus his attention on developing writers and singers, the job best suited to his gifts. Roy Acuff, of course, concentrated on his own singing career and business at the Opry, where, by the mid-forties, he was already a major force. Wesley Rose's contributions certainly helped catapult Acuff-Rose into its position as the most successful publisher of strictly country music.

Mr. Rose couldn't have been more cordial to us, and spent about two hours chatting with us, laughing about old Hank stories. Naturally, given his history with my father and his profession as a publisher, he was curious about music I had written. In fact, I'd written many songs, and I told him so. But I wasn't ready to share much with him, or sing for him just then. And Keith was not too sure whether or not Mr. Rose was—or would be—a source of support; in fact, he thought Mr. Rose might well have been one of my original problems.

Nevertheless, I left Mr. Rose's office thinking that I had made a friend. I felt certain that he would help me as his own father had helped mine. I also was beginning to see that a career in music wasn't quite so mysterious. Real people, nice people, seemed eager to help out.

Keith had scheduled a meeting with the recording executive that afternoon. I spent a few minutes explaining to him my feelings about my own talent and the dreams I had had since I was a child—way before I found out that Hank Williams was my daddy. I expected him to be skeptical, but I hardly finished talking before he launched into his ideas for me.

He loved the story of my life and believed that his company would be an ideal place for me to establish my career. Not only did he think he might produce a record, he thought my story could make a fabulous movie. It was almost as though he was selling us on his company, rather than the other way around. As we left his office, he said he would get back to us in a couple of weeks with a tentative proposal.

I was as thrilled with this meeting as I had been with my talk with Mr. Rose. Nevertheless, Keith had reservations about this man as well. He knew that this young executive was new at the Nashville office, and he wondered how long it would take before Hank Jr. made his influence felt. "Somebody's gonna yank his chain," Keith said. "I just know it." I was beginning to see that Keith could be not only a dreamer but also a hard-core realist. He had a sense—as did I—that Little Bocephus was not going to greet me with open arms.

That evening we went to a performance of the Grand Ole Opry in the new Opry House. On Friday, Saturday, and Sunday, the Opry presents two shows, one from 6:30 until 9:00 P.M., and one from 9:30 until midnight, so we arrived for the early show. The theme park adjacent to the Opry House was closed, but we strolled around for a few minutes looking at the carefully groomed grounds, Roy Acuff's beautiful house right next door to the Opry House, and the other buildings that made up the music complex.

Many of the people performing that night had been only famous names to me—like Little Jimmy Dickens, Porter Wagoner, and Hank Snow—and it was exciting to see them, especially since some of them had known my father. Through Keith's political friends, we were permitted to go backstage and be introduced to a man who had been an idol to me—and to my daddy—Roy Acuff.

As it happened, the night we were at the Opry was Mr. Acuff's first evening back after a minor heart attack, so I was reluctant to bother him, but he could not have been more gracious to me. Once we were introduced, he put his hands out and took mine and said, "Your daddy was a good friend of mine and he was a good man," which made me want to cry. At some point in our conversation, he looked at me closely and said, "You know, you look just like him," and although I still felt anxious about taking up his time, he insisted that we have our picture taken together before Keith and I left.

After the performance, Keith and I took a self-styled tour of the Opryland Hotel. We ate dinner in one of the restaurants and then spent an hour walking around a huge space called the Cascades, a sort of botanical garden with winding paths, trickling waterfalls, and fountains. We made it a point to throw shiny pennies—for luck—into every one of the fountains and pools.

Keith had booked a room for me adjoining his at the Radisson Hotel in downtown Nashville. By the time we got to the hotel, it was almost midnight, but we sat up until the early hours of the morning—as we had done a few weeks before in Washington—talking over the events of the day and the possibilities for the future.

Keith and I were growing very close very fast. We had talked to each other daily, we had spent five days together in October, and now we were together again in Nashville. I was beginning to realize that my relationship with Keith could be more than just that of lawyer and client, business manager and artist. Keith, who was divorced, made it clear that his feelings for me were growing, but, thank goodness, he was always a perfect gentleman and never pushed himself on me. I was flattered and moved that he felt as he did; nevertheless, I knew I needed time. Too much was happening too fast. My entire life—emotionally and professionally—was turning upside down, and I wasn't at all sure I could handle it. I told Keith that I was feeling all sorts of things for him, but I wanted to move more slowly with regard to our personal relationship, and he understood and accepted my terms.

For Saturday, December 8, Keith had made plans for us to meet Owen Bradley. Jerry Bradley had told Keith that he would call that day to set up the time, but we waited for several hours before we got the call. For a time, we were again afraid our luck had run out. Finally, in the late morning Jerry Bradley called and told us that we should meet Owen at The Barn, Mr. Bradley's studio, located in Mt. Joliet, Tennessee, about fifteen miles out in the country east of Nashville. We drove out Route 40, a wide interstate, and then got off at the Mt. Joliet exit and headed north. The outlying areas around Nashville maintain much of their country flavor—we even noticed a sign that advertised "Goats for Sale"—and under the bright blue sky and blanket of snow, the scene was particularly beautiful.

Despite the country setting and the humble name, Owen Bradley's "barn" is a large and extremely sophisticated recording studio. When we arrived, several engineers were working on the sound track for *Sweet Dreams*, and as we waited for Mr. Bradley, we were excited to get a sneak preview of the music, especially since Patsy Cline had always been one of my favorite singers. When Jerry Bradley arrived a few minutes later, Owen, Jerry, Keith, and I went into Mr. Bradley's office, lined with all of Owen's gold and platinum records, and started talking.

As Roy Acuff had done the night before, Mr. Bradley began our conversation with the comment: "You know, you're the spittin' image of your dad." Naturally, that remark never ceased to thrill me.

We played the demo tape for Owen, and then Keith got right to the point.

"Would you consider producing Cathy?" Keith asked. I knew he was apprehensive—and I, too, was scared.

Mr. Bradley didn't say no, but he didn't say yes; instead he deflected the question by explaining that he was still deeply involved with the *Sweet Dreams* sound track. At that point, Jerry jumped into the conversation and asked Keith if he couldn't show him around the studio. Keith figured that it was probably a good idea to leave Owen and me alone together, so he and Jerry left the room.

Then Mr. Bradley became very frank. He told me that he believed I had talent—certainly I was able to stay in tune and had a good quality to my voice—but he thought my voice was not strong and powerful enough yet. He also said that he thought I "made a nice appearance," and he suspected that I had charisma, which I found flattering. Ultimately, he said, I needed to do two things: I needed some serious coaching on my breathing control and other technical aspects. But more important, I needed to sing—a lot.

He made it clear that being the child of Hank Williams was as much a curse as it was a blessing. Because of who I was, people would expect more of me. They might come to hear me perform once, but they would leave in a heartbeat if I didn't show real talent of my own. He told me that he knew of a coach whom he admired a great deal, but she was out of the country for a few weeks and he didn't know her schedule. In any case, he thought it would be a good idea if she and I worked together for a time.

I felt good about this talk. Mr. Bradley wasn't telling me that I was the most wonderful singer since Patsy Cline, but he was taking me and my career seriously. He was talking to me as a professional, and I appreciated his honesty and thoughtfulness.

As we were talking, various people kept coming into the room to ask him questions and I could see that they were very busy. Mr. Bradley just wasn't going to say he would work with me right then and there, but I believed he intended to help me and that, alone, was precious to me.

As Jerry Bradley walked Keith and me out to our car, he told us that he very much wanted his dad to work with me and that he thought his dad would do it. Keith and I started driving back to Nashville. We were quiet for several minutes as we watched the soft, snow-covered hills fly by. Finally, Keith said, "Well, I guess we got the answer to at least one question— whether or not at least part of Nashville is ready for Hank's little girl."

I laughed and said, "I feel sometimes like Hank might be smiling on me."

Over the next couple of days we "toured" Nashville, old and new, public and private. We visited the Hermitage, the beautiful home built by President Andrew Jackson, and we walked up and down Music Row, browsing in all the shops and exploring the Country Music Hall of Fame. Finally, I very much wanted Keith to meet Patsy and Willard Jett. It had now been four years since I'd found the Jetts. We exchanged Christmas cards, I called them on their birthdays, and I talked fairly frequently with Jo out in California.

For an adoptee, finding one's "natural" relations is awkward, or at least I found it so. When it comes right down to it, you don't really have that much in common except blood, so after you've made the initial introductions and you've gotten to know each other a little bit, you go back to your regular life and you go on. At first I kept thinking or hoping that our relationship would be stronger or more intense—and I even felt a little guilty that it wasn't. But then I finally figured out that my relationship with the Jetts was no different from my relationship with any other set of cousins or aunts and uncles. You're related, but in fact, you lead totally separate lives.

Of course, I had told Keith all about Bobbie and Jo and the other Tippins kids, and how much I loved Willard and Patsy. I suspected that Keith and Willard would hit it off since Willard, as a former chief of detectives for the Nashville police department, would appreciate Keith's seven years of fighting crime on the Senate Rackets Committee.

I telephoned Patsy, and was upset when she told me that Willard, who suffered from painful, degenerative arthritis, had been in the hospital for several weeks. Patsy seemed a little vague about which hospital Willard was in—I suspected that she thought we might upset him with a visit—but she offered to meet us at the Radisson Hotel for coffee.

When Patsy arrived at the hotel, she still seemed reserved. During all my previous meetings with Patsy, she had been bubbly and talkative. I had not told Patsy anything about meeting Keith, his finding the contract between Bobbie and Hank, or my plans to pursue this case further. I also had told her nothing about my music career. On top of all that, I was up in Nashville accompanied by my lawyer. No wonder she seemed somewhat unnerved.

It took an hour or so for us to explain to her all that had happened since Keith and I had met in September. She seemed very interested, and slowly her reserve started to evaporate. In fact, before too long, Patsy was telling us stories that amazed me.

Patsy launched into an animated tale of the day Bobbie left Nashville with Hank in August 1952. I knew that Bobbie had lived with Willard in Nashville for a couple of years after coming back from California with Jo. I also understood that Bobbie had lived in Mrs. Stone's boardinghouse during the last months of her pregnancy. Now I was hearing the tale of how she got from Willard's home to Mrs. Stone's.

At this time, the Jetts lived in a large house on Acklen Avenue, a nice old residential street just a mile or so from what is now Music Row. By the summer of 1952, Patsy said, Bobbie had been living with the Jetts for two or three years, taking care of her grandmother, Ocie Belle, who was an invalid, and keeping house for Willard and Jo. Patsy, who was engaged to Willard at the time, would go over sometimes just to help out.

Patsy said that on this particular day, Willard had asked her to come over to take care of little Jo because Bobbie would be leaving for Montgomery with Hank Williams. She told us that she remembered Bobbie coming down the stairs dressed in a bright-colored dress and with a small suitcase in her hand. Bobbie waved and simply said "Bye," and off she went down the front steps of the house.

Patsy looked out the window, and Hank Williams was sitting in a big Cadillac not thirty feet away. Bobbie walked out to the car, got in, and the two of them sped off. She remembered that Hank was wearing a white cowboy hat and a light-colored suit.

"How did you know it was Hank Williams in that car?" Keith asked.

"Oh, everybody knew Hank Williams," Patsy said. "But also, Willard had told me that Bobbie was going off with him that day. That's why I was there in the first place. Willard wasn't too happy about Bobbie going off with Hank, I can tell you that. But I was under the impression that they were going off to get married."

"Did you know Bobbie was pregnant?" Keith asked.

I was a little shocked and unnerved by this question. I knew the Jetts were proud people, and, over the few years I had known them, I had avoided asking touchy questions directly. It also made me feel strange. Not only did I know these questions might embarrass them, but I, of course, also recognized that Bobbie's growing baby was me. These feelings were difficult—and even a little frightening—for me to consider.

Nevertheless, Patsy answered Keith in a very straightforward way.

"Oh, yes," she said. "Willard had told me."

I suspected Patsy had much more to say on this subject, but that reserve came over her again. She did tell us that Willard was in the Veterans Hospital, and she would talk to him and see if he felt up to having visitors. True to her word, Patsy called us later that day and told us that Willard would see us.

In retrospect, I can see that Patsy and Willard—and perhaps others in the Jett family—probably felt uneasy about the fact that I had found a lawyer who was obviously going to seriously explore my situation. I'm sure they were afraid that some aspects of Bobbie's life, if made public, might embarrass them.

We found Willard in poor shape at Nashville's Veterans Hospital. He was very thin and weak, and his arthritis had incapacitated him almost completely. Nevertheless, Willard talked with us about Hank and Bobbie's relationship in a more open way than he ever had before.

Willard confirmed what Patsy had told us—that he knew that Bobbie was pregnant, and that she was going down to Montgomery in August 1952. He never said he talked to Hank directly, but he related a funny little incident. He told us that after he learned that Bobbie was pregnant, but before she left for Montgomery, Hank had sent him a pair of pistols to keep.

"Why'd he do that?" Keith asked.

"Don't know," Willard said. "Guess he knew I was pretty mad about the whole thing." We suspected there was more to that story, too, but we didn't press him.

He also told us that, later that fall, Bobbie came back to Nashville and was staying downtown at a hotel. He heard she was there and telephoned the hotel. Bobbie picked up the phone and said: "Hank, honey, come on up," and Willard said, "This isn't Hank. This is your uncle." He implied that this exchange had triggered a big fight.

This was interesting to me because Marie Harvell had told me a story about being in a hotel room with Bobbie and Jo in the fall of 1952. Again, pieces of the puzzle were coming together. I tried to ask Willard more about it.

"Who was with Bobbie in that hotel room, Uncle Willard?" I asked.

"Oh, I don't remember, honey. It was a long time ago."

This was the answer Willard had given many times when I had asked him specific questions, and in the months to come he would say it again and again. Nevertheless, Willard and Patsy had been more forthcoming about Hank and Bobbie than they had ever been before, and I guessed Keith's presence as my lawyer had much to do with their initial reticence and later their openness. I suspected they were a little frightened, and yet saw that we were searching for the truth.

Both Keith and I could see that Willard was weak and tired, so we didn't stay too long that day. As I had suspected, Willard and Keith got along like a house afire. I believed that Willard was glad I'd found someone to help me—someone he could respect on his own terms—even though some aspects of our search might be painful for his family.

As we were about to leave, I decided to tell Willard straightforwardly that Keith and I had decided to explore this situation as intensely and as far as we possibly could. I also told him all about my plans for a singing career and our meetings with Owen Bradley, who turned out to be an old friend of Willard's and Patsy's. Willard lay quietly, listening to me and shaking his head.

I leaned down to kiss him good-bye, and he grasped my hand tightly and said, "Give 'em hell, girl." And I knew he was with us.

11
READING THE RECORD

In three short months, my life had taken a sharp turn. Thanks to Keith, I had discovered beyond a doubt that I was Hank Williams' daughter, that he had wanted me and intended to care for me. Now it seemed clear that those who had known Hank's wishes had gone to great lengths to keep that information from me, and with Keith's help, we were going to find out why, how, and if something could be done about it.

Thanks also to Keith, I had begun to take steps toward establishing a career as a singer, something I had always, secretly, wanted to do. To me, a career as a singer seemed to be part of my legacy, my fate. This was heady stuff for me, and it seemed right. I had total confidence in Keith's abilities as a lawyer and as a business manager, and his support made all of these ventures seem possible.

But another change was also evolving. I finally admitted to myself, without question, that I was falling in love with Keith. During our days in Nashville early in December, Keith had told me that his feelings for me were strong—that he loved me—

but I could not deal with his emotions, not simply because I was already married but because I felt these "life changes" were coming too thick and fast.

We left Nashville on December 9. I went back to Mobile and Keith went home to Washington. Our trip to Nashville had been incredible, and we had ended it with Keith giving me a beautiful white Stetson.

"You'll be needing it," he said. "Hank's daughter has gotta have a white Stetson."

We had planned to talk on Christmas Day, but he never called—or so I thought. Actually, Michael and I had gone out to dinner with my mother and my Aunt Helen. I later learned that Keith had telephoned while we were out. I missed him terribly, thought about him constantly, wished I was with him on Christmas Day—or, better yet, all the time. In other words, I was in love.

Once I admitted my feelings to myself, I was caught short. Michael and I had always been friends—best friends—but we had never "fallen in love." Certainly we loved each other very much, but as friends. I suppose I thought that a friendly marriage was about as good as one could hope for, and until I met Keith, I never questioned it. Now I had this terrible—and terrifying—feeling that I wanted only to be with the man I loved. And suddenly that man was Keith.

By New Year's Eve, 1984, the Christmas mix-up between Keith and me was long forgotten, and between Christmas and New Year's we talked on the telephone daily. Now that I was certain I was Hank's child, New Year's Eve took on special meaning for me because I knew that it was the night my father had died. Michael and I had invited several friends over for a New Year's party. However, as midnight approached, all I could think of was Keith and how I wished I was spending this moment with him. At 11:45 the phone rang and it was Keith. To my joy, he said he was calling to "talk me into the New Year." As Michael and our friends mingled at the party, Keith and I talked only to each other. The minutes preceding the New Year were very personal and belonged only to the two of us, and I almost forgot that anyone else was in the house.

During that telephone call, Keith said he wanted to do something special for my upcoming birthday. I had told him that my birthday had always been a "down" day for me, and Keith wanted to make this particular birthday a very special one. We decided that we would meet in Nashville, stage our own celebration, and then check back with the contacts we had made in early December.

I drove from Mobile to Nashville on my birthday, January 6. Keith, having flown in from Washington, was waiting for me at the Radisson Hotel that evening with flowers and cold beer. We went for a special dinner at one of the best restaurants in Nashville. Then, in what was also turning into a tradition, we went back to the Radisson and talked until dawn.

I still could not—and would not—admit to Keith my feelings for him. In fact, I had barely admitted them to myself. It may sound strange in this day and age, but I deeply value the vows of marriage. What's more, for me, sex is a deep and abiding expression of love. I was spending hours and days with a very handsome and sexy man whom I now knew I loved. At the same time, I was married to another man—whom I also loved. In addition, my life had turned upside down, and I was very vulnerable. Fortunately for me, Keith understood that, and when I told him I needed time—lots of time—he accepted my terms.

At breakfast on the morning of January 7, Keith started the day by nervously saying that he wanted to "drop in" on Jerry Bradley. This set off a couple of alarm bells in my mind.

"What's the matter? Do you think Owen Bradley is going to say no?" I asked.

"No," Keith said. "I just think it might be a good idea to let them know we're here."

Later Keith would tell me that he actually had been concerned, since we had not heard from Owen or Jerry Bradley in almost a month. Keith got on the telephone right after breakfast and found Jerry Bradley, who told us to meet him at his office a few hours later.

We had barely walked in the door when Jerry announced that Owen had decided to take me on.

"Dad's going to work with you," he said. "He has talked with the voice coach, and he wants to start in early March. He'd like you to move down here for a few months, and he has even asked one of the girls in our office to look for a place for you to live."

No sooner had Jerry finished telling us this exciting news than Owen Bradley himself walked in. Mr. Bradley seemed genuinely excited about working with me, and needless to say, I too was thrilled. This truly was the best birthday gift I had ever received.

That afternoon, Keith and I decided to visit the Ryman Auditorium. Neither of us had ever been inside the Ryman, although we had passed its looming presence many times as we drove or walked through downtown Nashville. After the Opry had moved out to the Opryland complex, the Ryman was turned into a museum and offers a nostalgic look at the Grand Ole Opry as it was in its heyday—during the days my daddy sang on its stage.

As I walked into the backstage left of the Ryman I could almost feel the ghosts of Uncle Dave Macon, Red Foley, Ernest Tubb, Patsy Cline— and most of all, Hank Williams— mingling around as they must have done all those Friday and Saturday nights in the forties and fifties. I stood in the center of the small stage and looked out at the Gothic windows that lined the back wall of the theater and the ancient sign on the balcony that read "The Confederate Gallery." Behind me hung the very same advertising signs that had decorated the stage of the Opry for decades, announcing the virtues of Pet Milk, Fender Guitars, and Goo Goo Candy Clusters.

I wondered what it must have been like for Hank on the night of June 11, 1949, when he made his debut. Surely it must have been hot as hell, as it often is in Nashville in June, and since the Ryman has never been air-conditioned and artists milled around the tiny area backstage, he must have been perspiring from the heat and nervousness. I looked out at the rows of old-fashioned pews and tried to picture the three thousand expectant faces and hear the wild applause as they called Hank back six times after he had sung "Lovesick Blues."

Hank's life had changed literally overnight. In a matter of two years he had gone from being a kid playing honky-tonks in south Alabama, to a regular on the Louisiana Hayride, to superstardom at the Opry. As we walked back through stage right and past the two or three little dressing rooms, I almost felt my father at my side.

Keith bought me a poster from Hank's last concert, the one Hank never gave in Canton, Ohio, which they sell as a souvenir at the Ryman. The sight of it, together with the ghostly feelings of the auditorium itself, almost brought me to tears. We walked through the alley to Tootsie's Orchid Lounge and toasted Hank.

Before we left Nashville, I felt a strong need to see Uncle Willard again, too. I was feeling very close to my natural parents, and Willard was the closest living soul I could connect with. We called Patsy's house and got no answer, and then telephoned the Veterans Hospital only to discover that Willard was no longer there. I started to panic for fear he might have died over Christmas, but finally we hooked up with the Jetts' maid, who told us Willard had been moved to a nursing home. We went out there briefly that afternoon, but Willard was so weak that we stayed for only a few minutes.

That night we drove down to Montgomery.

Keith was ready to launch into an aggressive battle to get access to my adoption files. He tried to prepare me for how tough this skirmish was going to be, but it didn't take much to convince me. I had already talked myself blue in the face with Miss Austin and Miss Pittman. If he was General Lee, I was Stonewall Jackson—and we both suspected we were in for a siege.

As part of our research, and prior to our approach to Pensions and Security, I wanted Keith to meet the rest of my "family," and on January 8 I took him to visit for an hour or two with Marie Harvell. She was talkative, telling Keith all her anecdotes about Hank, but ended our visit with her famous evasive line: "I wasn't at the havin' and I wasn't at the gettin'." Sometimes I would fantasize about buying Marie her tombstone and engraving those words right on it. For his part, Keith did not like her or trust her.

I also took Keith to meet Mama Cook. (Sadly, Daddy Cook had died in 1983.) Today, Troy Highway is a four-lane highway, so it takes only half an hour to drive the twenty-five or so miles down to Pine Level, which always amazes me, since I know that in 1955 Pine Level might as well have been on planet Neptune. Keith loved meeting Mama Cook, who greeted us with her usual gentleness and warmth. After we visited there for an hour, we went down the road to chat with Jimmy Cook and his family. Jimmy told Keith his tales of me at age two and of his adventure with Jewel into Montgomery on the day I left to go to my new home with the Deuprees. I could see that Keith was moved by Jimmy's lasting affection for me—and mine for him and his family.

On January 9, we decided we would see what sort of headway we could make at the Department of Pensions and Security. Of course, I had visited with them before, and aside from confirming a few incidental facts, they had always declined to give me much information. To them, giving me my files was unthinkable. Keith, too, had made inquiries about my files and had been told that claiming them was impossible.

That morning, we dropped by the office of Tommy Gallion, an attorney in Montgomery who at the time was a partner of Keith's friend Perry Hooper. (Keith had talked with them about serving as our Alabama counsel should we need one.) We told him we were in town to see about getting the files and he offered to call Pensions and Security to tell them we wanted to come by. Tommy had little luck getting through, and placed the call several times. Finally a person in authority called back and said Pensions and Security was ready to receive Keith and me. Mr. Gallion walked us over and a lady at the reception desk directed us to Miss Austin's office. When we entered, all my files sat on her desk in front of her.

Miss Austin, to our total surprise, said they had had their lawyers review the matter, and while they still maintained they could not give us the files, she was authorized to read from them if we wished. Keith and I immediately said, "Yes."

"Now, Cathy," she said, "are you sure you want to hear this?"

"Yes, of course," I answered. Her question suggested to me that whatever was in those files might be shocking and was certainly going to be intensely personal. When Keith gave me a sort of knowing look, I realized he understood, and I was glad he was there.

"One last question before I begin," Miss Austin said to Keith. "What do you intend to do with this information?"

"That depends on what the information says," Keith answered immediately.

Miss Austin sort of shook her head. Clearly, she was not at all convinced that the matter was going to end with the reading.

"So," she said, "what would you like me to read?"

I thought that was an odd question. Since I didn't know what was in the files, how could I possibly know what to ask her to read? So I answered the only intelligent way possible.

"All of it," I said. "Read all of it, please."

Looking down at the four-inch pile of files, she asked, almost pleadingly, "All of it?"

"Yes, ma'am," I said.

Miss Austin opened one of the files and pulled out a packet of typewritten sheets, about half an inch thick, typed single-space.

"This is a daily log," she explained. "Caseworkers are required to take notes and then record any meeting they have with regard to any foster care or adoption proceeding. I'll just start right in at the beginning. The first entry is dated January 28, 1953."

Miss Austin cleared her throat. I took a deep, nervous breath. Then she began to read:

1/28/53: Mrs. William Stone in office on this date . . . Mrs. Stone discussed her situation with ease, but cried during the time that she was talking. She said that she was in the office in regard to a child which was born on January 6, 1953. She explained that this child is the daughter of Bobbie Webb Jett and that the father of the child is her son, Hank Williams, deceased.

After all the mystery surrounding my paternity, I was shocked to hear such a bald, forthright statement: "She explained that . . . the father of the child is her son, Hank Williams . . . " I asked Miss Austin to repeat that sentence to make sure I heard it right. She did, then continued reading:

> Mrs. Stone brought with her a letter stating "to whom it may concern" and signed by Mr. Williams. It said that he would be responsible for the delivery of this child at the hospital where the mother desired. Mrs. Stone said that she took care of Miss Jett throughout the pregnancy in the boarding home which she rents and is located next to hers on North McDonough Street. She mentioned that her son took care of all the expenses during this time.

Although the meanings and complexities of this information had not quite sunk in yet, and it told me little more than I already knew from the contract Keith had found, it somehow seemed startlingly real. It was almost as if my grandmother was sitting next to me telling me the whole story herself.

Suddenly Keith jumped up and excused himself. I was shocked. He left the room for a couple of minutes and then returned looking harried and out of breath.

"I'm terribly sorry," he said. "I've totally forgotten a meeting we cannot miss. I can see this will take some time. May we come back tomorrow morning?"

Miss Austin seemed as surprised as I was by Keith's behavior, but she agreed.

"Good," Keith said, and took my arm as we left the office.

Once we were out on the street, Keith explained only that he had something to do for an hour or so. I said I wanted to come with him, but he said no, not this time. It wasn't until much later that I learned that he spent the next couple of hours stocking up on microcassettes and tapes.

The next morning we arrived at 8:50, and Keith, as I later learned, had three little tape recorders hidden in his pockets. We sat down again across from Miss Austin at her desk, and didn't get up again for the rest of the day. At least, *I* didn't get up for the rest of the day. Miss Austin must have thought Keith was juggling an awful lot of business or had a severe bladder problem. Every thirty or forty minutes he would apologize, leave the room, and come back with fresh tapes and ready to go.

The caseworker's log was a remarkable document because it seemed so immediate—as though we were back in 1953 watching these events unfold. Miss Austin began her reading the second day by finishing the log entry for January 28, 1953:

> The situation at the present time is that according to Mrs. Stone, Miss Jett had signed a paper stating that she wished for Mrs. Stone to keep the child until she was two years of age, and that Mrs. Williams would be responsible for this child's care until that time. She stated that . . . she does not wish to keep the child unless she can adopt her and that she would be tremendously interested in doing so.
>
> While crying, she stated that she knew that this is what her son would want her to do. Mrs. Stone seemed quite devoted to the child and it was apparent that she was very desirous to keep this child as it appeared that she would feel closer to her son.

I was absolutely overwhelmed with the fact that I was hearing a continuous recollection of events in my life—events now thirty-two years old. From these records, I knew exactly where my grandmother was on a given day, and even that she had been crying.

The caseworker's log itself was fascinating, but the files also contained scores of letters that supported and amplified the information. Most of the files concerned Mrs. Stone's efforts to prove her suitability to adopt me.

It became clear from the files that Mrs. Stone had been forced to go to great lengths to prove that she was a suitable person to adopt me. This was not an easy task for her since in 1953 she was fifty-five years old and suffered from heart trouble. (She had no trouble showing that she could care for me financially or even emotionally—which are, of course, common considerations.) However, because of her age and physical condition, the only way she could be deemed an appropriate adoptive mother was if she was a blood relative. As a result, she ended up having to prove that she was my paternal grandmother—or, to put it another way, that Hank was my father. The welfare department also required proof that my natural mother, Bobbie Jett, agreed to having Mrs. Stone adopt me. They also ultimately demanded a written statement from Bobbie declaring that Hank was my father.

In addition, Mrs. Stone had to satisfy the state that I would be cared for in the event she died before I was grown. They required an agreement that should she die, her daughter, Irene, would take care of me. All of this was complicated by the fact that, during the adoption process, Lillian got a divorce from her second husband, Bill Stone.

Given these terms, it took Mrs. Stone months to establish her suitability as an adoptive mother. In one letter, dated May 14, 1953, from the Child Welfare Service in Montgomery to the Davidson (Tennessee) County Department of Public Welfare, a caseworker summed up the situation—which at this point had been discussed and rediscussed for almost three months:

> We have several questions in regard to the suitability of this home for the placement of an infant. In the first place, we question the age of the grandmother as she is now fifty-five years of age and her health is not as good as formerly. Mr. Stone, the step-grandfather, is forty-two years of age. Then too, our references have made statements to the effect they feel that Mrs. Stone was lax in the training of her own children and allowed undesirable behavior on the part of her son.
>
> On the other hand it is felt that both Mr. and Mrs. Stone strongly desire that the child be legally adopted to them and they seem to express warm interest and affection in her. Because of the apparently accepted blood ties so far as everyone connected is concerned and with the natural mother's definite and clear-cut statement that she will not surrender the baby for adoption unless she is assured that Mrs. Stone will adopt the child, we feel that it would be best to proceed on this basis.

Mrs. Stone's problems were evidently complicated by the action—or lack of action—of her lawyer, Robert B. Stewart. In a log entry dated March 11, 1953, the caseworker wrote:

I telephoned Mr. Robert Stewart, lawyer on the Stone case, in regard to this matter. Mr. Stewart . . . told me that . . . he did not think that Mrs. Stone should have this child. He said that is one of the reasons he has not worked any harder on the case. He pointed out that she is ill and is getting old, and furthermore is not actually able to give the child the things she needs.

However, the biggest obstacle Mrs. Stone faced, based on the caseworker's log and other letters in the file, turned out to be getting Bobbie Jett to cooperate. It wasn't that she did not want to give me to Mrs. Stone—clearly, she did. The problem had to do with her emotional state and pressures she was experiencing in her home, particularly from Willard. She made her problems clear in a handwritten letter to Mrs. Stone dated February 10, 1953, just six weeks after Hank's death and my birth. In part, Bobbie wrote:

Dear Mrs. Williams,
Can you ever forgive me for not writing you as I should. Honestly, I haven't had a chance to even breathe. Mama and Jo have both been very sick. So, I have had to take care of them—cooking, house and all.

Bobbie had just given birth to a child, suffered the death of that child's father, and was responsible for a three-year-old. But when she returned to Nashville, apparently, she was obliged to take on heavy household responsibilities. However, after apologizing for not writing, she addressed the point of the letter—which was to assure Mrs. Stone that she would sign the papers, acknowledging that she wanted Mrs. Stone to have me:

I would like very much to see you all so I will come down there just as soon as I can and sign the papers. Yes, I want to do the right thing and am going to. You and I made a bargain. I will stick to mine.

Bobbie's letter also provides a feeling for Mrs. Stone's maternal qualities, and Bobbie's—and Jo's—apparent emotional attachment to her:

So, you see those talks you would give me did some good. Jo and I both miss you very much. When she gets mad here, she says she is going home to "Liddy." She will never forget you. I won't either. You were so good to us—Mama said you were a fine person—said you were never too busy for me when I needed you.

Bobbie closed the letter by restating that she wanted Mrs. Stone to have me, but made it clear that she was emotionally distraught—which is hardly surprising:

You take good care of yourself, and the baby, and let me hear from you when you can. Just believe and trust in me and know I will do what is right. I want you to have the baby, couldn't be in better hands, and loved any more. So just give me a little time to get things straight here. I get so lonesome and blue at times I can hardly go on, but know I have to. I have Jo, and now you have something to look forward to.

Please take care of yourself and know Jo and I love you very, very much—Till I see you—

Love, Bobbie & Jo

This letter was followed by another, dated just two days later, February 12, 1953, from a child welfare worker from the Montgomery Department of Public Welfare to the "chief" of the Bureau of Field Service in Nashville. In it, the caseworker outlined the entire situation:

According to Mrs. Stone, Miss Jett left the baby at her home and returned to Nashville. She has not told Mrs. Stone of any definite plan she has in mind for this child; however, it is our understanding that it was originally agreed that Mr. Williams would assume financial responsibility for two years after the child's birth. Mrs. Stone told us that she would like to have the baby herself provided she could legally adopt her, but otherwise, she is very anxious that Miss Jett take the baby back. Mrs. Stone pointed out that she is becoming more attached to the baby and unless consideration can be given to her permanently keeping the child, she wishes to be relieved of this responsibility at the earliest possible convenience. She indicated a strong desire to keep the baby.

Several letters were exchanged between the Montgomery and Tennessee authorities in an attempt to analyze the situation with regard to "the baby." The social workers in Nashville attempted to get a written statement from Bobbie declaring what she wanted done with "the baby." In a letter dated March 27, 1953, a social worker described Bobbie's history and situation in detail:

Bobbie Jett was born 10/5/22 in Nashville, Tennessee, the only child of Pauline Jett. Since infancy she has lived with her maternal grandparents. According to Mrs. Jett, when Bobbie Jett was three years old her mother went to Cincinnati for a course in nursing. After she became a nurse, she lived in California. Mrs. Jett made the statement "Bobbie's father was killed when she was three years old." . . . she said his name was Miller. Mrs. Jett told us that when Bobbie was ready for school "they" wanted her legal name to be Jett, and an attorney advised adoption.

The home seems to be an odd mixture of personalities. It is composed of Mrs. Jett, Bobbie Jett and her child Josephine, Colonel Jett [Willard], a handsome friendly person, and another son of Mrs. Jett's who appears to be somewhat taciturn. "The Colonel" seems to be the dominating figure in the home . . . we gained the impression he has supported both Bobbie and her daughter Josephine.

Miss Jett is an attractive blonde, small in build. We gained the impression that she is a nervous, disturbed, repressed person. It would seem that her behavior stems from her background and the domination of her uncle, whom she also designates as "the Colonel."

Miss Jett has a difficult role to fill; she feels a deep sense of responsibility for her grandmother, who is unable to dress herself. She has the care of her own child and prepares all the meals for the family.

Miss Jett informed us she is ready to sign a surrender in Nashville in the presence of her uncle. She "cannot sign any paper without the Colonel's consent." We assured Miss Jett that she alone has the right to make such a decision. She will surrender the baby for adoption only with the assurance the baby is to be adopted by Mrs. Stone. Miss Jett expressed the idea that the care of the baby will in some measure compensate Mrs. Stone for the loss of her son. Miss Jett rationalizes by saying, "I am keeping the baby in the family circle."

During our interview we realized Miss Jett was repeating for her baby her own experience of being adopted by a grandmother. Miss Jett was definite in her refusal to surrender the baby except for adoption by Mrs. Stone.

We have included a lengthy description of Miss Jett's situation since it appears to be an abnormal atmosphere for a child or young person. If you desire a surrender from Miss Jett within accordance with her provision that the baby be adopted by Mrs. Stone, we will attempt to assist the mother. Miss Jett said as we terminated the interview, "I can't tell you how relieved I feel."

These letters were like "snapshots" of my mother's family and her life, and I was completely enthralled by them. Clearly, Bobbie was willing to give me up for adoption only if, in fact, Mrs. Stone was to be the adoptive mother. The problem, as it turned out, had to do with obtaining a notarized release or statement from Bobbie—and this problem was not solved for months.

The primary obstacle to obtaining the release seemed to be Willard Jett. Many times, the Nashville caseworkers referred to Willard's total domination over Bobbie, "to such an extent she is unable to make any independent decision." It appeared that Bobbie was ready to give me to Mrs. Stone in her letter of February 10, 1953, but in a letter from the Nashville caseworker to the Montgomery caseworker dated June 22, 1953, four months later, Bobbie had still not signed the appropriate forms.

Willard's resistance had to do with the fact that he was reluctant—perhaps embarrassed or ashamed—to reveal to a notary—who would undoubtedly be someone he knew personally or who was acquainted with the Jett family—that Bobbie had an illegitimate child, one that she was giving up. What's more, with Jo present in the household, it would be clear that Bobbie had yet another child with no visible father. I knew, based on my relationship with Willard, that he was a very proud man. I also could see, as much as I loved him, that he could be a domineering one.

The Nashville caseworker, in the same letter of June 22, seemed to understand the situation:

> Miss Jett said "the Colonel" would arrange with a Notary for the signing of the forms. The Colonel hoped to find someone he could trust not to reveal the information on the surrender. Miss Jett told us that she has never been married.

The fact that Bobbie's previous (or current) marital status was in question posed another problem not only for the welfare department but for Mrs. Stone—and, most of all, for Bobbie herself. In a letter dated August 24, 1953, from the Montgomery people to the Nashville people, the welfare worker laid out the sticky points:

> We wondered if Miss Jett has been previously married or if her other child was born out of wedlock. In the event she has been married, would you verify this divorce for us. Should she not be divorced, please explain to her that it will be necessary to have the consent of the legal father although he is not the natural father of this child. We are also asking for a statement from Miss Jett as to whom she says is the father of her child.

The Nashville caseworker responded to this request in a startling letter dated September 1, 1953:

> In response to your letter of August 24, Miss Jett reluctantly agreed for us to see her on August 31.
>
> When we arrived, Miss Jett seemed to accept the visit and was in a fairly good humor. She became quite indignant over the request to make a written statement as to the identity of the father of the child. Miss Jett feels that she has met all the requirements for the adoption of her child and should not be approached again concerning it.
>
> We thought she would refuse to write any word, finally she hurriedly and with much nervousness or anger wrote out the en-

closed statement. We accepted it, since we realized it was possibly all she was willing to say.

The "enclosed statement," which Miss Austin read to us, was only a photocopy of the original note, which seemed to be missing from the file. Nevertheless, its contents were extraordinary:

Hank Williams is the father of the baby Mrs. W. W. Stone of Montgomery, Ala. now has—Bobbie Jett.

I was dumbfounded, not only over the note itself, but because the original was missing from the file. Keith gave me a knowing nod; this was exactly the sort of material Keith had feared would be "missing."

However, the letter from the Tennessee authorities went on to describe Bobbie's almost hysterical rage at being asked whether or not she had been married before.

In our correspondence to you on 6-22-53 we reported the information we had received from Miss Jett, that she had "never been married . . . "

When we said, "I believe you told me during one of our visits you had never married," she was quite angry and denied saying it. She said, "Alabama is just prying into my affairs . . . this is my private business giving my baby to Mrs. Stone, they ought not to mess with it." She was unable to accept any interpretation of the concern of Alabama to protect the child and her future security.

We asked, if she had married, had she obtained a divorce in Tennessee. Would she tell us what name Josephine uses, if not Jett? She could not recall where she obtained the divorce, which she said was granted two and a half years ago, nor would she give us the child's name other than Josephine. She began to threaten Alabama with dire activities on her part, if Alabama did not stop "messing" with her and her past.

We do not believe we can obtain more definite information for your report.

Ultimately, Keith and I never found proof of whether or not Bobbie was ever married to Jo's father. Frankly, I suspect she was not.

The other issue that required clarification before Mrs. Stone could complete adoption proceedings had to do with my fate should Mrs. Stone become incapacitated or die. Marie Glenn (Harvell) was referred to frequently in the files, and it was clear that Marie was my caretaker or nursemaid. However, Mrs. Stone chose her daughter, Irene, as the most responsible member of the family to take over in the event of her death.

In 1953, Irene Williams Smith and her husband, J.T., were living in Portsmouth, Virginia, where J.T. was serving as a chief yeoman in the U.S. Navy. In order to assure the Montgomery welfare department of Irene's suitability, the Norfolk (Virginia) Department of Public Welfare was asked for a report. In a long response, dated September 23, 1953, the Norfolk department summed up Irene's personal life at that time:

> The Smith household consists of J. T. Smith, age 32, Irene Abby Williams Smith, age 31, Irene LaNora Smith, age 7, and John T. Smith, age 10. The family lives in a three-bedroom apartment . . . and it appears clean and "lived in."
>
> Mrs. Smith describes Mr. Smith as being a "quiet, easygoing person" who allows her to make decisions on family matters.
>
> Mrs. Smith is a friendly, talkative individual who seems to be content in her role of wife and mother.
>
> She states that she will be willing to assume responsibility for Antha in the event this becomes necessary. She had inquired about adopting the child prior to Mrs. Williams' adopting her. She feels that adoption of the child in her mother's community, where the child's parents are well known, may present upsetting situations later, but she seems to be delighted that her mother and stepfather have a child. She seems to have positive feelings toward the child's mother and the child. She seems to maintain a close relationship with her mother.

The letter goes on to describe Irene's children in some detail and the financial situation of the Smith family, which was sound. Then the report concludes with a fascinating statement—a remark that proved to be one of the more telling observations in the entire file:

> Mrs. Smith stated that she understands that Antha will share any inheritance with her and she is glad to share with her if the child brings her mother happiness as she has done in the months her mother has had her. She stated that she is glad that this child will in this way be able to share the family's estate.

Even Miss Austin appeared to be taken aback by this statement, since, of course, she was well aware of the subsequent suit between Irene and me that went on from 1955 to 1959, the suit that prevented me from inheriting from Mrs. Stone's estate. I thought it was shocking that Irene had gone so far as to say she was "glad this child will be able to share in the family estate." Keith, whose mind could jump to the legal ramifications of Irene's remark, found it enraging.

The files revealed that the adoption proceedings lumbered on for another year. During 1954, Lillian and Bill Stone were divorced, but the file indicated that the welfare department believed that their separation did not adversely affect Mrs. Stone's ability to care for me. It appeared that their divorce was so amicable, in fact, that Bill Stone agreed to pay child support (ten dollars a week) to Mrs. Stone for my care. What's more, after the divorce, although Mrs. Stone went back to using the name Williams, my name remained Stone when the adoption became final. I wondered why, but I settled on the fact that since Bill Stone was my adoptive father, I was a Stone.

The Probate Court granted the final decree of adoption on December 23, 1954, one month short of two years after Mrs. Stone had started working toward that end. A birth certificate in my adopted name of Catherine Yvone Stone was issued to her about seven weeks later, on February 7, 1955. (Curiously, "Yvone" was spelled wrong on my birth certificate, just as "Hiriam" was spelled wrong on Hank's.) Two weeks later, on February 25, 1955, Mrs. Stone died of a heart attack in her sleep.

All her work had been in vain. On March 10, 1955, the log indicated that the wheels were already well in motion to get me out of the picture. Ironically, the forces behind that "railroad train" were Irene Williams Smith, who had promised to care for me, and Robert B. Stewart. As the log stated:

3/10/55: Mr. Bob Stewart, lawyer for Mrs. Stone, called on this date and stated that Mrs. Stone's daughter, Irene Smith, would like to come to the office and discuss what would be best for Cathy Stone, the adopted daughter of Mrs. Stone who is supposedly Hank Williams' child.

Later:

Mr. and Mrs. Smith in office by appointment. Mrs. Smith stated that she felt that it would be for the best interest of Cathy if the child was placed for adoption and was no longer associated with Hank Williams' family. She . . . feels that there would always be publicity and gossip connected with this baby. They plan to return to Montgomery each year for the Hank Williams Memorial and Mrs. Smith stated that she could just hear the tongues wagging now when Cathy would ride down the street in an automobile as part of the parade to commemorate Hank.

Irene worked quickly. She explained to the caseworker that Bill Stone wanted the Smiths to take me, but that he understood Irene's point of view. According to the log, she brought Bill Stone into the office on March 11, and he agreed that it would be best for me to be placed for adoption. However, as the log stated:

Mr. Stone was quite emotional and cried, but after a lengthy discussion, stated again that he could see nothing else to do but have the child placed for adoption.

On March 15, Bill Stone met the social worker at Juvenile Court and signed the petition for me to be taken to a boarding home. Again, the log stated that Mr. Stone "was very emotional and cried."

Of course, I already knew that on March 15 I was taken from Mrs. Stone's boardinghouse screaming and shunted down to Pine Level, Alabama. Nevertheless, the file continues:

3/17/55: Mrs. Smith in office by appointment as we explained that we would like as much background information on the alleged father of Cathy as possible as it would help in finding the most suitable home for the child. Mrs. Smith seemed to thoroughly understand and was quite willing to give any information and cooperate in every way.

Mrs. Smith was quite talkative and seemed to want to talk in detail regarding her family, herself, and the placement of Cathy for adoption. She told us that someday Cathy would be eligible to inherit money from Mrs. Stone. Mrs. Smith explained that she had been appointed as administratrix of the estate, but it would be many years before it would be settled and any money would be realized from it. Mrs. Smith stated that she and Cathy would share in a certain percentage of the royalties received from the sale of Hank Williams' records and sheet music. Worker assured Mrs. Smith that we would call Mr. Stewart and talk with him as to who the Court appointed as Cathy's guardian and what the possibilities were for her inheriting any large sum of money.

Again, Irene's statement was absolutely breathtaking. It was not yet clear precisely what had happened, but we knew one thing for sure: I never received any "royalties."

Keith and I spent the entire day with Miss Austin listening to her read from my files. Already I had a much clearer picture of what had happened to me and why—at least as far as my adoption by Mrs. Stone was concerned. The files confirmed, over and over, what the contract had already stated: that Hank Williams was my father and he had wanted me, and I was expected to inherit from his estate. Everyone involved—from Mrs. Stone, Bobbie, and Irene, to several members of the Montgomery and Nashville bureaucracy, said so at one point or another.

For me, the most painful part of the files had been the reports on Bobbie. Any last fantasy I may have had that she had secretly wanted me—or perhaps had been somehow "forced" to give me up—was eradicated. I had to face reality. I remembered my fistfight with Jo, and realized that I had always known the truth. But I could never deny it now.

And yet, I felt sympathy for Bobbie. Bobbie's early life experiences paralleled mine—or so it seemed. Although I did not know all of the details, I could see that Bobbie's separation from her own mother must have been painful to her. Although apparently she was confused and upset, I suspected she was trying desperately to do what was best for me.

As Keith had suspected, the facilitator of all the deception was quite clearly the Williamses' lawyer, Robert Stewart. He had drafted Hank and Bobbie's agreement, then kept it hidden for many years. He had purported to represent Mrs. Williams in her efforts to adopt me, yet had dragged his feet, telling the state he did not want his client to succeed. Then, after Mrs. Stone died, he showed up again helping Irene in her efforts to make me a ward of the state—and to place me as far out of the Williams sphere of influence as possible. We now knew more about what happened, how it happened, and who was responsible, but we still had many unanswered questions. In fact, each new bit of information raised a score of unsettling issues.

As Keith and I walked down the steps of the Department of Pensions and Security late that January afternoon, we felt both drained and elated. We had taken a major step forward. But slowly I began to feel angry.

"It just burns me to be so close to my files and not have them," I said. "It's the worst of all worlds now. I know what's there, but I can't have them."

"Look," Keith said, as he put his arm around me, "I promise you those files. If they'll read them to us, I guarantee we can get them to turn them over."

"Promise?" I said, knowing that if he said he'd get them, he'd get them.

"Promise," he said with a hug. "It's meant to be."

12
LOVE AT LAST

After our second trip to Nashville and our remarkable days together in Montgomery, Keith and I knew that all the things we had once thought were fantasy could now become reality. The mechanism for change in my life had been set in motion. Owen Bradley had said that he wanted me to move to Nashville within the next several months in order to work with him. After hearing the contents of my adoption files, Keith could tell that something was amiss with regard to how I had been treated, and although we were still unclear on the details, he intended to push the legal issues aggressively.

Keith and I also knew that something deep and powerful was developing between us. On January 10, Keith went back to Washington and I went back to Mobile, but we recognized that it was only a matter of time before we would be together on a more permanent basis. For the next week after we returned from Montgomery, we continued our daily telephone calls. More and more frequently, Keith discussed my coming to Washington, ostensibly to work on my singing and to talk about legal tactics, but we both knew that what he had in mind was more than just another brief visit.

Finally, Keith told me he was sending me a one-way ticket to Washington for a plane leaving from Mobile on January 19. I knew in my heart that by sending me a one-way ticket Keith was saying that he wanted me to come to Washington to stay forever, but I wasn't quite ready to admit to anyone that I was leaving my old life. I could barely admit it to myself. Nevertheless, I knew I was going, and I made my plans, telling Michael, my mother, and Aunt Helen, that I was going up to Washington to continue working on my singing.

The weather in Mobile conspired to make my nerve-racking departure even more difficult. On the nineteenth, it turned frigid, which is rare, and Mobile was hit with an ice storm. After I boarded the plane, we sat on the runway for hours, waiting for the sun to melt the ice that had formed on the wings. The waiting only added to my nervousness. I'm a "white-knuckle" flyer anyway, the result of a couple of rocky flights I'd been on in the past, and tales of dangerous maneuvers I had heard from Michael. Finally, the airlines canceled the flight altogether, and I had to go home to wait until the next day. When I showed up at the airport the following morning, we experienced some additional nerve-racking delays, but finally the plane took off.

Again, Keith had his driver meet me at the airport in the Rolls-Royce, and by the time I got to Keith's office, around midafternoon, everyone was in a dither because—to my amazement—we were all going to one of the Presidential inaugural balls.

"Why didn't you tell me?" I asked Keith, instantly realizing that I had not brought anything to wear to such an event. I wondered if I even owned anything suitable.

"I knew that the prospect of going to a Presidential ball would make you even more nervous than you already were," Keith said, and turned me over to Angie, his secretary.

Keith had told me that he had made arrangements for me to live at Angie's apartment—as I had done in October—for the next few weeks until we went to Nashville. Angie and I had gotten to know each other a little bit in October, and I liked her, so this arrangement sounded great to me. Angie also had the inaugural situation well in hand. Late that afternoon, Angie and I drove over to her apartment, she presented me with a glittering black gown that she had borrowed from a friend, and fortunately, it fit perfectly.

At seven o'clock, Keith picked me up in the Rolls. We were spending the evening with clients of his from California, Steve and Janice Tavera, and it eased my nervousness to see that this couple was just as dazzled as I was about attending an inaugural event. The particular ball we were attending was at the Washington Convention Center, and was attended by two or three thousand people. I had been to many formal balls in my life, particularly the Mardi Gras balls that are the highlight of the year in Mobile, but this party was certainly more high-powered than any I had ever attended.

"You look gorgeous," Keith said the moment he saw me, and I could see by the expression on his face that he meant it. Looking gorgeous had always been Mother's domain, but I must admit, I felt wonderful and suspected that my "starry-eyed" feelings showed.

We milled around the ballroom, drank champagne, danced, and chatted with scores of people. I recognized several famous senators and congressmen—faces I had seen on the front pages of newspapers—and they looked incredibly dignified and glamorous in their black ties and dinner jackets. The women all wore beautiful gowns, not unlike Mobile ladies dressed for a Mardi Gras ball, and glowed with power and sophistication. When President and Mrs. Reagan made a brief appearance and danced for a few minutes, I shook my head in disbelief. Here I was, partying with the President of the United States! It was like a dream.

We left the ball about 10:00 P.M. and went for a late dinner with Steve and Janice to one of Washington's best restaurants, the Jockey Club. After dinner, Keith took me for a drink at the Embassy Hotel, a handsome hotel on Massachusetts Avenue near Embassy Row, where Keith's friends from California were staying.

By then it was after 1:00 A.M., and I was exhausted. Only

twelve hours had passed since I had left Mobile, but it might as well have been twelve years. I had never dreamed I would attend a party with the President of the United States, but I felt surprisingly comfortable in my new position as a "Washington lady." I had never thought I would be living in Washington, D.C., but here I was, at the other end of Keith's one-way ticket—and I intended to stay.

As Keith's friends said good-night, Keith suddenly made an interesting announcement.

"Look," he said, "I can see that you are really tired. Another couple was supposed to have joined us this evening, from Texas, but they couldn't make it. I booked a room for them—and it's all paid for. Why don't you go up there and get some sleep?"

I suspected that perhaps Keith had something more romantic in mind than just a night's sleep, and, truth be told, so did I. But, once again, I had to think about this clearly, and to consider an affair at this point—particularly when I was so exhausted that I could hardly stand—was too much for me. My emotions were still too confused.

"I'd love that," I said to Keith, meaning that I thought the idea of a warm bed and a good night's sleep sounded perfect. I didn't know quite what I would say to Keith about my ambivalent feelings.

But Keith read my mind. I didn't need to tell him that I still felt vulnerable; he knew it intuitively. He took me to the room, tucked me in bed, kissed me tenderly, then quietly left.

The next morning, I woke up with a start. I found myself in an elegant room, snuggled down in a beautiful bed. Sunlight was streaming through the windows, and the room was bathed with a cheerful white light, the likes of which I had never seen in my life.

I remembered vaguely Keith telling me that the Rolls would be waiting for me in the morning to take me back to Angie's apartment. I recalled that he had taken me to the window, pointed out the car, and assured me that it would be in precisely that same place when I woke up.

I pulled myself out of bed and went to the window and

looked out. I smiled, realizing that the unusual "white light" I had observed was due to the thick blanket of snow that covered the street, the grass, the fences, the cars—everything. I had never seen so much snow. Then I looked down to the spot Keith had pointed out the night before, and sure enough, there was the black Rolls, waiting for me.

With the help of Keith and Angie, my life in Washington immediately settled into a routine. Each morning, I practiced religiously, and every two or three days, I would spend a couple of hours working with Jim Morris on my singing. The rest of the time, I worked with Keith, planning how we were going to proceed or helping out at his office.

Keith had believed from the start that my story would make a fascinating book and great movie. We spent hours together, drafting a "narrative" of my life that Keith wanted to show to another lawyer he knew who specialized in various sorts of entertainment deals.

But most important, given the information we had gleaned from my adoption files and Keith's exploration in the Montgomery courthouse, Keith believed that there was a very good chance that I should have shared in the income generated from Hank Williams' songs, and certain people or businesses may have conspired to prevent me from receiving my rightful share.

It was also very clear that my case was a complicated one, and Keith wanted the most knowledgeable lawyers—experts in copyright issues—to associate with him. But more, Keith needed someone who could hang tough with him for as long as it took to win. Fortunately, Keith knew the best man for the job: Milton Rudin.

Mickey Rudin is one of the most renowned figures in entertainment law in the country. Over the years, he has represented such celebrities as Frank Sinatra, Groucho Marx, and Lucille Ball, as well as many powerful entertainment executives. He has encountered difficult situations and fought complex cases, and more times than not, conquered the problems and won the suits.

Keith had worked for Mr. Rudin at the Beverly Hills firm of Wyman, Bautzer, Rothman and Kuchel, as a young associate in the late sixties and early seventies and thought of Mr. Rudin as a mentor. Keith was very proud of this relationship. Mr. Rudin was very demanding on those who worked for him, expecting only the best, and Keith had survived under his tutelage. Keith would say over and over to me that he had learned more about law from Mr. Rudin than from any other lawyer he ever worked with. Keith also said that Mr. Rudin had forgotten more about copyright law than most lawyers would ever know.

In fact, Mr. Rudin had argued major copyright cases before the United States Supreme Court and won. One classic case he was involved in, *DeSylva* v. *Ballantine*, concerned an illegitimate child who claimed the copyright renewals on his father's compositions. This case had been argued successfully, and was considered a landmark decision in copyright law. The details of this suit fascinated me because they sounded so similar to my own.

Finally, Keith said that Mr. Rudin's firm employed several lawyers who specialized in copyright litigation. If we were able to obtain Mr. Rudin's support, we would be getting not just one of the best copyright lawyers in the United States but a whole team of experienced partners and associates.

All this was enough for me. I didn't need to be convinced any further that having Mr. Rudin working with us would be ideal. However, Keith felt that securing Mr. Rudin's help would be at least as difficult as convincing Owen Bradley to work with us—and for many of the same reasons. Mr. Rudin was an extremely busy man, Keith was certain he was loaded down with other commitments. In addition, like Mr. Bradley, he was no longer a young man, and might not be interested in taking on another long-term project at this point in his career.

Nevertheless, Keith felt optimistic. We had succeeded in persuading Mr. Bradley to work with us, and we hadn't known him before we asked for his help. Keith had known Mickey Rudin for years, and they were friends. At the very least, Keith knew that Mr. Rudin would agree to take a look at the material we had put together so far and give us an honest and knowledgeable assessment of my case.

Keith called Mr. Rudin's office in Beverly Hills and asked Mr. Rudin's executive assistant, Helen Montrose, who was also an old friend of Keith's, if a meeting could be arranged. As it turned out, Mr. Rudin was planning to be in Washington on other business in early February, and his assistant promised that Mr. Rudin would give us a call when he was in town.

Over the next couple of days, Keith worked up a detailed twenty-page memo outlining my situation. One afternoon less than a week later, the telephone in Keith's office rang, and Mickey was on the other end of the line. He said that he was sitting in a room at the Hay Adams, one of Washington's finest hotels, without a thing to do for the next few hours. Could Keith come over for a chat?

"I'll be there in five minutes," Keith said, then slammed down the phone, pulled on his coat, and ran out the door.

I was well aware of how important this meeting was, and was almost as nervous as Keith was about Mr. Rudin's response. But when Keith returned two hours later, I could tell by the look on his face that all had gone well.

"Well, B.J.," he said, hugging me. "We've got co-counsel. As a matter of fact, we've got one hell of a co-counsel."

Then Keith gave me a play-by-play account of the meeting.

"We talked for a few minutes . . . you know . . . pleasantries," he said. "Then he just launched in and asked me what I had wanted to talk about. I handed him the memo and he started reading. The phone rang just as he turned the page, and I was afraid I'd lose him, but he did something amazing. He told the front desk to hold his calls until he buzzed them back."

As Keith said, he could almost see Mr. Rudin's legal mind kick into gear as he finished the memo.

"Anyway," Keith went on, "after he read it, he put his glasses down and said what a great story he thought it was."

Keith said that at this juncture he expected a "pregnant pause," or an awkward moment. He didn't want to have to ask Mr. Rudin outright for legal help on the copyright issues. But of course Mr. Rudin had read between the lines—both on the memo and probably on Keith's face.

"So, who are you working with on the copyright issues?" Mr. Rudin asked.

Keith said he smiled and admitted that he had consulted with no one as yet.

Then Mr. Rudin uttered the desired words: "May I associate with you on the copyrights?"

"We'd love it," Keith answered, thrilled.

After that, the meeting went quickly—as it always did with Mr. Rudin when "business" was settled. Mr. Rudin related to Keith several stories about copyright cases he had won. He explained that all of his cases had been argued under the old copyright law, which had changed in 1976. (The copyright law was revised in many ways in 1976, but the issue most relevant to me involved the specific eligibility of illegitimate children to inherit from their natural parents. Under the old law, illegitimate children were not specifically addressed; under the new law they were.)

According to Keith, Mr. Rudin seemed especially intrigued with the idea of arguing another potential landmark copyright case under the revised law. At this point in his career, Mr. Rudin had said, such a suit would be a challenge and a pleasure.

Now it looked as though we had two of the most knowledgeable and talented men in their fields to help me: Owen Bradley to coach my singing; and Mickey Rudin to provide the knowledge and the wherewithall to bring suit against the folks who had prevented me from obtaining my legacy. Both Keith and I were delighted. This was working out better than we had hoped. As yet, we'd had no disappointments, although we would eventually encounter them. We began to feel so confident that we established a little buzz phrase every time something worked out as we hoped: "It was meant to be."

Keith and I also now believed without question that our relationship was "meant to be." As the last weeks of winter sped by, I stayed in Washington, living at Angie's apartment, helping at Keith's office with secretarial chores, and practicing. I would talk to Michael occasionally on the telephone, and told him that "the work" was going well and I could not say when I would be coming home. The truth, of course, was that I knew I would never be "coming home," but I didn't yet feel ready to spell that out to Michael.

Toward the end of February, we decided it was time to move down to Nashville so that I could begin work with Mr. Bradley and the coach that he had lined up. Keith found us a marvelous old farmhouse way out in the country east of Nashville with a view of the surrounding hills, and even a swimming pool. By an accident of fate—again, it was "meant to be"—Keith arranged his schedule so that he could conduct most of his work from the farm, so he would spend more time in Nashville with me.

The rest of the time I worked hard on my singing. I practiced every day, as I had done in Washington; twice a week, Arlene, the coach, would work with me for several hours. Often I would go visit with Mr. Bradley and the guys who worked with him at the Barn, and toward the end of our months in Nashville we worked up another demo tape. Mr. Bradley had said when we first met that the most important thing for me to do was sing, sing, sing, and, of course, he'd been right. I had improved tremendously.

Keith's and my personal relationship was also deepening. One weekend in early March, Michael came up to Nashville to visit. This was the first time we had seen each other in six weeks, which, in retrospect, doesn't seem too long, but at the time I felt I had lived a whole other lifetime. By now, Keith and I were deeply involved with one another, professionally, emotionally, and sexually. But I still found it impossible to tell Michael the truth: that our marriage was over; that I was never returning to Mobile.

Somehow, however, I suspect Michael knew, although I'm sure he was not admitting it to himself. No sooner had he arrived when he came down with a virulent case of the flu. He was so ill that he spent most of the weekend in bed, and his illness, to my relief, prevented me from having to confront our situation.

Michael returned to Mobile late that Sunday night. Over the next three months, we talked on the telephone a couple of times a week, but we never managed to get together, and as was our way, we never talked about anything deeply personal. In June, Keith had some business in Gulf Shores and I joined him there. It seemed to me that this was a good time to make a stopover in Mobile, to explain to Michael the reality of our situation.

I had tried to give Michael some warning, but nothing could shield us from the pain we both felt. I could see that he was upset, but, as always with Michael and me, we talked calmly. I told him I wanted a formal separation and then a divorce, that I was taking my belongings, and I would probably be living in Nashville or Washington from now on. It would take a year before our divorce was final, but the break was now clean and complete.

By midsummer 1985, news of my musical work in Nashville and Keith's research into my paternity and the related legal problems was beginning to trickle out, particularly into the country music establishment. Keith, Mr. Rudin, and Mr. Rudin's associates had been working day and night putting together my copyright suit against the copyright owners and publishers, and after five months they were almost prepared to file the complaint. At the same time, Keith had also decided, after several requests for their release, that it was time for me to sue the Department of Pensions and Security for my adoption records.

As all of these factors were simmering—and close to coming to a full boil—Keith came to the conclusion that it was also time for me to make a public statement about my existence, to make it clear that we were serious about learning the truth about my past, to put some heat on Pensions and Security to give up those files—and to let the world know that I was Hank Williams' little girl.

13
GOING PUBLIC

Like every other aspect of my story, making a public statement that I was Hank Williams' daughter involved both my new dreams for a career in music and my legal claims. As it turned out, "going public" was also very upsetting to me personally.

By late June 1985, Keith and I had been working in Nashville for over four months. We had made many acquaintances in the press, they knew something was about to happen, and they kept pushing us for a comment and for interviews. But more important, the legal issues surrounding my situation were also firming up quickly.

By June it was clear that we would have to sue the state of Alabama Bureau of Vital Statistics (which held my birth certificates and my formal adoption records) and the Department of Pensions and Security (which had monitored my placement) for my records. We also needed the sealed file, which contained the original copy of the agreement between Bobbie and Hank, as well as the record of the proceeding acknowledging the document.

By late June, Keith's office had received a number of phone

calls from various newspapers and magazines requesting confirmation of the rumors that were circulating about me around Nashville and Montgomery. At the point that Keith decided to sue for my adoption files, he also figured it would be useful to hold a press conference in Montgomery. Not only would the reporters then get their answers, but Keith surmised that the public attention would help assure that no files—or parts of files— would "disappear."

We decided to hold the press conference at the law offices of Perry Hooper and his partner, Tommy Gallion. A few days before the proposed date, July 11, Keith called back all the reporters who had contacted his office, as well as the newspapers and television and radio stations in Montgomery, and informed them of the time and date. We decided that I would not appear at the press conference in person for fear that my presence might dilute the impact of my story. If all went well, we were certain that we would have numerous opportunities for me to tell my story, but, for now, we wanted to test the waters first before submitting me to a personal invasion. I would wait for Keith at the Holiday Inn in Prattville, Alabama, nine miles north of Montgomery.

Frankly, I was afraid that Keith and I might be the only ones who cared who I was, and for a moment we weren't sure whether anybody would come. I couldn't have been more wrong. Perry Hooper's office was packed. Later, many people would say that the only other time they had witnessed the press turn out in such numbers was when the governor spoke.

News reporters from almost every major newspaper, radio station, and TV station in the state of Alabama were there. Keith said later that he could see cameramen and photographers searching around, looking for me, and he was glad we had decided that I not attend. I would have been overtaken.

Keith had put together a press release that outlined the details of my life, and closed with the announcement that we had joined forces with Milton Rudin and his firm, and intended to sue for the portion of the copyright renewal royalties that was rightfully mine.

By evening, news of my existence was the lead story of every

TV and radio news program in the state. By morning, the story of the press conference was on the front page of not only every newspaper in Alabama but many newspapers throughout the South—including, of course, Nashville. Within the week, the news had been picked up by the wire services and appeared in such far-flung places as Canada and Alaska. Over the next few weeks, many national journals, including *Variety*, the *New York Times*, the *Washington Post*, and the *Boston Globe* all ran sizeable pieces.

I had been afraid that no one would believe me, but not only did all of the reporters accept my story as gospel, they seemed sympathetic to my goals. For example, the *New York Times*, one of the most important newspapers in the country, devoted five columns to my story and ran a large photograph of me. They said: "At stake, in economic terms, are millions of dollars, but in the human elements of the story are the very themes of country music and of Mr. Williams' songs: heartbreak, rejection, loneliness and blues."

Before the press conference, we were worried that reporters loyal to Hank Jr. might work against us, but as it turned out, some of them inadvertently helped us dig up information that might have been exceedingly difficult for us to find by ourselves. For example, a reporter from Montgomery's *Alabama Journal* tracked down Richard Emmet, the judge who had presided over the 1967 court case, the one who had declared that it didn't make any difference whether or not I was Hank's daughter—I could not inherit from the Williams estate. By 1985, Judge Emmet was retired and living in California, but he offered up some very interesting observations that were of great help to us.

Under the headline FORMER JUDGE SHEDS LIGHT ON WILLIAMS PATERNITY QUESTION, he said, "I think that it's common knowledge that Hank Williams Sr. was the father of an illegitimate daughter." He went on to say, "Montgomery was a small place in the 1950s, and Williams was a well-known person. The community knew Hank, and they knew that a child due to be born would be Hank's child."

The *Alabama Journal* also interviewed Maury Smith, the attorney who had represented Acuff-Rose in the 1967 proceedings, and reported that "he couldn't recall seeing the alleged hidden contract." He added, however, that another Montgomery lawyer who represented the Williams estate, "the late Bob Stewart, may have told him about the contract."

At first this *Alabama Journal* article had thrilled us, because, obviously, here was the same judge who had ruled in 1967 that I couldn't inherit stating flat out that my existence was "common knowledge." However, when we got to the paragraph concerning "the late Bob Stewart" we were a bit unnerved. Robert Stewart was the one person who knew everything, and, as we quickly confirmed, Mr. Stewart had died in January 1985. Now the records would have to speak for themselves.

Overnight, I became a celebrity in Alabama. People would come up to us in restaurants and wish me well; others would wave from their cars, give us a thumbs-up sign, and smile. Even more surprising was the extent of national attention my case created. Within days of the press conference, we were contacted by a writer from *People* magazine, Lois Armstrong. Lois spent four days with us, and *People* ran her long piece, complete with a photograph of me by Hank's grave, in its September 2, 1985, issue.

That same week, the "Today" show also asked me to appear. I had never been to New York City in my life, but Keith and I flew up the night before the program, and showed up at the studio like troupers at 5:00 A.M. I was scared to death, and pleaded with Bryant Gumbel not to embarrass me, and he smiled and assured me that he wouldn't—and he didn't.

For the most part, I was relieved and flattered at the response we were receiving. It gave me the confidence to forge ahead—a confidence Keith warned me that I might need when things got rough.

However, throughout all of this publicity, one of my biggest worries was my mother. Three years before, she had called me on the telephone and screamed that I had "betrayed" her by finding and befriending the Jetts. Since that time, I had not confided much in her, although I called her regularly.

Therefore, I was surprised to discover that Mother had agreed to a lengthy interview for the *Mobile Register* in September 1985.

In the article she went into raptures about my singing abilities, saying that I "loved music and was always very talented. She has wanted a music career for a long time." This was a statement by somebody who had never even mentioned my singing to me in her life.

When I got to the end of the story, however, I began to get a true picture of her real sentiments. She told the reporter: "She stayed with that life for 10 years. I was hoping that she would be happy in that pretty little house." Mother was, of course, referring to my marriage. Then, to my amazement, she said, ". . . but I support her 100 percent" (referring to my pursuit of my rightful portion of the Williams legacy). "I hope she makes it. It will open doors that would have taken years to open for her to have a singing and music career."

The entire article was vintage Louise Deupree. First of all, I'm sure she loved the attention, but it was fascinating to me that publicly she could say that she supported me 100-percent, when privately she felt—at least, at times—that by seeking my roots I was betraying her. It was like everything else that had ever gone on between us. I never knew where I stood in her eyes.

Within four weeks of Keith's press conference, the Bureau of Vital Statistics and the Department of Pensions and Security decided to give up the files. From Vital Statistics, Keith received a telephone call that could only have come from a native Alabamian. The official said: "What do you think Ol' Hank would want us to do?" With that down-home remark, Keith knew that the files were ours. Keith made an arrangement with both agencies whereby we would drop the suit in exchange for the files, and they agreed.

On August 12, Keith and Tommy Gallion headed over to the courthouse to literally pick up the files. To their amazement, they were met by a fleet of lawyers representing Hank Williams, Jr., who demanded that the presiding judge, Joseph Phelps, not hand over my files. Keith was incredulous. True, we had made it clear that we were preparing to sue for my portion of the copyrights, but this particular action concerned only my adoption records and had nothing whatsoever to do with Hank Jr.

It didn't take Junior's lawyers long to realize that, under the circumstances, they could not stop me from claiming my files, but they then insisted that they should receive copies of the files on behalf of their client. In addition, the other outstanding issue before the judge was the so-called sealed file, the court-held file containing the original contract between Bobbie and Hank, together with the transcript of the hearing that was held in 1967 confirming the contract's validity. Needless to say, we wanted it; and naturally, of course, so did Junior's lawyers.

Judge Phelps' court resolved this battle by ordering Keith to have me show up, in person, on September 11, when he—Judge Phelps—would deliver the sealed file to me by hand. Keith agreed, and we planned to be in the Montgomery courthouse on the eleventh.

However, Judge Phelps had no choice but to honor the agreement between the two agencies and Keith, and after paying $44.50 for copying charges, Keith was given copies of the adoption files.

Keith was working on another case in Florida, and that evening, as we drove down, I was in a state of off-the-wall rage. Keith, who had been surprised to find Junior's lawyers at the courthouse, was equally furious, but saw it as a preview of things to come.

"Remember when we first started on this thing I said that we'd run up against some sons of bitches?" Keith said. "Well, darlin', they're here. I probably should have seen 'em comin', but they're a little ahead of schedule."

"Why?" I asked. "Why should we have seen them now? These are my files. My adoption was not, and is not, Junior's business. It's so unfair."

"I know," Keith said, trying to soothe me. "And, of course, he could not care less about your being adopted—back then or now. His lawyers just want to see what we've got."

I tried to be rational—and I knew Keith was right. Also, deep in my heart, I knew that Junior had had nothing to do with my birth, my adoption by our grandmother, and my rejection by our mutual aunt, Irene Smith. He had been only four or five years old at the time.

But by 1967, he sure as hell knew about me; I was one of the reasons he and his mother lost that litigation. I could see that, without my knowing it, I had been a potential legal problem to him for at least twenty years, and I'm sure he hoped I'd just stay lost. He knew I existed. His own mother told him, our aunt told him, the Alabama courts told him, and "the late Bob Stewart" told him. It just made me furious that he wanted something as personal as my adoption files.

"Remember," Keith said as we drove, "this has been unjust from the start. We sure as hell can't expect them to be fair now that we're after them. Junior is gonna bring out every big gun he can find."

When we got settled into our Tallahassee motel, Keith brought in the files. "This is your life," he said, handing me the thick packet of files. "You should be the first to see it. As for me, I'm going to take a walk."

I lay down on the bed and opened the sealed package and started reading. All of it, from the first day Mrs. Stone walked into their office in January 1953, through Irene giving me away. This portion had been read by Miss Austin, but I read it again. It meant more to see the correspondence—especially a copy of Bobbie's handwritten note acknowledging that Hank was my father.

But there was much more. The files that Miss Austin had read to us the previous January were from the Department of Pensions and Security. Now we had files from the Bureau of Vital Statistics, as well as papers from the welfare department. For example, I found, buried in those files, a log of my year with Mama Cook, kept by welfare workers charged with my case. It went on for twenty or thirty pages, a remarkable, grainy "film" of the life of my subconscious. It started on March 15, 1955, the day I arrived at Mama Cook's home, and ended on February 21, 1956, the day I left Montgomery with the Deuprees. Here are a few excerpts:

3/15/55
Graham
    County Child Welfare Worker picked up Cathy and took

her to Mrs. Cook's boarding home in [Pine Level] Alabama. She cried the entire way. She could not be quieted. She screamed when we left the boarding home. Mrs. Cook forcibly took her from the worker. Worker took her hi-chair, a large car in which she could ride, a huge box of toys and a large suitcase full of clothes.

3/22/55
Graham

County Child Welfare Worker visited with Cathy and Mrs. Cook and the minute Cathy saw worker she started crying. Mrs. Cook explained that the first two days she had Cathy she cried continuously, then she was almost at the point of calling the worker. However, Mrs. Cook related that her son played with her the second afternoon and finally persuaded her to get in the blue [toy] car and she smiled the sweetest smile that encouraged Mrs. Cook and the entire family to keep working with her. Since that date, Cathy has been very happy.

These entries shocked me—although they should not have. They confirmed what Marie Harvell, Mama Cook, and Jimmy had told me, although it was fascinating to read it from another point of view. The little car was obviously the toy car that my grandmother had bought me, the same one Mama Cook laughingly said I continuously drove off the porch. Clearly, I had loved that car!

The worker, however, was wrong. I was not happy. For some reason, the worker named Graham left the case, and another worker named McWhorter became my social worker. (I never could find out their full names.) She came about once every two weeks for the next eleven months. According to Miss McWhorter, my progress was slow. Obviously, I had been traumatized and was very fearful of being taken away again.

5/3/55
McWhorter

Worker and the County Child Welfare Worker went to the boarding home on this date to see Cathy. Boarding mother had the children down in someone else's yard swinging. When Cathy

saw that someone was coming, she began to cling to the boarding
mother and to cry.

Boarding mother said although Cathy would not talk when
strangers were around, she could say a number of words although
it is difficult to understand her. Boarding mother described Cathy
as being a very alert child and one who caught on to things quickly
and easily.

Cathy . . . is usually a responsive child until there are
strangers. Since the child welfare worker had taken her to the
home, she has always cried when she has seen her car and recognized her.

Worker told the boarding mother that Cathy is going to be
difficult to get friendly enough to place.

5/26/55
McWhorter

Cathy remembered worker and talked to her until worker
decided we would go and get some ice cream. She began to cling
to boarding mother but worker told boarding mother that perhaps if she took her once and let her cry that Cathy would understand the next time that we were coming back. Cathy cried
all the way to the store saying she wanted her mama. When we
got to the store and got some ice cream, she ate her ice cream,
but would cry between every bite.

There was a gap in the reports, which may have been due
to the summer holidays, or perhaps the reports were lost. In any
case, when the reports pick up again, I seem to have grown
much more comfortable and secure with my surroundings.

9/22/55
McWhorter

Cathy is growing and improving. On this date, as worker
went in, Cathy was coming into the living room and came right
up and began talking to worker. She said they were going to town
and that they were going to the doctor. Cathy did not show any
of the shyness that she has previously shown. She even sat in
worker's lap and seemed to be perfectly happy.

10/18/55
McWhorter

Worker went to the boarding home, got Cathy and brought

her into town. She was dressed attractively in a little navy blue skirt and sweater. She was perfectly willing to go with worker and was well-behaved during the entire trip.

10/27/55
McWhorter

Worker took Cathy for a ride to get ice cream. As we passed the school, Cathy pointed it out as being a school and very excitedly began to tell worker a story. She kept making a motion about her clothes as if she were tying a tie and she would throw back her head and laugh. Later, boarding mother told worker that Cathy had been to see a hillbilly program and one of the men had on a bow tie and picked a guitar, and Cathy thought he was very funny.

On the trip to town, worker had begun to talk with Cathy about getting her a new mama and daddy and she was not opposed to the idea, although she would say "no" when worker would talk about her going home with them to live.

11/3/55
McWhorter

Worker picked up Cathy on this date to take her to the doctor. In the waiting room Cathy was very quiet and sat close to worker. When we got into the doctor's office, she didn't seem to be at all frightened.

When we left the doctor's office, worker said we were going to have to go and get Cathy's finger stuck. Worker said we had to do this so she would be ready to go to her new Mama and Daddy. Cathy showed worker her thumb and told worker she wanted that finger stuck.

Cathy walked into the hospital without showing any fear at all. When the nurse stuck her finger, Cathy did not flinch or change expression. The nurse said she believed Cathy was the best child she had ever seen. When we left, Cathy kept showing worker her finger and saying she was going to tell her mama that they got some "bleed" out of it.

We told the boarding mother we hoped we could make some plans for Cathy in the near future.

11/13/55
McWhorter

Worker talked with Cathy about the fact that she was going

to get her a new mama and daddy but that it would be a little while. Worker has brought up the subject a few times before, and the idea is beginning to appeal to Cathy. She always insists that she is going to come back to her old mama.

1/9/56
McWhorter

Worker took Cathy for a ride to get ice cream, and talked to her quite awhile about getting a new mama and daddy. Since Christmas, Cathy has almost gotten out of the notion of getting a new mama and daddy but worker talked with her about how nice it would be and she agreed rather hesitantly that she would go.

2/6/56
McWhorter

Boarding mother has been talking with Cathy about getting a new mama and daddy and she is more enthusiastic about it than she was. However, she still says she is coming back to see her old mama and is a little uneasy. She understands about the placement and knows unless worker has told her that this is the day she is going, she does not have to be fearful each time she goes out with worker.

2/13/56
McWhorter

Worker went to the boarding home to get Cathy to bring her up to the office again. During the trip, however, worker did talk with her more about getting her a new mama and daddy and told her she was going to come for her the following week and she would go into town and meet some friends of hers, but worker would bring her back to the boarding home that night. Worker told Cathy this over and over a number of times with Cathy repeating it. Worker assured her she was just going to visit with her friends on this first date, but the next day she might go home with them.

2/20/56
McWhorter

Worker went to the boarding home to get Cathy early in the morning. She was dressed and ready when worker got there, but

205

she began to cry as soon as she saw worker. It was necessary to leave the boarding home with her still crying and she sobbed and cried all the way to town. She was very disturbed about something she had left at the boarding home, but worker could not understand what it was. Cathy repeated over and over that she had left it, but worker could not understand. Worker kept assuring that we should be going back and would get it later, but Cathy continued crying about it and about the fact that she was leaving. Worker kept assuring Cathy that she was not going anywhere on this date, but was just going to meet some of her friends and play with them.

Just as soon as we got out of the car, Cathy, still crying, told worker to wipe her tears away. When we got into the building, Cathy cried only for a few more minutes. She met the foster parents without too much difficulty, and stayed with them after worker left the room.

Later:

On the way back to the boarding home, worker told Cathy over and over that she would come for her the next day, and she would go home with the people with whom she had had a good time. Cathy kept saying that she wanted to stay with her boarding mother, but worker felt that since she did make a good adjustment during the day, and that she would later also.

After we went into the boarding home, worker asked Cathy if she could show her what she had left behind that morning that she was so anxious to have. Cathy said she could not bring it, but would take the worker to see it. When we got back into the bedroom, worker found that it was her suitcase that she had forgotten which had all of her things in it. Worker assured her that we would not forget her suitcase on the following day.

2/21/56
McWhorter

Worker went back to the boarding home to get Cathy. Her suitcase was packed and she was dressed and ready, but she began to cry as soon as worker got there. She did not resist going with worker, but she cried all the way into town heartbrokenly. She kept saying that her old daddy would come and get her and take her back home. She just could not be consoled during the entire trip.

Cathy was still crying when we got there, however, when

we went in the motel, she did go to the foster father and began to tell him that her old daddy was going to come and get her. The foster father took her outside to walk around, and she stopped crying momentarily. However, she began to cry again when worker left and worker had to leave her crying.

By the time I finished reading these entries, I was awash in tears. I didn't remember any of these details, yet, at the same time, they somehow seemed familiar, as if out of a dream.

One of the files was labeled "Deupree" and in it were detailed reports on Daddy and Mother describing their backgrounds, their efforts to adopt a child, and their suitability to become adoptive parents. The same Miss McWhorter whom I had apparently come to know so well had also spent a considerable amount of time with the Deuprees. Because I had a lifetime of experience with my parents, I was better able to understand the contents of Miss McWhorter's report on them. It made me very sad, but her observations only confirmed what would become a lifelong behavior pattern.

2/20/56
McWhorter
Mr. and Mrs. Deupree were in the office on this date by appointment.
Worker told them she knew they had been given the background information, but that we would like to go over it again for them and try to clear up any questions they might have. Most of their questions seemed to be about the child herself, although they did ask about the age of the mother and something about the [previous] living arrangements.

Miss McWhorter then outlined, in great detail, the details of the suit I was involved in with Irene Smith, including the fact that I was not entitled to inherit from Mrs. Stone's estate according to the lower courts, and that the suit was being appealed to the Alabama Supreme Court. None of the real names were mentioned; the Deuprees knew only that I had been adopted by my grandmother, who had died without including my name in her will. Apparently, Daddy and Mother preferred to know nothing about my past. As Miss McWhorter reported, they wanted only the barest details, "except that if there were money coming to her from the estate, that they really would prefer that it be handled without their knowing anything about the former family. Mrs. Deupree said they did not even want to know what her name was."

This was interesting to me because it had never been clear to me when my parents first knew I was Hank Williams' child— and, as odd as this may sound, I was afraid to ask them. Now I could assume that they had not known this fact until the 1967 trials.

Miss McWhorter then went on to describe the extreme agitation Mother experienced as I left the Cooks and came to live with them. The following excerpts describe Mother's feelings before she had even seen me:

> Mr. and Mrs. Deupree both indicated that they were very happy to be approached about a child of this age as they had hoped to get a young child. Mrs. Deupree was a little threatened by the fact that she would probably remember and talk about the boarding parents for quite some time. She said she just did not think she could stand it if the child grieved for them.
> Worker tried to impress upon them that time is the only thing that is going to help the child in her adjustment, but that, of course, patience and understanding will help a great deal.

From the moment I entered the Deupree home, I had been discouraged—to put it mildly—from mentioning Mama and Daddy Cook. I clearly remember Mother's displeasure if I spoke of them. It sounded to me as though the social worker was urging them to exercise patience and understanding, but clearly they didn't— or couldn't.

Miss McWhorter then told of that first day that Daddy, Mother, and I had spent together. They had taken me out to lunch and then on a shopping expedition. I apparently enjoyed myself and behaved well. In the late afternoon, they had taken me to their motel, clearly hoping that they could take me home that night and not experience another traumatic day. They asked Miss McWhorter to meet them at the motel.

When worker got out to the motel, they were very pleased with the way she had responded to them. Mr. Deupree had taken a very active part in caring for her and entertaining the child and worker was able to see that he was probably the stronger of the two and the child seemed to be more identified with him than she did with Mrs. Deupree. He took the initiative in taking her around and showing her things and loving her and talking to her.

Neither Mr. nor Mrs. Deupree could see the value of the child going back to the boarding home. Worker said we still had a real conviction that it was the best thing for the child to go back to the boarding home overnight. Worker said we had found in working with many children that they feel a great deal better about leaving if they can go back to the boarding home and talk to the boarding family about their new mama and daddy and get the sanction of the boarding family. Worker said the child would feel very guilty later if she left without going back to tell the boarding parents goodbye.

In spite of worker's interpretation, Mr. and Mrs. Deupree were not able to see this.

2/21/56
McWhorter

Worker took the child to the motel on this date to go home with Mr. and Mrs. Deupree. The child was upset and crying when worker took her in. Mr. Deupree at once took the child and began to love her and talk to her. Mrs. Deupree was obviously very upset and said she just did not think she could stand it if the child cried. Mr. Deupree took the child outside and worker talked with Mrs. Deupree for quite some time.

Mrs. Deupree said it was very upsetting to her for the child to be hurt over the change, and she cried herself as she talked to worker. She said she was an emotional person, and she really did not know what to do.

Worker reminded Mrs. Deupree that this was a perfectly natural reaction. Worker said if they had wanted the child the day before and if her being upset was the only thing that would keep them from taking her, she thought they would be making a mistake not to take her just because she was upset over leaving the boarding home. Worker said this had been home to the child for a year, we could not expect her in a day's time to substitute other parents for the boarding parents.

Mrs. Deupree said she could understand this, because she knew how she felt when her parents got a divorce when she was four years of age. She said later, when she was seven, she went to a convent and each time her mother would come to see her, she would cry for a day or two, then would get adjusted and would just have it all to do over again the next time her mother came.

She said she believed this child would always remember something about it, and worker agreed that she might have faint recollections as she grew older but we certainly hoped these would be replaced by a good, secure home.

Mr. Deupree brought the child back in and indicated that there was no question in his mind but that he did want to take her and he was sure Mrs. Deupree would be very happy with the child after they all got adjusted.

Mr. and Mrs. Deupree were ready to leave by the time worker left and said that they thought when they got her home, things would be better.

To me, these last two entries by Miss McWhorter were very telling. From day one—it is really quite extraordinary—the die was cast. I "identified" with Daddy fifteen minutes after I met him, and our relationship never changed. He was the one who was attentive and loving. He was the one who could cope with a child. He was the one with "no question in his mind" that he wanted me.

He was wrong about only one thing: Mother would never be "happy" with me after we "all got adjusted." She was never happy with me—and never would be. Miss McWhorter seemed genuinely sympathetic to Mother's feelings, given the abuse and neglect she had experienced as a child. And yet, I read a certain amount of impatience and fear in her tone when she said that neither Daddy nor Mother could see the importance of my returning to the Cooks' for one last night. On that last day, Miss McWhorter tried to assure Mother that I would gradually forget sad memories, and she "certainly hoped that these would be replaced by a good, secure home." It's almost as though Miss McWhorter felt the need to tell Mother that she should love me—that it is imperative that a mother love a child.

I had felt a sadness when I read the entries about my life with the Cooks. I had been that little girl and I had lived through it. Now, looking back as an adult, I could finally allow myself to really experience the loneliness and terror I had felt as a baby— emotions I, of course, could not even begin to understand or articulate at the time. Yet, with Mama Cook, I had grown up and gone back and found that she loved me so much and I had loved her.

But with the entries about Mother, as pathetic as they are, my tears were not ones of sadness; they were vinegary and bitter. As Mother said from the get-go, she really didn't think she "could stand it if the child cried." And she was right; she couldn't.

So, I didn't cry. I stopped crying during that drive from Montgomery to Mobile on February 21, 1956, and, for Mother's sake, in the hope that she would love me, I didn't cry again until that moment in September 1985, and then I just lay on that bed in that motel room in north Florida and cried until I could cry no more.

But this time, I was lucky. I was glad Keith had gone out and left me alone, let me cry all my tears by myself. I knew I could cry and cry and cry some more, but I also was absolutely stone-cold positive that, for once in my life, somebody was coming back for me and that he loved me. I realized that it was the first and only time I could ever remember when I had felt secure enough to face my feelings and weep for my past because somebody was there to catch me.

Sure enough, when he came back a few hours later and saw me lying on that bed in a sea of faded papers and tears, he lay down beside me and just held on.

14
DISCOVERY

Keith and I had seen our first legal skirmish on August 12, when Keith and Tommy Gallion went to the Montgomery courthouse to pick up my files. On September 11, 1985, when I showed up, at Judge Phelps' request, to pick up the sealed file, war was declared.

As we had been instructed to do, Keith and I arrived in Judge Phelps' anteroom at 1:00 P.M. on September 11. Although Keith had warned me that Junior's lawyers might attempt to block my receiving the file in some way, I was stunned to find three lawyers already seated in the office. I felt the same rage I had experienced a month before when these guys had tried to stand in Keith's way and prevent me from getting my adoption files.

Keith and I stood in the room for a moment, wondering what was going to happen next. We didn't have to wait long. Just a minute or two after we arrived, the door opened again, and a Montgomery County deputy sheriff walked in carrying a copy of *People* magazine, open to the full-page picture of me.

"Which one of you is Cathy Stone?" he called out. Two

middle-aged secretaries sat at their desks and I stood in the center of the room. He couldn't miss me.

"That's her," all three of Junior's lawyers called out. If the situation had been less serious, these guys could have seemed like Keystone Cops. Instead, they frightened me.

Keith tried to step between me and the deputy sheriff, but not before the man had handed me a notice informing me that I was being sued by Hank Williams, Jr. At first I couldn't figure out quite what was happening. I had never been sued in my life, and I felt humiliated being confronted with this summons in such a public manner. Clearly the deputy had known precisely where I would be, at exactly the right time.

At least the deputy was human. "I'm sorry," he said to me, and I could see that he meant it.

"That's all right," I told him. "You're just doing your job."

In fact, I felt like crying. I also felt like gunning down the three lawyers who were sitting there, self-satisfied as hell, just waiting to eat me alive.

This was precisely the scenario I had wanted to avoid. I did not want a legal battle in the state of Alabama, whose laws, lawyers, and judges seemed to have been successfully conspiring against me literally since the day I was born.

What's more, their suit said I was making a claim against the estate of Hank Williams, and I had done no such thing. They were saying that the entire issue had been decided in 1967, and I had no recourse. As Keith said, they, of course, wanted a battle in the state of Alabama for the same reasons I didn't. These lawyers were hooked into a well-oiled good-old-boy network, looking for a fight on their turf, by their rules.

Basically, Junior was suing on two issues. He stated that my "claims" to be Hank Williams' daughter intruded in his ability to carry on his business. Therefore, he wanted it decided: (1) that he was the only natural child of Hank Williams, Sr.; and (2) that he was the sole heir to the estate of Hank Williams, Sr. In fact, as Keith would explain to me, the entire issue was much subtler than it seemed. These lawyers weren't stupid—not by a long shot—although they played a good country lawyer game.

They knew we were about to sue in a federal court, and they wanted issues that would be important in that federal action decided in their local arena, where they hoped they had more control.

Keith was absolutely furious. First of all, the issue for which we had appeared that day, the current "suit" at hand, had to do with my receiving the sealed file. (As it turned out, Judge Phelps, within minutes of my being served, handed me the sealed file.) This action had nothing to do with the estate of Hank Williams, and Keith wanted the suit dismissed.

Keith put in a call to Mickey Rudin, and they decided to proceed with haste with our suit, which we planned to file in New York Federal District Court. (We were suing for my child's portion of the copyright renewal royalties generated by Hank Williams' songs. We took the position that since this was a copyright issue, which is covered under federal law, it had to be heard in a federal court, not a state court.)

Keith and Mickey also decided to appeal to the Alabama Supreme Court to get Junior's action against me thrown out. Since I had not sued the estate, Keith argued that no "justiciable controversy" existed—that is, there was nothing before the court to be decided.

It was a mess. Now we had a fight on two fronts. Hank Jr. was suing me in Alabama, and by noon the next day I was suing him—as well as others who shared in the copyright renewal royalties of Hank Williams' work—in federal district court in New York City.

We'd fought the Battle of Bunker Hill (so to speak) on that September day in Montgomery and it was a bloody fight. Now we were moving on to Valley Forge—and it was going to be a long, cold winter. For the next twenty-three months, Keith, Jim Goodman (the attorney from Mickey Rudin's California office), and I lived and breathed what is called "discovery."

Jim Goodman was a young associate whom Mickey had assigned to work with Keith on the case. In his early thirties and smart, Jim had an easygoing way about him. He was thorough, methodical, and an excellent wordsmith. Besides, Jim loved the case and was devoting most of his time to it. He and Keith worked easily together, and he made me feel comfortable.

We had been required to prepare a list of anyone who claimed to know anything about me, Hank Williams, or Bobbie Jett, or who might have some knowledge of my situation. The opposition subpoenaed that information and then scheduled most of the depositions themselves. (Over fifty depositions were taken altogether.) Of course, even if the opposition took the initiative in deposing certain people, we were always present to ask our own questions.

We deposed several Williams family members, including Hank Jr. himself. (Hank Jr.'s deposition was notable for its brevity and its blandness. He claimed to know nothing about me or anything that related to me—including the 1967 court proceedings.) We also questioned Irene Williams Smith, Billie Jean Eshliman Berlin, Taft and Erlene Skipper (Lillian Williams' brother and sister-in-law), and Marie Harvell.

Irene's deposition, which we took in March 1986, was fascinating. Naturally, she said that she did not believe I was Hank Williams' natural child, and she even went so far as to say that Bobbie had told her that she didn't know who the father was. In response to statements she had made to the Department of Pensions and Security—for example, that I was her brother's natural child!—she said she had no memory of ever saying such a thing.

During the deposition, which took place in Nashville, Irene and I were staying in the same hotel—and although Keith and Jim decided that I should not attend her deposition, I hoped we might run into each other. Nevertheless, we never met. As she finished her deposition, she began weeping, saying how difficult it had been for her to give me up. Keith said to her, "Well, if you'd like to see Cathy, she's in the next room," whereupon Irene's tears disappeared instantly. No way did she want to cross paths with me.

Both sides also talked to various members of the Jett family, including Patsy and Willard, Jeannie Jett (Bobbie's niece), and Jo Tanguay. They interviewed folks from the Nashville music world like Owen Bradley, Eddy Arnold, Roy Acuff, Wesley Rose,

Ray Price, and Don Helms and Jerry Rivers, two of the original Drifting Cowboys. Ultimately, of course, they insisted on deposing my mother, Louise Deupree.

Over the months we worked on the depositions, we began to resemble one big traveling circus. Naturally, lawyers for each of the parties involved were equally interested in deposing these people, so in the interest of time and money, we often combined efforts. Junior's New York lawyers were joined by his Nashville lawyers. The lawyers for Acuff-Rose, Opryland, and Billie Jean Eshliman Berlin and her publisher—all of whom were named in my suit against the copyright holders—all joined forces. At times, we had more than eight lawyers participating in each deposition.

Needless to say, I, too, was deposed—which turned out to be a very sticky and disturbing situation. Back on September 11, when I had first been sued, Junior's lawyers had asked to depose me immediately. We managed to get out of that situation, but Junior's lawyers still insisted on taking my deposition—even before Keith's appeal to the Alabama Supreme Court was decided. (In other words, we still didn't know whether Junior could force me to litigate in Alabama or not.)

Judge Phelps insisted that I be deposed sooner rather than later, and in December 1985, I was subjected to six hours of intense interrogation in front of a host of lawyers in Montgomery. As with the other deponents, I was confronted by at least eight lawyers from the opposition, one of whom was designated to ask the questions for their side. He just hammered away for hours. Before they were finished I felt like a rape victim. As often happens in such situations, the opposition made me feel that it was all my fault.

I begged Keith and Jim Goodman to assure me that I would not have to go through another deposition, and they tried very hard to get an agreement to that effect. (In other words, an agreement that my initial deposition, taken in Alabama in Junior's suit against me, could be used by the lawyers dealing with my suit against the copyright holders in New York.) But, unfortunately, that didn't work out. As it turned out, over the course of the next few months, I was deposed several more times. By then, any lawyer in the room could ask whatever questions he wanted, so they just took turns with me.

We did, on occasion, have a little break in the tension. For example, at one point during one of my New York depositions, an attorney for the opposition began badgering me about the various names I had had over the years and when I had used them: Antha Belle Jett, Catherine Yvone Stone, Cathy Louise Deupree, Cathy Mayer. Then he said, rather snidely: "Have you ever heard the name Jett Williams?"

"Yes," I answered, realizing that I had failed to include that name in the list I had just rattled off, and I knew it had been widely reported in the press that I would be using the name Jett Williams professionally, as a tribute to both my mother and my father.

"Just when do you use that name?" he asked sarcastically— hoping, I suppose, to ruffle my feathers.

I stared at him for a minute, then answered, "Just whenever I want to."

Keith told me later that one of Hank Jr.'s attorneys leaned over to him and said: "Perfect answer."

Of course, one of the major areas of initial interest to the opposition had to do with precisely when I first learned of the existence of the now-famous contract between Bobbie and Hank. As it turned out, one of Hank Jr.'s Alabama attorneys turned out to be none other than Maury Smith, who had represented Acuff-Rose in the 1967 trials, and who had first announced my existence to the press.

Although another lawyer in his firm was taking the lead in asking me questions, Mr. Smith jumped in now and then. On one particular occasion, the lawyer turned, in a forceful manner, to the subject of the contract. He wanted to know how I had first learned about the contract.

"Mr. Smith told me," I answered, not even thinking twice.

Maury Smith's face turned scarlet, and the veins on his neck began to throb. He was stunned, and said that he had never met me before.

By then, I had memorized those lines from the yellowed news clips Wayne Deupree had sent me, and now I calmly recited them.

" 'The question arose on Tuesday when attorney Maury Smith, representing Acuff-Rose Publishing Company, told the court that Hank Williams had recognized "in a written contract" that a child had been born to a woman in Montgomery.' "

Of course, I had not seen the article until years after its publication, and even then I had no idea what Mr. Smith was referring to.

Maury Smith just shook his head.

By the end of 1985, Keith's and my personal life had solidified. Although my divorce from Michael would not be final until March 1986, and we didn't have a proper home and often ended up staying at Keith's aunt's home in Maryland, we were very happy together.

Unfortunately, however, our labor on the two cases was taking its toll on my work with Mr. Bradley. After Junior sued me in Alabama (and I countersued him in the New York federal court) in September 1985, the legal side of my life began to take up all our time, and I found it necessary to put my intense musical work on hold for a while. Besides, the music industry wasn't quite sure what it wanted to do with the woman who was possibly the daughter of Hank Williams—especially since, by now, I had sued a number of its "legends." I began to feel like a pariah in Nashville. Owen Bradley comforted me a bit by saying that Nashville was waiting to see which way the wind would blow, and I hoped he was right.

Most people in Nashville were still friendly and sympathetic, but the lawsuits frightened them, I guess. There were just too many key players involved who were all interwoven too closely together in the music business. There had been a time when the record labels Keith had approached had expressed interest in signing me. Now no one was offering a contract. When I sang, it was just to Keith—or to myself when I felt blue. At least Keith was there to wipe my tears away.

———

One chilly Friday afternoon in early spring 1986, I'd been working in Keith's office since morning getting some things organized, and Keith had been out at a meeting most of the day. When he returned to the office, he was carrying a six-pack of Coors Light, my favorite brand of beer, and had a bottle of George Dickel, his favorite "sippin' " whiskey, under his arm. He closed the door behind him and locked it, then began to take off his coat.

"Are we having a party for two?" I asked.

"No," Keith said, dialing the answering service to tell them to hold our calls. "We're going to play detective. It's time we pulled out all the pieces on this case and started to refine our theory."

"What is our theory—exactly?" I asked.

"I don't know yet," Keith answered. "But by Monday morning, we're going to have something. We're going to take this mountain of material we've collected and we're going to plow through it until we make some sense out of it. . . ."

"So I'm about to spend a lost weekend with Sherlock Holmes?" I asked.

"Right," Keith said, laughing. "This isn't going to be a leisurely weekend curled up with a book, but don't worry. By the time we're done, we may have solved a mighty good mystery."

So we poured ourselves a couple of drinks, pulled out our boxes of papers, and started in. That Friday, we worked until late into the night, slept in the office on the floor, got up before sunrise on Saturday, and started sorting again. Keith kept pulling papers, making notes on a legal pad, and instructing me to stack them in one pile or another. I couldn't follow his train of thought at first, but after several hours Keith isolated a very particular issue.

"B.J.," he said. "Go through those stacks and pull out any piece of paper signed by, addressed to, or mentioning Robert Stewart, Esquire."

For the next several hours, I did just that. Meanwhile Keith kept sorting and taking notes. Finally, he sighed deeply and said: "Okay, let's go back to the beginning. What is the earliest document we have bearing Robert Stewart's name?"

"Hank and Bobbie's contract," I said.

"Okay. Then what?"

"Well, he represented my grandmother in my adoption by her. We have references to that," I said.

"Yes . . ." Keith said. "Including the part of your adoption file saying he didn't think his client should prevail. Remember that entry? Then what?" he asked.

"Stewart represented Irene Smith in her efforts to turn me over as a ward of the state," I said.

"Yes," Keith said. "And then what?"

"Well, I guess he represented Irene in the suit over Mrs. Stone's estate when I was two—to keep me from getting any of Lillie's estate."

"Right," Keith said. "That's when Drayton Hamilton enters the scene as your guardian ad litem. What next?"

"He represented Irene in the 1967–68 proceedings," I said.

"Right, and . . ."

"And there was Drayton Hamilton again," I said.

"Right, and you lost again. What was that trial about?"

"It was the suit where Audrey Williams sued Irene to void the copyright renewal contract on Hank's songs and to close the estate with Junior as the only heir," I offered, rather tentatively, since that part of the story was still confusing to me.

"When, to your knowledge, is the first public mention of you?" Keith asked.

"During that trial, I guess. Why?"

"Okay, let's go back to the beginning again. After making Hank and Bobbie's contract, what is the next thing Robert Stewart did?"

"The adoption thing?" I asked.

"No. Look at this," Keith said, showing me a copy of Lillian Stone's will, dated January 13, 1953. "Stewart prepared a will for Lillie to sign within days of your birth, leaving everything to Irene."

"Okay," I said.

"Look who witnessed it," Keith said.

"Drayton Hamilton!" I exclaimed.

"Also, on the day you were born, Stewart brought Lillie the

papers he had prepared for her to sign so she could be the administratrix of Hank's estate."

"Yes," I said. "So what?"

"Look at it."

I read the document he handed me, a paper entitled "Application for Letters of Administration." It listed potential claimants to Hank's estate.

"Other relatives are listed," Keith said, "but you are not. But is there a name included with a notation that strikes you as strange?"

"Billie Jean Eshliman. She claims to be the widow."

"Right! Remember those words: 'Claims to be,' " Keith said.

Keith continued. "Okay, now let's go to the famous '67 trial. What happened?"

"They decided I couldn't inherit and that Junior was the sole heir to Hank's estate."

"That's true. That's what every record you might have found would tell you. But the subject of that trial was a contract between the estate and Acuff-Rose that gave them the copyright renewals to Hank's songs—a contract negotiated years before those renewals would start coming up for a twenty-five-thousand-dollars signing bonus. Stewart negotiated it and Irene signed it, as administratrix of Hank's estate. And Audrey and Junior sued because the signing bonus was so low. Also, he could have negotiated his own agreement himself if they had waited until the renewals came up. He might have negotiated with another publisher, leaving Acuff-Rose—and Irene—out in the cold."

"And that's how I got into the act. Robert Stewart, Irene, and the Acuff-Rose people raised me as a potential claimant to justify their own actions! Everybody won but me!" It was also becoming clear to me now.

"Exactly," Keith said. "It's the ole 'straw man' principle. They set you up, then they knocked you down. In this case, they also buried you."

"But why did the judge rule against me, since they all knew about me?" I asked.

"Well, he covered the waterfront, but let's focus on adoption—he said you lost because you had been adopted, and the judge ruled that, by law, adoption precluded you from being an heir."

"But what about in 1953? I wasn't adopted then."

"Now you've hit it. You weren't born adopted. And what would have happened if you had been listed as a claimant and a guardian had been appointed for you then?"

"We have no way of knowing, do we?"

"No, and neither do they. But you weren't encumbered by adoption then; and your guardian could have challenged the constitutionality of the damn adoption laws, anyway," Keith said. "The point is, Stewart had an obligation to list you as a potential claimant in 1953—he certainly knew about you. If he thought enough to let Billie Jean 'claim to be the widow,' he surely should have listed 'Antha Belle Jett—known to be daughter.' He had the proof—the contract—locked in his desk. The court was the one to decide what to do next. Hell, you could have claimed support and maintenance under the conditions of Hank and Bobbie's contract."

Then he moved on to another aspect that was troubling. "It gets better—or worse," he said. "One would expect that the Hank Williams estate would have closed when Randall reached his majority, when he turned twenty-one. That would have been in 1970. But it didn't. They didn't close it and make a final accounting and distribution until 1975."

"Why? They had the '67 order, didn't they?"

"Here, read this," he said.

It was a letter dated December 26, 1972, from Robert Stewart to Richard Frank, Junior's lawyer in Nashville. It said: "I am enclosing a check on the Williams Estate in the amount of $112,000 along with a copy of Judge Emmet's order authorizing this distribution. He is not pleased with Randall's heavy withdrawals this year. I do not believe that he will authorize any further distribution until the Jett child reaches her twenty-second birthday, which will be in January, 1975."

"In other words," Keith said, "they waited to close the estate until the statute of limitations had run out on you. Of course, by then Robert Stewart was administrator of the estate, since

Irene had gone to jail. In other words, they knew—or feared—that the 1967 order wasn't worth the paper it was written on."

"Did they know all along?" I asked, astonished.

Keith handed me two other pieces of correspondence. The first was a letter from Robert Stewart to Mr. Frank, dated April 4, 1974. It read:

> This morning I got out my old files relating to Baby Jett to work out a plan to turn over to her the money being held by the Court here. After getting all the facts back in mind, I called the Court to find out exactly how much the Court was holding. Much to my surprise, she had already come up from Mobile, and has now gotten it.
>
> This relieves me of any further responsibilities in the matter, but after all the strong statements the family made during the 1967 hearings, I am surprised they let her get anywhere near the Montgomery County Courthouse. I hope this doesn't lead to a further claim for renewal rights.

I was astonished, but moved on quickly to the second letter, which was Richard Frank's response, dated April 15, 1974:

> This will acknowledge your rather disturbing letter of April 4, 1974. I am much afraid that if Baby Jett has personally come up with a lawyer [they thought Uncle Stanley was a lawyer] to get the money from Mrs. Stone, her ancestry may well be reasonably obvious to her, and further trouble may ensue. We will just have to await the event.

"They knew all along," I screamed. "And Stewart didn't even notify me that I had any right to a claim when I reached twenty-one—and he didn't tell me the estate was still open."

"Stewart didn't notify you. Irene Smith didn't notify you. Drayton Hamilton didn't notify you. Pensions and Security didn't notify you. The court didn't notify you." Keith was thoroughly disgusted. "They all knew you had a right to a claim, and nobody bothered to help you. They just sat on the information, hoping you would never figure it out."

"Isn't that fraud?" I asked.

"It's looking that way," Keith answered.

"Wait a minute," I said. "When did Randall first know about me? In 1967?"

"No, he would have known about you at least as early as 1963, around the time the publishing contract was renewed," Keith said.

"Then he's been part of it all along . . ."

I noticed that Keith was now rummaging through some old press clippings we had generated. He found one from the September 16, 1985, *Atlanta Constitution* that had run a feature on me. In it, George William Koon, author of *Hank Williams: A Bio-Bibliography*, is quoted as saying: "If there actually is a trial on this thing, it's going to be the wildest show there is. Hank Jr. was born on the first anniversary of his parents' divorce, and what's going to be interesting is to see who the illegitimate child is."

Keith got out some more files that contained the old divorce records. Hank and Audrey were divorced on May 26, 1948, and Randall Hank was born on May 26, 1949, in Louisiana. His birth certificate itself appeared irregular, listing his father as Randall. The divorce was amended August 9, 1949, in Montgomery, Alabama, in an unusual action called nunc pro tunc, which nullified the operative provisions of the divorce decree retroactively—in effect "undivorcing" them, and making Hank Williams, Jr., legitimate in the eye of the law. Audrey then, of course, divorced Hank again in 1952. But the nunc pro tunc proceedings were based on affidavits from Hank and Audrey executed in Louisiana. It was a fill-in-the-blank typed page where the child's name—Randall—had been added in a scrawling print. And in it, Hank said he refused to remarry Audrey, even though, he says, his lawyer had suggested it.

"You know the theory on all that, don't you?" Keith said. "Audrey pushed ole Hank into that, saying he'd present a better image as a newcomer to the Grand Ole Opry as a family man with a child."

"I just don't understand why Junior has never been interested in meeting me. Heck, normal folks would want to meet their long-lost sister."

"Unless he went along with or benefited from losing you," Keith said.

We finally left the office late Sunday night, after an entire weekend of work. Keith's "paper chase" hadn't come to an end yet, but he'd pulled down enough of it—and now we had put it in order—so that it was starting to make sense. We decided to take a walk, get some fresh air, and buy ourselves a trashy hamburger and some fries at a local hangout around the corner from the office.

We braced ourselves against the harsh wind, and I took hold of Keith's arm.

"Well, Sherlock, do we have a theory for our case now?"

"Absolutely, Ms. Watson," he said. "And it fits the facts perfectly."

In late spring 1986, we came to a plateau in the discovery process. We had already interviewed thirty or forty people and would interview many more before we were finished, but for the first time ever, Keith and I found that we could focus just on each other and our life together.

One evening we were having dinner at La Rivage, a lovely restaurant overlooking the Washington waterfront, enjoying the warm evening and the boats as they bobbed up and down on the Washington channel. A huge yacht floated by, and we commented on how beautiful it looked. Suddenly I had an inspired idea. We still had not set up a home of our own, and I deeply believed that anything was possible—my own life proved that!

"Keith," I said, "have you ever considered buying a yacht?"

"Right," Keith said, and laughed.

"I'm not kidding," I said. "We love antiques. I'll bet there's an old boat somewhere. We could fix it up. We could even put the office on the boat."

Now the idea started to take hold with Keith. We spent the remainder of dinner dreaming, and the next day, in typical Keith form, he called various marinas, repair facilities, and yacht owners whose names were given to us. It took weeks, but finally we found her, and, as it turned out, she had been docked right under our noses the night of our "inspirational" dinner.

Her name was *Wampeter*, she was fifty years old, seventy-two feet long, and in dismal shape. She had been built in 1936 by American Car and Foundry, the same company that built Pullman Railroad cars, and she had once been known as the Queen of the Potomac. Now, however, after years of neglect, people were taking bets on when she would sink.

We took possession on July 1, 1986, and as soon as we walked on board as her owners, we were evicted from the marina. The owners of the marina had been waiting for her to be sold so that they could throw her out. They claimed she was too big for their marina, but mostly she was just an embarrassment.

We found a secluded, old marina several miles downriver, and we took her there to begin a major overhaul. One of the first things Keith did was rename her the *Jett Stream*, which made me very proud. We did much of the work ourselves; the physical labor of stripping and varnishing old wood, polishing brass, installing new doors, replacing rotten wood, and the hundreds of jobs large and small that needed doing, were a welcome relief from all the mental stress and aggravation of the case.

We also had a goal. We had decided to get married on September 28, two years to the day of our first meeting, and we wanted to have our wedding reception on the boat. We wanted her polished and gleaming, and back in an "uptown" marina in time for the festivities. We met our deadline, and in mid-September we steamed back up the river and docked her in sight of the Washington Monument and the U.S. Capitol.

Keith reveres Thomas Jefferson more than any other man in history. Keith had taken his undergraduate and law degrees from the University of Virginia, which had been founded, designed, and built by Jefferson. He had proposed to me, on bended knee, at a place called Jefferson's Rock in Harpers Ferry, West Virginia. (Actually, Keith proposed to me three times during our months together; and I accepted all three times.) Our life together was infused with "the law" and the quest for justice. It seemed right that we should be married in some place that evoked Jefferson, so we landed on the idea of marrying at dawn in the Jefferson Memorial.

Naturally, we met with a few problems. We had to obtain a permit to use the site of the monument, and we had to find a minister who would agree to marry us. I was a divorced Catholic and Keith a divorced Methodist without a church to call his own, so we had to find a willing, licensed, early-rising minister. We ultimately found a pastor from the Waterside Brethren Church in the Shenandoah Valley. Finally, we secured a permit that allowed us to be married in the woods close by the monument, but we were not allowed in the actual monument itself.

"I don't want us to be married in the woods," Keith told Larry Finks, a retired deputy chief of the park police and an old friend of his from his crime-fighting days. "We want to get married standing at the feet of Mr. Jefferson himself."

"No one is allowed to desecrate the monument," Larry said.

"Hell, we're not going to desecrate it," Keith said. "All we want to do is hold a wedding."

"I'll see what I can do," Larry said.

The day before the wedding, many friends of mine began arriving from Alabama. Lenore and Sally both came; two pals from college, Kemper Franklin and Joanie Williams, came from Alabama; and my best friend from Montgomery, Connie Buckalew, was to be my matron of honor. Having my friends travel all this way to our wedding was a special gift to me. None of my friends had come to my first wedding, thanks to Mother's machinations, and having them present this time meant the world to me. Mother was very ill at the time, so she did not come, and Aunt Helen declined to come, too.

But I refused to let their absence spoil our day. Keith and I hosted a large cocktail party on the *Jett Stream* the night before the wedding, and I felt like a queen on my floating palace, at the side of a very special king. He had also ordered eight roses—one for each letter in the expression "I Love You"—for me to carry the next morning.

Just before sunrise on September 28, 1986, we drove to the gates of the Jefferson Memorial in the black Rolls-Royce. My friend and matron of honor, Connie, rode with us, and Keith's friend and best man, Clifton Dinneen, drove. We decided to "give each other away," which seemed appropriate.

When we arrived, the gates at the Memorial were unlocked, and Larry was conveniently absent—or at least out of sight. Slowly we drove around to the front of the Memorial by the Tidal Basin, and looked up the long steps to the statue of Thomas Jefferson. At the top stood the chief of the park police. He beckoned us into the Memorial, and there, at the feet of Mr. Jefferson, before God, man, and our friends, Keith and I became man and wife just as the sun was coming up.

Now all the paper we had collected was starting to make sense, our depositions began to take on a different coloration as well. I'm not quite sure why this happened or when exactly it started, but by the winter of 1986–87, we had come across a number of "eyewitnesses." People were turning up who had actually known or observed Bobbie and Hank together. What's more, people were coming forward who knew I was Hank's child—because he had told them so himself. And many of these people had actually known me when I was a baby. Their courage at coming forward made me feel loved and connected. It was as though this whole exploration was starting to have some perspective, and some of the mystery of my life was beginning to dissolve.

Our first big break came when Keith was contacted by a man named Neal "Pappy" McCormick from DeFuniak Springs, Florida, who said he was trying to locate "Hank's little girl" and that he had tried to adopt me years before. At first we were skeptical, but on one of our trips to Alabama, we dropped down to see him, since DeFuniak Springs is just a few hours' drive from Mobile.

Pappy had been a well-known local bandleader in the late thirties, and had given Hank Williams one of his first jobs as a musician. Pappy and his wife took in young musicians and treated them like their own children, and Hank was no exception. Over the years, Pappy and Hank had kept up their friendship, and Pappy had also remained good friends with Lillie.

Pappy had known Hank since Hank was thirteen. More, it seemed as though Pappy had been something of a father figure for Hank, and Pappy said that Hank confided in him when he had troubles up until the end of his life. As a result, Pappy was knowledgeable about Hank's personal life. To my amazement, he said that the had met Bobbie on at least two occasions—once at a show in Greenville, Alabama, and once at Mrs. Stone's boardinghouse. He said, "Miss Jett, Mrs. Stone, and Hank was all talking about how she was fixin' to have a baby. And Hank went out to the hospital to make arrangements for her to have it. Hank just said the baby was his. He said it more times than one to me, because he would always come to Pappy."

After Hank died, Pappy made a habit of dropping in on Lillie whenever he was up and around Montgomery, and he told me he had seen me there several times when I was a baby. He also told me that after Lillie died, he came to see if he and his wife could adopt me. He said that Marie told him "they didn't want nobody to have the young'un that knowed anything about Hank."

Pappy's stories made me feel real good, and I could readily understand why Hank had cared for him. I also felt more secure knowing not only that somebody had wanted me after Lillie died, but that Hank himself had been so open with the fact that I was "on the way." He hadn't been ashamed of Bobbie—or of me.

Pappy holds a special place in my heart because he never once wavered in his support of me. It would slowly become clear to me that people who had been close to Hank were, in some cases, reluctant to get involved—even people who actually knew the facts of the situation. Not Pappy. From the beginning, he was on my side and he stayed there.

A couple who proved to be as special and dear to me as Pappy showed up in the December 7, 1986, edition of *Wiregrass Today*, a newspaper published in Dothan, Alabama. The headline read: JETT WILLIAMS: BOB AND CONNIE HELTON HELPED RAISE HANK'S DAUGHTER. The lead sentence went on to say: "If Jett Williams wants to find her roots, she should talk to Bob and Connie Helton," and the article was accompanied by a large photograph of me as a toddler playing in Mrs. Stone's yard on McDonough Street with Marie's son, Louis, and another little boy.

We first learned of the article late that Sunday night when we received a call in Washington from a man who said he was looking for "the attorney for Hank's daughter." He told us about the article and the Heltons. Within hours, we got Connie and Bob on the telephone. As soon as I started talking to them, they began to cry—first one and then the other. Clearly, these people had known me, and had seen me many times during the two years I lived with Mrs. Stone. Like Pappy, they too had wanted to adopt me when Mrs. Stone died, but, in their case, they were told they were too late—that I had already gone into the welfare system.

It turned out that both Bob and Connie had been old friends of Hank's. In the thirties and forties, Bob had formed a band, the Blue Ridge Mountain Boys, and they used to play with Hank at clubs throughout Alabama. Later, Bob became a well-known disc jockey in Montgomery. Bob married Connie in 1940, and they were both close to Hank.

Like Pappy, they remained quite friendly with Mrs. Stone, and grew very fond of me, after Hank died. They had no children of their own, and had offered to adopt me even before Lillian died, thinking that, as a young couple, they could offer a long, secure life for me. Lillian refused.

The Heltons, however, played a pivotal role in my legal proceedings as a result of a fascinating encounter they had with Hank and Bobbie in August 1952. In late August, Hank had been visiting his mother and then had disappeared for a couple of weeks. Lillie called Bob and asked him if he would mind driving her up to Lake Martin, a beautiful resort place and fishing spot northeast of Montgomery, to see if they could find Hank. For some reason, Lillie thought he was there.

They drove up to a cabin on Lake Martin and parked the car in front. Hank came out, and leaned against the window talking to them. Suddenly, a blond lady came out on the porch wearing white shorts and a "hatchin' jacket," as Connie described it.

"Is that Bobbie?" Mrs. Stone asked Hank.

"Yes," Hank answered.

"Ain't she pregnant?" Lillie asked.

"You ole eagle eye," Hank said. "You just don't miss anything."

"Is it your child?" Lillie asked.

"Hell, yeah," Hank said. "And I'm gonna keep it, too."

Bob and Connie stayed at Lake Martin only about thirty minutes and never got out of the car. They drove Mrs. Stone back to Montgomery.

Four months later, in December, Hank spoke with Bob again and mentioned that he was going to Ohio to perform, and asked Bob to drive him, but Bob and Connie had already planned a trip to Texas to visit Bob's brother, so he was unable to help out. They heard about Hank's death while they were in Texas. Mrs. Stone asked Bob to serve as a pallbearer, which he did.

Connie and Bob remained close to Mrs. Stone. In the spring of 1953, they drove Mrs. Stone to New Orleans, and on that trip she discussed Bobbie quite a lot. Mrs. Stone said that Hank had planned on finding a nurse in Nashville who would care for the baby. She also mentioned that Bobbie had received five thousand dollars to go to California.

The Heltons, on at least one occasion, took care of me when I was an infant while Mrs. Stone was out of town. After her death in 1955, Marie called the Heltons and told them that I had been taken away and put in a foster home.

Like Pappy, Bob and Connie Helton were absolutely loyal to me—and to Hank. As Bob said during his deposition, he wanted only to set the record straight and let Hank rest in peace.

As a result of finding the Heltons—or their finding us— we also were able to track down another interesting source, Bob McKinnon, a disc jockey who worked in Alexander City, Alabama, in the early fifties and who was also an old friend of Hank's. (McKinnon was apparently the person who tipped off Mrs. Stone that Hank was at Lake Martin that August.)

McKinnon, too, had seen Bobbie with Hank. In fact, he had been introduced to Bobbie and had talked with her. During the time Hank and Bobbie were at the cabin at Lake Martin, Hank went on a drinking spree and got thrown in the tank. McKinnon bailed him out and took care of Bobbie during the spree. At one point, Bobbie went into the bathroom, and McKinnon heard her being sick. When she came out of the bathroom, she was crying, and Bob asked her if she was all right. She told him she was pregnant.

As a side note, Bob McKinnon maintains that he was an "eyewitness" to the writing of Hank's famous song "Kaw-liga." The area where he was staying at Lake Martin was known as "Kowaliga," and Hank mentioned to Bob that he felt the place was steeped in Indian lore and he felt there was a song in it. At some point, Bob saw Hank pull out a pad of paper and a pencil and write down the song in fifteen or twenty minutes.

In a curious—and a really rather amusing—way, Uncle Willard, who I long suspected knew more than he had ever told me, finally spoke up. We asked him if the lawyers could depose him, and although he was extremely ill, he agreed. However, on the day before his deposition, he asked to speak with Keith alone.

"I've got a problem," he said. "I just don't want to get in trouble. Can you give me some legal advice?"

"What's the problem?" Keith asked.

"Well," Willard said, "I threatened to kill him."

"What do you mean?" Keith asked. "Kill who?"

"Williams. Hank Williams," Willard said. "He called and I told him if he came around my house I'd kill him."

Keith knew Willard was dead serious—and clearly a little frightened, since now he was going to be testifying under oath.

"Remember I told you that Williams sent me his pistols?" Willard said. "I guess that was his peace offering. He knew I was mad as hell about Bobbie. And I threatened to kill him if he came 'round here. Can they get me on that now? That's what I want to know."

"No," Keith said. "They can't get you on that—never could. Anybody would understand how you felt."

Willard felt better, and after that he loosened up considerably. He told us that after he'd threatened to kill Hank, Hank had gone down to the police station to complain. Of course, Willard was friendly with every cop in town; what's more, the cops in Nashville didn't take too kindly to the Opry people—especially ones who had been drunk and disorderly a time or two.

Apparently, Hank had spoken to a senior officer. According to Willard, Hank had said flat out: "Willard Jett has threatened to kill me if I go by his house. What should I do?"

"Well," the cop said, "if I were you I wouldn't go by Willard Jett's house."

My cousin Jeannie Jett had another story about Bobbie and Hank. Jeannie was Bobbie's cousin, a couple of years younger than Bobbie, and worshipped her. One afternoon in the summer of 1952, Bobbie had asked her to take a little ride because Bobbie wanted Jeannie to meet somebody. They got in the car and drove over to a little stone house a few blocks away on the Natchez Trace. Bobbie walked right in as though she lived there. Suddenly from the back of the house came a tall, skinny man dressed just in his pajama bottoms—looking kind of tired and worn out.

"This is Hank Williams, Jeannie," Bobbie said.

Hank said hello to Jeannie, chatted for a minute, telling Jeannie that he was upset about being "on probation" from the Opry.

Jeannie also remembered lots of conversation among various family members about Bobbie and Hank's relationship. She remembered vividly that Willard was particularly angry, and Ocie Belle, their grandmother, was very upset. Late in the summer of '52, Jeannie's own mother had said to her: "Jeannie, pray for Bobbie. She's going to have Hank Williams' baby."

"I'll pray for Bobbie, all right," Jeannie had said. "I'll pray that baby don't look like Hank Williams."

Apparently Jeannie wasn't too impressed with the looks of the skinny guy in his pajama bottoms.

Another person we found who proved pivotal to our case was a nurse named Jean Davis. In early 1953, Jean was working as a student nurse at St. Margaret's Hospital in Montgomery. On the day of my birth, she was on duty in the labor room, and the only woman in labor on that day was Bobbie Jett. Someone told her that "the lady in the delivery room was supposed to bear the child of Hank Williams."

She remembered that while Bobbie was in labor she was given a sedative that alleviated some of the pain, but did not knock her out completely. At that point, Bobbie started singing, and, according to Jean Davis, "she sang every song Hank Williams ever wrote." Bobbie got particularly attached to "I Can't Help It If I'm Still in Love With You," and sang it over and over. "We couldn't shut her up," Jean said, "and it like to drove us crazy."

Bobbie stayed in the hospital for several days after my birth, and during the hours she was in labor and the days following delivery, she and Jean must have chatted quite a lot. Bobbie told Jean that she and Hank "had been lovers for a long, long time," that she and Hank had spent time at Kowaliga, and that she had been staying with Mrs. Stone during the last weeks of her pregnancy, at Hank's request.

The day Bobbie left the hospital, she told Jean that she was on her way to the airport, and that the baby would be picked up. A few days later, Hank's mother, Mrs. Stone, did, in fact, come for me, and my odyssey began.

Over the months of preparation for the trial, I had noticed an interesting phenomenon among our witnesses. The more comfortable they became, the more they remembered—or were willing to say. Willard Jett was a perfect example. What's more, most people who were deposed were unusually kind—even those who were speaking on behalf of Junior. There was one noticeable—and to me disappointing—exception, and that was Roy Acuff. He recanted everything he had ever said to me. I remembered the thrill of standing with him backstage at the Grand Ole Opry and hearing him speak so kindly about my daddy, about what a "good man" he was.

At his deposition, Acuff said: "I wouldn't tell anybody that Hank Williams was a good man. When he first came to Nashville maybe he was all right. But he was bad when he left. He let himself drag out."

It was just as disappointing to have him deny even meeting me. He was shown the photograph of the two of us together, but he just wrote it off. He claimed he had his picture taken with people all the time, and he had no memory of that particular occasion—one that had been so important to me.

Thus, the process of discovery turned out to be not unlike many other journeys. Some of the stops were fascinating, some were instructive, some were baffling and disillusioning. But after two years, we were ready to move ahead.

15
My Day in Court

By fall 1986, we had a theory to our case—that information had been fraudulently kept from me—and piles of paper to back it up. We also had witnesses who knew my mother and my father, had seen the two of them together, and had heard Hank admit that he was the father of Bobbie Jett's child. We even had an eyewitness to my actual birth.

Now all we needed was a legal arena in order to present my case. Our objective was to make sure that trial was in the New York federal court over the copyright renewal royalties, not in Alabama over my daddy's closed estate. But the Alabama Supreme Court, which was deliberating our appeal of Hank Jr.'s suit against me, had a different idea.

It took over a year, but finally, in the fall of 1986, after sitting for a year on the docket, the Supreme Court of Alabama ruled against me. They declared that since my claims on the estate were having a "chilling effect" on Hank Jr.'s ability to conduct business, a trial should be held to decide the issue once and for all. My worst fears were coming true, and to make matters worse, they sent the case back to Judge Joseph Phelps in Montgomery for trial, and Judge Phelps thought both sides should be able to go to trial within days.

We had a different idea about that, and this time we won. We did have to go to trial, but again it would take months before we worked out certain problems. As the first order of business, Keith wanted Judge Phelps off the case. Then he wanted to join all the issues. If we were ordered to litigate Hank Jr.'s position, in his arena with his players, then we were going to litigate the hell out of everything. So we countersued for fraud.

By now, our original Alabama counsel, Tommy Gallion, was having second thoughts. He was coming to the realization that his career and practice might not necessarily be enhanced by working with us, since Keith was suing Robert Stewart's estate, and his old firm, alleging fraud. Keith had come to a similar conclusion, but for different reasons. He wanted the toughest and most respected local counsel he could find, and he thought it might be smart to look outside Montgomery. He found his answer in Birmingham in the form of David Cromwell Johnson.

David Johnson had worked with Keith on several legal matters in the past. Also, since he had been married to the sister of Keith's good friend Clifton Dinneen, David was part of our extended family. Keith believed David was a fearless lawyer—and therefore our kind of guy.

With a new Alabama legal team in place, we turned our attention to a problem we discovered with regard to Judge Phelps. Keith and Mr. Rudin, in preparation for the copyright trial in New York, had microfilmed every piece of paper in the Alabama courthouse that dealt with the Hank Williams estate. Jim Goodman, our lawyer on the West Coast who worked with Mr. Rudin, uncovered an obscure report that interested him, and he promptly called Keith about it.

"Did you know that Judge Phelps had once been Hank Jr.'s guardian ad litem?" Jim asked.

"No!" Keith said, startled.

Armed with that discovery, Keith and David Johnson demanded that Phelps recuse himself from the case as a result of his prior representation of Junior. At first, Judge Phelps refused, but then agreed to allow the Alabama State Bar Ethics Commit-tee to decide. It didn't take the Ethics Committee long to insist that Phelps get off the case. Our battle still loomed, but we felt we had won a major skirmish—and one that could be critical in days to come.

Our relief at having Phelps removed quickly turned to dis-tress when we learned that Judge Mark Kennedy had been as-signed to preside over the trial. Once again, I saw all the signs of an Alabama conspiracy. Judge Kennedy had been appointed to the bench the moment he finished law school because, I assume, he happened to be the son-in-law of former governor George Wallace. To complicate matters, Hank Williams, Jr., had cam-paigned tirelessly on behalf of George Wallace and later for George Wallace, Jr.

As I kept saying repeatedly, all I wanted was a fair shot. But it seemed to me that I kept getting knocked out of the game before I even got a chance to play. This time, however, we got lucky. As it turned out, Judge Kennedy was a fair and honorable man, although this did not seem obvious to us at first.

In July 1987, Judge Kennedy ruled, without calling a single witness, that under Alabama law, which prohibited an adopted child from inheriting from its natural father, Hank Williams, Jr., was the sole heir to the estate of Hank Williams, Sr.

I had lost.

But before I could become too depressed over this part of his decision, Judge Kennedy turned his attention to the "other issue" before him. As Hank Jr.'s lawyers had asked, he needed to rule on the issue of whether or not Hank Jr. was, in fact, the sole child of Hank Sr. Judge Kennedy said, in the same ruling, that he could not make that decision without a trial. So, without hesitating, he set a trial date of August 27, 1987, on that issue, and that issue alone.

"Those bastards misjudged this one," Keith said, grinning. "Now let's see if we can make them pay for it."

David Johnson agreed, and was all for litigating even though there was no money in it, since Judge Kennedy had already ruled that I could not have any. The issue had been distilled down to one: Was I the child of Hank Williams? This was the only issue

I really cared about anyway, and somehow it seemed like "divine justice" that we were going to trial on it because Junior's lawyers' had overreached—they had asked for more than they needed to win.

Keith got a betting pool going based on how long it would take Junior's lawyers to realize their miscalculation and come roaring back, demanding that I be denied my day in court. It took about twenty-four hours.

Hank Jr.'s lawyers were up in arms, telling that judge that he had misinterpreted their pleading originally filed before Judge Phelps. Judge Kennedy insisted that he had ruled on the exact two points they had asked for. They demanded to be allowed to withdraw that part of their pleading, and Judge Kennedy said, "Too late." They fretted, fumed, and argued long and hard, but Judge Kennedy turned a deaf ear to them. We were going back to court.

Keith and David now focused their attention on proving paternity, a luxury none of us thought we would ever have. They developed a basic concept to pursue during the trial, and wrote down their remarks summarizing their position and my feelings:

> Cathy's father was and is a national resource. That she even exists is of incalculable value to her, his fans, and his memory. That he wished to raise her is of incalculable value as a reevaluation of Hank Williams, the man . . . This court has within its sole province to address an issue long avoided, to right a wrong her daddy never intended be visited upon her head.

They then talked about all the "what ifs" I had experienced over the years, including "what if" I were again cheated out of my heritage. They concluded by outlining all the facts we had uncovered.

As we geared up for the August 27 trial, we gathered documents from Mr. Rudin's office and asked our witnesses to make their way to Montgomery. We were ready to roll.

But on August 25, we were presented with one more hurdle to jump. We received a call from Judge Kennedy's secretary asking us what we "understood" the upcoming proceeding to be. "A trial on paternity," was of course Keith's answer. Although Judge Kennedy understood the same thing, Maury Smith, one of Junior's lawyers, was under the impression that it was only to be a "status conference." According to the secretary, Junior's boys weren't ready for a trial. We reluctantly agreed to the status conference, knowing full well it was just a delaying tactic.

At the conference Hank Jr.'s attorneys immediately began hammering on the judge. They insisted that since he had already ruled that Hank Jr. was the sole heir, there was no reason to go to the trouble of proving whether or not he was the sole child. I'd heard this song before: Even if I was the daughter of Hank Williams, I couldn't inherit anything, so why bother to prove my relationship.

Luckily for us, Judge Kennedy was not cowed. He set the trial for September 4.

Maury Smith immediately launched into another round of stalling tactics. He complained that he had a prior commitment on September 4. Kennedy then suggested September 3, but again Maury Smith was busy. Fine then, Judge Kennedy moved it to the second. Just as Maury Smith was about to object again, a young associate tugged on his sleeve and probably suggested that Maury sit down before Judge Kennedy scheduled the trial for that very afternoon.

Once again, we had a trial date, this time for September 2, 1987. Keith and I were so sure the trial date would be pushed far into the future that we had packed up to head home after the hearing. We were delighted to turn around and head back to Birmingham, unpack all the files, and get ready.

As the days passed, we heard no commotion at all from Hank Jr.'s attorneys. It was not like them to be so quiet, and Keith began to get nervous. He didn't trust this sort of calm—something was happening.

Again, Judge Kennedy's secretary called us with the bad news. Maury Smith's firm had again asked the judge to stop the trial. The judge had refused, and Maury had gone over Judge Kennedy's head, straight to the Supreme Court of Alabama in an effort to stay the proceedings. His request was pending, and they would determine whether or not we would have a trial.

Keith and David rushed to get a copy of Maury's petition, then worked all night to write and file our reply. We did not want any more delays, but Keith knew that it could take the Supreme Court months to rule on such a petition. He—and I— also realized that they could rule against us.

To our amazement, on September 1, we got an incredible call. The Alabama Supreme Court had ruled— and we were going to court at 9:00 A.M. on September 2.

We had decided that I would attend every proceeding. Keith felt it was important that I be sitting there, that the judge see the flesh-and-blood person everyone was talking about. Of course, no one and nothing could have kept me away.

Hank Jr.'s lawyers introduced only one piece of evidence, the 1967 order ruling that Hank Jr. was the sole heir of the estate of Hank Williams, Sr. They also said that they were willing to stipulate that there might be other children by Hank Williams, Sr., but Junior was the only heir. And then they rested their case.

My greatest fear was the possibility that Judge Kennedy could simply dispose of the matter by saying, "This court finds that Hank Williams, Jr., is not the sole child," and leave it at that. Clearly, Hank Jr.'s lawyers had considered the same possibility.

I begged Keith and David to make Judge Kennedy finish the sentence—to state flat-out that I was Hank Williams' child. I did not want to be cheated again, especially after all I had gone through, by some mealymouth ruling. I did not want to be "maybe another child." I was Hank's daughter, and I wanted everyone to know it.

Just as we put our first witness, Pappy McCormick, on the stand, Sterling Culpepper, Maury Smith's partner and another of Junior's lawyers, rose and once again began telling the judge that he had made a serious mistake by allowing the trial to begin.

I could see that Judge Kennedy was angry. He called all the lawyers into his office and, as Keith got up to leave, I again begged him not to allow things to end here. As he told me later, Judge Kennedy raged at Culpepper, and finally said that if he wanted to stipulate that Cathy was also a child of Hank Williams, then they wouldn't go to trial. Culpepper declined, and back they all came. Keith was grinning; he knew we'd won.

Judge Kennedy allowed us to bring all our witnesses to the stand. I sat almost motionless and listened as Pappy McCormick, Bob Helton, Jean Davis, Jeannie Jett Byrnes, and even Miss Austin from Pensions and Security, all got up and related their stories. Every time we called a witness, one of Junior's lawyers would jump to his feet and object. And every time, Judge Kennedy would say, "Proceed."

Jean Davis, the nurse from St. Margaret's Hospital, ended up being the star of the proceeding. She told all about her conversations with Bobbie Jett while she was in the hospital, how Bobbie had said that she and Hank had been lovers for years, and how, during the delivery, she just kept singing and singing. When David asked her the name of the song Bobbie was singing, Sterling Culpepper objected adamantly. This time the judge agreed with Culpepper, and Jean got up to leave the witness stand. But as she walked toward the door, she looked over at the crowd and said, "It was 'I Can't Help It If I'm Still in Love With You.' "

I watched and listened as the lawyers fought over the introduction of our exhibits—the documents that I knew so well and had treasured for so long—and I sighed with relief to hear Judge Kennedy order their admission. I watched with tears in my eyes as the famous contract was admitted into evidence, followed by information from my adoption files and the other papers that told the story of my life.

These documents—documents we had fought for long and hard—had been hidden for thirty years, and now were going on the record. My life history and years of work were slowly and methodically building the case of Baby Jett. I stared at Keith, but I could no longer see him because tears blurred my eyes.

Finally it was over. We retired from the courtroom, feeling confident we had won, yet not absolutely secure until we heard the judge's ruling. We drove back to Washington and started to wait.

Fortunately, we didn't have to wait too long. On the afternoon of October 26, 1987, as Keith and I were lounging on the deck of the *Jett Stream*, the telephone rang. It was David Johnson.

"Touchdown," David yelled into the phone. Then he read me Judge Kennedy's ruling:

> The court upon consideration of the evidence does hereby find that Hank Williams, Jr., is not in fact the only natural child of Hank Williams, Sr., in that defendant Catherine Yvone Stone is also a natural child of Hank Williams, Sr.

16
HANK, THE MAN

By the time Judge Mark Kennedy declared to the world that I was Hank Williams' child, Keith and I had spent three full years researching my mysterious past. In some instances, I knew to the day where I had been, what I had been doing, and what others had been doing on my behalf or to my detriment. Because of all the research, I got to know myself better than I could have ever imagined.

As it turned out, as a result of all the depositions and the comments from people I met as a result of my own publicity, I got to know someone else remarkably well. That person was my daddy, Hank Williams.

The Hank Williams I came to know was a very different man from the fellow George Hamilton had portrayed in the film *Your Cheatin' Heart*. He was a complex flesh-and-blood human being, an extremely intelligent man, a man gifted beyond the comprehension of most of the people who knew him intimately. He was also a man whose real life, especially during his last four years, was fraught with insurmountable problems.

244

Curiously, after we'd deposed and interviewed scores of people who had known Hank, we discovered that his life was riddled with contradictions. Every fact we uncovered raised scores of questions. What was his marriage to Audrey Williams really like? What was his relationship with Bobbie Jett? Why did he sign an agreement with Bobbie, admitting his paternity and assuring that he would keep me, and then, three days later, marry Billie Jean Eshliman? What was going on in his career during the last months of his life? Was he fired permanently from the Grand Ole Opry or was he just suspended until he could pull himself together? What caused his death? Where did he die? Why did he die at that particular moment?

One fact that seems irrefutable: During the last thirteen months of his life, Hank Williams lived with great pain, both physical and emotional. I suspect that his pain started long before the last year of his life, but certainly after his major back surgery in December 1951, he spent much of his time in physical agony.

His back injury itself is typical of the sort of myth that sticks tenaciously to the story of Hank Williams. Many stories circulate about the source of Hank's back trouble. Some say he was born with congenital spina bifida. Others tell of a brief adventure as a cowboy in Texas and a fall from a bucking bronco. In his book, *Hank Williams: From Life to Legend*, Jerry Rivers tells of a hard fall Hank took in a little creek one morning when they were out hunting. Someone else claimed that Hank said that his mother once beat him with a baseball bat.

Hank himself spoke at length about his back problems in one of the few recorded statements he ever made that was not part of a radio show or other entertainment. In January 1952, he was scheduled to appear in Baltimore, but when the date arrived, he was still laid up in bed from his surgery a month before. As a result, his message was played at the concert, and in it he apologized for his absence and explained the history of his back ailment.

By Hank's own account, neither he nor his doctor knew exactly why his back was so weak. He certainly doesn't mention a fall from a bucking bronco, and questions whether or not he was just born with a weak back or, as he put it, "it just wore out or somethin'." Nevertheless, he founded philosophical and closed with the thought: "I sure wished I could slough this bed here today for the stage in Baltimore . . . but that's just one of those things that happens that you can't get by."

Hank's back surgery marks the beginning of the final disintegration of his health, which resulted in the loss of his position at the Opry and ended with his death a year later.

In the full message regarding the Baltimore engagement, Hank mentions that his wife, Audrey, showed up with his boys (the Drifting Cowboys) and several people from the Opry to do the show. Audrey did go to Baltimore, but on January 3, 1952, Hank moved out of their house on Franklin Road, and on January 10, 1952, Audrey filed for separate maintenance.

Audrey Williams was probably the most striking contradiction in Hank's life. Hank and Audrey's marriage had been in trouble for quite some time before their 1952 divorce—if not from the moment they wed. Audrey sued Hank for divorce, alleging physical abuse, early on in their marriage. Their May 26, 1948, divorce, Randall's birth a year to the day later, and the peculiar nunc pro tunc amendment to that divorce, were symptomatic of the turmoil. One thing was certain, their second divorce became final on May 29, 1952. Although Hank was advised by his lawyer, Robert Stewart, to remarry Audrey in 1949, he refused. Nevertheless, until the day she died in 1975, Audrey would have the world believe that she was the love of Hank's life. Others, including Lillian Stone, would help her perpetuate that myth.

Hank's feelings toward Audrey were always ambivalent. By all accounts, Audrey was a belligerent, pushy woman—not popular with Hank's friends or fellow musicians—and possessed a volatile temper and a roving eye. As with his mother, Hank needed her aggressive support and control, yet probably resented it deeply. At the same time, he was apparently obsessed with her, believed he loved her passionately, and, according to many sources, was profoundly jealous of her.

From a pragmatic point of view, they both had good reasons

to try to stick it out after the 1948 divorce. She now had a child—
something Hank wanted, as he would later want me. (There is
no getting around the fact that Hank adored Randall. He closed
every performance with his famous line: "If the Good Lord's willing
and the creek don't rise, I'll be seeing you." After Randall was
born, he would add: "I'll be home soon, Little Bocephus.") Since
Randall was conceived after their first divorce, he would have
been illegitimate regardless of whether or not Hank was his biological father, and the nunc pro tunc was an effort to assure
his legitimacy.

Professionally, by the time Randall was conceived, it was
obvious to one and all that Hank was on the fast track. By February 1949, when Audrey was six months pregnant, Hank's first
megahit record, "Lovesick Blues," was racing up the charts. By
June 1949, two weeks after Randall's birth, Hank had arrived at
the Grand Ole Opry to the sound of six standing ovations. Success at the Grand Ole Opry depended upon the illusion of a
stable, loving family life. With Audrey and her daughter, Lycretia—and now Little Bocephus—Hank could present and maintain that image.

For her part, Audrey wanted to be married to a star. She
wanted the money, she wanted the trappings, she wanted the
prestige, she wanted the glory. She pressured him into buying a
big new house on Franklin Road in one of Nashville's newer and
fanciest neighborhoods. She dressed them both in expensive
Western gear designed by Nudie of Hollywood (and clothed herself in designer dresses, furs, and expensive jewelry). She opened
a store in downtown Nashville that sold Western apparel and
Hank (and Audrey) Williams souvenirs. Hank loved big cars, but
Audrey insisted on her own yellow Cadillac to match Hank's
version, which, during his last year, was baby blue. They also
bought a farm near Franklin, Tennessee, at the urging of Hank's
banker, for investment reasons, but the status of a "country estate" would not have been lost on Audrey.

Hank Williams was an intelligent, ambitious man, and surely
he recognized the importance of "image" and its effect on success and "stardom." The Nudie suits and the big cars probably
appealed to him. He also loved horses, and apparently enjoyed,

to some extent, their country house. But, for the most part, he could not have cared less about money and the accoutrements of success.

Given Audrey's actions, both during her marriage to Hank and after his death, it was obvious she desperately wanted to be a star herself. Audrey apparently thought she possessed musical gifts, and insisted on being part of the performing entourage. The truth was, she had a grating, strident singing voice, and Hank knew it. Nevertheless, he allowed her to perform with him and the Drifting Cowboys on stage, on radio, and on many recordings. On some records, Hank even seems to be holding his own voice down so that hers predominates. (One of the Drifting Cowboys, Don Helms, claims that he did this in order to "carry" her—to help keep her on key.) Hank even managed to persuade Decca to give Audrey her own recording contract. Jerry Rivers, the fiddler from the Drifting Cowboys, says Audrey's singing drove Hank crazy. Every now and then, according to Jerry, Hank would say, "Boys, the only thing worse than having a wife who wants to sing is havin' one who can't."

Part of the "Hank myth"—no doubt nurtured by Audrey—professes that Hank's feelings for her inspired some of his greatest songs. "Cold, Cold Heart" was supposedly written while Hank sat in the waiting room of a Shreveport hospital while Audrey was in labor during the birth of Randall. Some people believe "Your Cheatin' Heart," written just before their divorce in early 1952, reflects both his jealousy and a certain finality of feelings with regard to his relationship with Audrey. Even less well known songs like "I Can't Escape From You," one of the few songs that mentions his drinking, is thought to have been inspired by Audrey.

In any case, Hank was characteristically generous toward Audrey in their divorce settlement. Audrey apparently received the house on Franklin Road and other things. But, most startling, Hank gave her half the royalties due from Acuff-Rose and MGM Records, both at the time of the divorce and for all time, unless she remarried.

Audrey had also retained custody of Randall, who was three at the time of their 1952 divorce. After Hank's death, Randall was considered the sole heir, so until Randall turned eighteen in 1967, Audrey probably ended up receiving Randall's share of the estate. Audrey and Randall ultimately fell out over her management of his affairs—and his money—but the fact remains that, from 1953 until 1967, almost all the revenue from the Hank Williams estate flowed through Audrey's hands whether she received it directly as his ex-wife or for Randall through Robert Stewart and Irene Smith.

After his divorce from Audrey, Hank moved into a little stone house out on the Natchez Trace with Ray Price, a young singer who was new at the Opry. I don't know precisely when Hank met Bobbie Jett, but I do know, based on Jeannie Jett's account, that Bobbie spent time with Hank in this house.

As far as I can make out, Bobbie met Hank Williams in late 1951 or early 1952. She liked to socialize, and possibly through friends or through Willard, who was well known around Nashville, she met many people from the Opry, who of course were the most glamorous folks in town. According to an entry in my adoption files, Mrs. Stone said that she first met Bobbie in early 1952, which would indicate that she would have known Hank for at least a while prior to that if they were friendly enough for her to visit him at his mother's home.

In February, 1952, [Bobbie] came to Montgomery and at that time, her son was at home sick. [Mrs. Stone] mentioned that she made her leave as her niece was waiting on him.

By the time Hank moved into the Natchez Trace house, he had been recuperating from his serious back operation for only four weeks. Several people, including Mrs. Stone, allude to the fact that Bobbie was his "nurse" at some point. Although I have no record that she had any formal nursing training, her own mother, Pauline, was a trained nurse, and Bobbie had spent the preceding two or three years nursing her grandmother, Ocie Belle. Bobbie was working full-time during these years for the Selective Service, but it is not inconceivable that she offered to help look after Hank while he was laid up. She lived a few short blocks away from the Natchez Trace house, so "looking in" on him would have been "neighborly."

In any case, it is easy to see how they could be attracted to one another. Hank was the biggest star in Nashville, and Bobbie liked "stars." Bobbie was, of course, a very attractive woman, and according to her friends was fun-loving and easygoing. Also, Hank seemed to gravitate toward women with children. Audrey had had another child before she met Hank; Billie Jean Eshliman, whom Hank would marry the following October, had a child by an early marriage; and Bobbie had Jo. The fact that Bobbie had a child, I suspect, had a powerful effect on him.

By April 1952, Bobbie was pregnant. Apparently Bobbie was not a person who readily confided in other people. Her friends of later years in California knew nothing of me or her relationship to Hank Williams, and even most of her Nashville friends during that time were unaware of her pregnancy. I can only imagine how painful and frightening the months of May, June, and July 1952 were for Bobbie. She already had one child, Jo, and now she was pregnant with another—by Hank Williams, no less.

Those months were no less painful for Hank. He was drinking heavily, showing up drunk for performances, and, in some cases, missing performances completely. Ray Price found living with Hank in the Natchez Trace house impossible, and he moved out. Also, according to many sources, Hank seemed to be taking drugs.

Jerry Rivers believes strongly that Hank's "drug taking" must be taken in context with his time and place. Hank was not a "recreational" drug user. (Actually he was not a "recreational" drinker either.) He took drugs to kill pain. But, as with alcohol, he ended up abusing himself. According to Jerry: "Hank would say, 'If it helps to take one pill every four hours, it must be even better to take four pills every one hour,' whereupon Hank would throw back a handful of pills." During 1952, Hank was in and out of the hospital innumerable times. Some say it got to the point where if he wasn't on the road performing, he was either in the hospital or at his mother's home in Montgomery recuperating.

Hank Williams in 1937, strummin' on the streets of Montgomery.

Hank, Audrey, and the Drifting Cowboys, at the height of their fame. From left: Cedric Rainwater, Sammy Pruett, Audrey, Hank, Jerry Rivers, *and Don Helms.*

Hank Williams, circa 1951, singing his heart out. Sammy Pruett and Don Helms are in the background.

Nobody could capture an audience the way Hank Williams could.

(THE BETTMANN ARCHIVE)

A publicity photo taken on October 9, 1952, at Hank's and Billie Jean Eshliman's blow-out wedding in New Orleans.

The cottage at Kowaliga where Hank and Bobbie spent two weeks together in August 1952. Bobbie was pregnant with me at the time.

Bob Helton paying his last respects to Hank in the parlor of my grandmother's boardinghouse.

*Hank Williams, Jr.,
1977.*

*Owen Bradley and me
on his houseboat at a
lake outside Nashville,
summer 1985.*

Keith and I approach the Jefferson Memorial at dawn on our wedding day, September 28, 1986.

Our magnificent home, The Jett Stream.

Laying a wreath at Hank's grave to launch the Hank Williams Memorial Celebration, June 1989.

Don Helms (left), Jerry Rivers, and me getting to know each other—and liking it a lot, summer 1989.

Jett Williams and the Drifting Cowboys Band, fall 1989. Clockwise from top left: *Jerry Rivers, Don Helms, Bobby Andrews, and Frank Evans.*

(PHILIP HIGHT)

Singing my heart out in Birmingham, Alabama, October 1989.

Sometime in 1952, Hank hooked up with a quack doctor named Horace Raphol "Toby" Marshall probably in Oklahoma City. Marshall claimed to be a respectable physician who specialized in alcoholism when in fact he was a high school dropout and an ex-convict who was out on parole at the time he met Hank. According to George William Koon in *Hank Williams: A Bio-Bibliography,* "Toby was a reformed alcoholic who claimed that he could help Hank. Actually, though, he was little more than a drug contact who, with a series of fraudulent prescriptions . . . kept Hank in amphetamines, Seconal, chloral hydrate, and morphine."

Both Hank and his mother believed in Toby's expertise, and apparently leaned on him quite a bit during the last months of Hank's life. Koon notes that Toby's "last prescription for Hank, probably written when the singer was in Oklahoma in December 1952, was for . . . chloral hydrate, a sedative that depresses the central nervous system. Within much less than a month [Hank] would be dead and his family would receive a bill for $736.39 from Dr. Marshall."

But while all that may have been true, Hank also produced some extraordinary music during that same period. On June 13, he recorded "Jambalaya," "Settin' the Woods on Fire," and "I'll Never Get Out of This World Alive." On July 11, he recorded "You Win Again."

Hank was at Lake Martin with Bobbie on August 15, was arrested for being drunk and disorderly on August 17 in Alexander City, and appeared on the Louisiana Hayride on September 20, 1952. On September 23, he did a Nashville recording— his last— which included "Your Cheatin' Heart," "Kaw-Liga," and "Take These Chains From My Heart." He would be dead in a little over three months, but at the last session, he recorded some remarkable songs.

To complicate his already complicated life, sometime in the spring or summer of 1952, Hank met another woman, Billie Jean Jones Eshliman. Billie Jean was a nineteen-year-old divorcée, and "so pretty you couldn't look at her," as one man described her. She was a sexy redhead from Bossier City, Louisiana, who first showed up in Nashville as the girlfriend of another Opry newcomer, Faron Young. Again, Hank's and Billie Jean's first meeting is the stuff of legend. Some say he went out for a drink with Faron and Billie Jean, took Young aside, pulled a gun on him, and said he wanted Billie Jean for himself.

In August 1952, Hank was suspended—or fired—from the Grand Ole Opry. Again, many different interpretations of the firing float around. Wesley Rose dubbed it a "leave of absence" that would be "better for Hank"; others thought that it was only an effort to shake Hank up. Still others believed that the powers-that-be at the Opry were fed up with Hank's unreliability, although it's difficult to believe that the Opry would not have taken back one of their biggest drawing cards had Hank pulled himself back together.

In late August 1952, just after Hank was let go, he and Bobbie Jett left for Alabama, and in late August, they spent two weeks at Kowaliga. I have tried to analyze Bobbie and Hank's relationship a million times, turning it around and around in my head, looking at it from every angle I can think of, playing it out in every possible way. Did he love her? Did she love him? Did they consider marriage?

By August, Bobbie was almost five months pregnant, and undoubtedly disturbed about her situation. I think it is fairly obvious that Hank Williams was a "marrying" kind of man. He got married for the first time when he was only twenty-one; he would get married again in October 1952, less than six months after his final divorce from Audrey. Bobbie, on the other hand, evidently hadn't married Jo's father, and was still unmarried as she approached her thirtieth birthday. Many of her friends have described her as a "one-man woman"—that is, when she was "with" a man, she didn't run around on him—nevertheless, unlike Hank, she apparently wasn't the "marrying" kind.

Did they consider marriage? Possibly, but the fact is they didn't do it. On October 15, 1952, they signed a contract where Bobbie agreed to give up custody of her baby—me—to Hank. As painful as this is to me, I can only conclude that she did not want to be tied down with a second child—and very possibly didn't want a husband either. The contract states clearly that Hank very much wanted the baby for himself.

Three days after signing his agreement with Bobbie, Hank married Billie Jean Eshliman, not once, but three times. Did Hank think that Billie Jean would "mother" me? Apparently not, since the contract states clearly that Mrs. Stone would care for me for the first two years of my life. Nevertheless, in a crazy kind of way, Hank seemed to be trying to establish a family life for himself.

Did Hank and Bobbie love each other? Perhaps, but they must not have been "in love," although I find it odd that a man who was supposedly madly in love with another woman (Billie Jean) would spend two weeks in a secluded cabin with a beautiful woman—who happened to be carrying his child. I think they must have genuinely cared for each other. During the months they were together, they were both in states of extreme agitation and confusion. Yet, they managed to consider each other and the situation—that is, me—to the extent that they contracted for my care. They struck an agreement requiring that they be in constant contact with one another for the rest of their lives, rather like an amicable divorce where the partners share custody and visitation rights of their child.

Even after Hank married Billie Jean, Bobbie continued to live with Mrs. Stone at the McDonough Street house. Granted, it would have been difficult for her to return to Nashville while she was so obviously pregnant, but if she felt "jilted" by Hank, she certainly could have gone to either Nashville or California— where Hank had agreed to send her. In any case, I don't think Bobbie behaved like a "woman scorned."

Hank's marriage to Billie Jean is another topic riddled with conflicting points of view. Mrs. Stone and Irene Williams Smith made no bones about their dislike for Billie Jean. Billie and Hank spent Christmas in Montgomery with Mrs. Stone, but apparently they were fighting. After Hank's death, Mrs. Stone would tell Connie Helton that Hank had sent Billie Jean home to her family—for good. For him, their marriage was over. Billie Jean denies this, saying that Hank left for his Canton, Ohio, date and she headed for Shreveport and was going to meet him the following week in Nashville. No one has come forward joining her in support of that proposition; however, it wouldn't be the first time a man told his mother one thing and his wife another. Audrey Williams also always maintained that she and Hank were going to get back together. But Pappy McCormick says Hank wouldn't have taken Audrey back "on a Christmas tree."

The stories surrounding Hank Williams' death are the most confusing and conflicting of all. One fact is certain: Hank had accepted a date to play in Canton, Ohio, on New Year's Day, 1953. Beyond that is chaos, and George William Koon, author of *Hank Williams: A Bio-Bibliography*, offers the best-researched account of the hours preceding Hank's death:

> The thirtieth of December brought snow to Montgomery, and that meant no flying for Hank. He hired Charles Harold Carr, an eighteen-year-old Auburn freshman who sometimes worked for his father at the Lee Street Taxi Company, to drive the baby-blue Cadillac convertible for the twenty hours it would take to get to Canton.
>
> He and Carr took Highway 31 to Birmingham, where they spent the first night. Then it was up Highway 11 to Chattanooga and on into Knoxville. Hank was drinking beer and taking chloral hydrate while Carr drove. In Knoxville, Hank and Carr caught a 3:30 P.M. plane for Ohio. But bad weather forced the flight back to Knoxville, where it landed at 5:57 P.M. The two travelers then headed for the Andrew Johnson Hotel, where Carr checked them in at 7:08. Assistant hotel manger Dan McCrary talked to a nervous Charles Carr but did not see Hank, who was carried up to a room by porters.
>
> Carr ordered two steaks, but Hank was unable to eat. Dr. P. H. Cardwell arrived and noted that Hank was extremely drunk and that he was carrying several capsules. Cardwell gave Hank two B_{12} shots; each contained one-quarter grain of morphine. The B_{12} was probably for the vitamin deficiency standard in alcoholics. The morphine could have been for Hank's back pain, but it is also a recognized treatment for pulmonary edema— excess fluid in the lungs. Hank's fight [Hank had been in a brawl during the Christmas holiday] might have caused the edema, but the condition is symptomatic of drug overdose as well. It seems that Hank was subject to the problem on both counts. Carr still seemed intent on getting Hank to Canton in time to rest before the show; he was well aware that Hank's contract carried a one-thousand-

dollar default penalty. He got the porters to help dress Hank and then carry the singer back out to the Cadillac convertible. Hank showed no sign of life except for a slight cough when he was picked up. Carr checked them out of the Andrew Johnson at 10:45 P.M.

At 11:45 P.M. Carr was stopped for reckless driving near Blaine, Tennessee. He had been trying to pass a car and had nearly run head-on into Patrol Corporal Swann H. Kitts. The patrolman questioned Carr about the lifeless-looking man in the back seat. Carr explained that Hank had been drinking and had taken a sedative. Kitts seemed to accept the explanation and led the travelers to Rutledge, Tennessee, where Carr paid his $25 fine to Magistrate Olin H. Marshall. Carr then drove on toward Canton until about dawn on New Year's Day when, in Oak Hill, West Virginia, he decided to stop and check on Hank. He pulled into Glen Burdett's Pure Oil, now a Union '76 station, and reached back to find his passenger cold. Patrolman Howard Jamey came to the scene and arranged for Hank to be taken to Oak Hill Hospital where he was pronounced dead on arrival. The body was taken to the Tyree Funeral Home and embalmed.

The details of the events in and around Knoxville are fortuitously available to us for one reason: When Captain John Davis of the Tennessee Highway Patrol heard of the death and of the involvement of Patrolman Kitts, he ordered Kitts to investigate the details of Hank's passage through Knoxville. Kitts made a thorough investigation and filed a handwritten report, which was made public in a *Knoxville Journal* story of 15 December 1982.

In the last part of his report, Kitts makes these interesting comments:

> Carr said he was driving Hank Williams. I noticed Williams and asked Carr if he could be dead, as he was pale and blue looking. But he said Williams had drank 6 bottles of beer and a doctor had given him two injections to help him sleep.
>
> He asked me not to wake him up as he was very sick and looked that way. I had him (Carr) to stop at Rutledge. I wrote him a ticket (for reckless driving) at 12:30. He was tried before a Justice of the Peace, O. H. Marshall, and was fined $25 and costs.
>
> I talked with him about Williams' condition in the

presence of Sheriff J. N. Antrican and Marshall. I thought
he (Carr) was a little nervous over paying the fine and he
asked us not to bother Williams.

Carr had a soldier with him at the time he was in
Rutledge. He paid the fine, thanked us and left about 1 A.M.

After investigating this matter, I think that Williams
was dead when he was dressed and carried out of the hotel.
Since he was drunk and was given the injections and could
have taken some capsules earlier, with all this he couldn't
have lasted over an hour and a half or two hours.

A man drunk or doped will make some movement if
you move them. A dead man will make a coughing sound if
they are [sic] if lifted around. Taking all this into consideration, he must have died in Knoxville at the hotel.

Patrolman Kitts' report, which is the most detailed of any
describing Hank's death, raises as many questions as it answers.
Of course, the first and most stunning question is: Why was his
report not made public for twenty-nine years? But beyond that,
the questions are unending.

Who was "Dr. P. H. Cardwell" of Knoxville? How did Carr
find him and convince him to come to a hotel and give a famous
celebrity a vitamin shot laced with morphine? Realizing that Hank
needed medical attention, why didn't Carr just take Hank to a
hospital? More to the point, why didn't Dr. Cardwell put him in
a hospital? Kitts' report also contains the note that Carr made
two phone calls from the hotel. If one was to Dr. Cardwell, who
received the other?

Why did Carr leave the hotel in Knoxville less than three
hours after he checked in, especially since Hank was so ill? If
Officer Kitts' analysis is correct, Carr must have known Hank
was already dead and spent the next six hours driving with a
dead man in the back of his car. The image of this scenario is
gruesome, terrifying, and of course, brings up the obvious question: Why?

And what about Kitts himself? He saw Hank looking pale
and blue in the back seat of the car, and therefore must have
been standing within inches of the body. Carr was an eighteen-
year-old kid, driving around "recklessly" on New Year's Eve, in

a great big baby-blue Cadillac with a dead-looking singing star in the back seat. Wouldn't a cop shove an eighteen-year-old kid aside and investigate such a suspicious-looking matter thoroughly? Kitts even reports that he discussed the situation with the local sheriff and the Justice of the Peace who tried Carr on the reckless driving charge. Incredibly, nothing was done.

Most bizarre of all, who was the "soldier" with Charles Carr in the blue Cadillac at the time he was picked up in Rutledge? Why did Kitts neglect to take his name?

Where did Carr pick up this man—and more to the point, why? Carr's excuse for taking Hank out of the Knoxville hotel was because he was intent on getting him to Canton, Ohio. If so, why would he take the time, especially when he thought Hank was ill, to pick up a hitchhiker—if that is, in fact, who the "soldier" was? By the time Carr got to the hospital in Oak Hill, West Virginia, the "soldier" was gone. Where did Carr drop him off—and why?

And there is more. Press reports around the time of Hank's death say Hank actually had two bookings—one on December 31 in Charleston, West Virginia, and then another on New Year's Day in Canton. The *Memphis Commercial Appeal* reported on January 2, 1953, that Charles Carr was to pick up a relief driver in Bluefield, West Virginia, named Donald Surface.

Toby Marshall also made a mysterious claim against Hank's estate for expenses he supposedly incurred at Mrs. Williams' behest. A memo he wrote from the Oklahoma State Penitentiary where he was an inmate dated January 8, 1954, addressed to the Circuit Court of Montgomery County, says:

At approximately 4:30 P.M. on December 30, 1952, Mrs. Lillian S. Stone, mother of the decedent and administratrix of the estate, telephoned the Doctor's Bureau in Oklahoma City, Oklahoma, where I was registered as an Alcoholic-Narcotic Therapist . . . and requested to speak with me . . . [I took the call from Mrs. Stone] whom I knew. Upon answering the phone, it became immediately obvious that Mrs. Stone was greatly upset, however, she was able to convey the information to me that the decedent had recently gone through a highly upsetting emotional incident which had caused him to resume his drinking. It had also caused him to take off in his car with a hired driver for Charleston, West Virginia, where he had an engagement scheduled for the evening of December 31, 1952. Mrs. Stone continued to stress her worry over his condition and what might result from it and requested that I immediately leave Oklahoma City and intercept the decedent at Charleston to care for him, stay with him and return him to Montgomery at the conclusion of his engagements.

I accepted the assignment without reservation. . .

If the court will review the expense account attached to my filed claim in the matter, the court will note my actual traveling and personal expenses amounted to some $763.39.

We'll never know whether Toby Marshall actually traveled to West Virginia to help Hank, but rumors about these and other inconsistencies have run rampant since New Year's Day, 1953. Frankly, I suspect they will circulate forever and no one will ever know the truth. Certainly Charles Carr isn't talking, never has, and probably never will. No charges were ever made against him or anyone else, and so Carr has never been forced to make a full statement.

When Lillian Williams Stone arrived in Oak Hill to pick up Hank's body, she demanded an autopsy. The autopsy revealed that Hank died of "alcoholic cardiomyopathy," or heart disease directly related to excessive drinking. The coroner found alcohol in Hank's blood, but no sign of drugs.

By Saturday, January 3, Lillie had brought Hank's body back to Montgomery. She held a wake at her house and hundreds of friends filed through, paying their last respects to Hank. Staying at the house, over the next few days, were Lillie, Audrey, Billie Jean, and Bobbie Jett. I can't imagine that the extreme tension and grief of Hank's death wasn't exacerbated by the presence of these particular women—together—under the roof of one small house on McDonough Street. The only comment that survives was one reflecting Lillian's disgust that Billie Jean showed up at the wake wearing red slacks. But I suspect that Billie Jean's red slacks were the least of it.

Lillie had hired A. V. Bamford, a Nashville promoter who

had booked Hank into Canton, to arrange the funeral, which took place on Sunday afternoon, January 4. Twenty-five thousand people showed up for the 2:30 service, and for an hour prior to the service, mourners were permitted to file past Hank's open casket.

Later that afternoon, Hank was buried at the Oakwood Cemetery Annex, just up the hill from the majestic Alabama State Capitol Building. He died without a will and without life insurance, but he left a remarkable legacy, not the least of which included a very determined mother, a very shrewd lawyer, and a couple of very scrappy wives.

Both Billie Jean and Audrey decided immediately to "go on the road," booking themselves as "Mrs. Hank Williams." By late spring 1953, based on a ruling that Billie Jean and Hank's marriage was illegal because her divorce from her first husband was not final, Audrey and Lillian bought out Billie Jean's claims to widowhood as well as her use of the name Mrs. Hank Williams. Billie Jean accepted a thirty-thousand-dollar settlement, which must have looked like a fortune to a nineteen-year-old girl who had been married for just over two months. Within a year, she would be married again, to singer-songwriter Johnny Horton.

As for Lillie, she worked hard to perpetuate Audrey's version of the myth, for reasons that escape me. In April 1954, she signed a movie deal with MGM on the condition that MGM not mention Hank's divorce from Audrey or his marriage to Billie Jean. The idea was shelved when Lillie died the following year.

For the next fifteen years, Audrey promoted herself as an entertainer and worked hard to develop the talents of her son, Randall. She trained him to sing Hank's songs in Hank's style, she booked him around the country, and even at the Grand Ole Opry at the tender age of eight. After more than ten years of difficulty, she finally was able to get the movie *Your Cheatin' Heart* made and released. Audrey served as a consultant on the film. As a result she got the opportunity to rewrite history, including the myth of their love and her widowhood. Hank Jr. sang on the sound track.

In 1966, Randall and Audrey sued Irene Smith (by then the administratrix of the estate) for the return of some of Hank Sr.'s possessions, including the baby-blue Cadillac in which he died. They won this battle. In 1967, they were battling with Irene again, this time over the copyright renewals, and Audrey's desire to close the estate with Hank Jr. as sole heir. But by this time, Audrey and Hank Jr., now eighteen years old, were fighting between themselves, and by the late sixties life began to seriously unravel for Audrey.

In the early 1970s, Billie Jean, the little girl from Bossier City who had been married to Hank Williams for ten weeks, reappeared on the scene. In 1960, she had been widowed for a second time when Johnny Horton was killed in an automobile accident, and a few years later she was married for a fourth time, to a man named N. Kent Berlin, and divorced. In 1972, she sued MGM over her portrayal in *Your Cheatin' Heart*—or, rather, her lack of portrayal—since under Audrey's "technical advice," the movie contained no mention of Audrey's divorce from or Billie Jean's marriage to Hank.

In an unusual decision, the court declared that Billie Jean was the "common law wife" and therefore the "legal widow" of Hank Williams, but gave her no damages. However, ultimately, this decision worked out exceedingly well for Billie Jean. She sold her prospective interest (as the legal widow) in Hank's copyrights to Hill and Range, a music publisher, and together they sued for a share of the copyright renewal royalties—and together they won. After 1975, Billie Jean, and not Audrey, received the widow's portion of the royalties. Today, Billie Jean Jones Eshliman Williams Horton Berlin collects half the royalties from the copyright renewals on all Hank Williams songs. Hank Williams, Jr., collects the other half.

Audrey Williams died on November 4, 1975, less than two weeks after Billie Jean's successful suit was decided, in the Franklin Road house she had bought with Hank Williams in 1949. Officially, she died of natural causes, but like Hank, she suffered from the damages of alcohol and pill abuse. According to her daughter, Lycretia, Audrey died virtually destitute.

So what about Hank Williams, the man?

Hank Williams granted very few interviews. I would guess

that it wasn't that he refused to be interviewed, or set out to create a mysterious picture of himself. He was much too honest and down-to-earth to waste his time with such effort. Perhaps, as Bill Koon suggests, he worked so hard that it was difficult for interviewers to catch up with him. Perhaps he was so young that it didn't occur to anyone that he might not be around long enough to tell his story his own way.

In any case, most of the information about Hank's life comes down secondhand and accounts, in part, for the mythical aspects of his life story. Of course, after his death his mother and his ex-wife, Audrey, went to great lengths to mythologize him. As for me, given the contradictions in the stories I've heard, I trust his music to give me the best picture of the real Hank.

In many ways, Hank did tell his life story through his songs. For example, he rarely spoke of his years growing up, which undoubtedly were tough, but in a few of his songs, he evokes images of his early years that, to me, are revealing. "The Log Train" tells of his father's life as a logger in "Chapmantown." Hank sings of his poignant memories of his daddy "grabbing his lunch bucket" and going off to work, his mother "gettin' supper on the table" in anticipation of Lon's return home, and his vision of Lon "sweatin' and a swearin'" while on the job. This is a nostalgic song, perhaps a wish on Hank's part to return to a more secure time, or maybe just an expression of a desire for a simple, stable life that, in reality, never existed.

Hank recorded several songs about his mother that also tell something of his personal life. "I Dreamed About Mama Last Night," written by Fred Rose, tells how a mother can't sleep until her nearly grown children are home in bed, safe and sound. Hank recorded this song as Luke the Drifter, and though the words are Fred Rose's, they could easily have been Hank's.

Hank wrote a song about Lillie titled "Message to My Mother" that seems to reflect not only his feelings toward his mother but certain attitudes he held about himself. It is a song about a young man who is lying on his deathbed in "dyin' anger," which, in itself, is an interesting phrase. Apparently, Hank didn't think of death with resignation, but with rage. He speaks of the regret he feels about the "tears of sorrow" he may have caused her. He tells of her fears for him—which were undoubtedly true—and closes with the incredible lines: "Soon I'll cross death's dark river. Please let her know that I was saved."

Hank was only twenty-eight years old when he wrote these lines about death, an extraordinary concern for so young a man. I suspect that he knew in his heart that he would die young— and probably soon. But just as Hank's life was full of contradictions, so were the messages he revealed through his songs. One of his last songs was "I'll Never Get Out of This World Alive," and although, again, he expresses anger about dying ("Now you're lookin' at a man who's gettin' kind of mad"), the song itself is upbeat and ironic—almost humorous.

Hank Williams is best known for his "lonesome, lovesick" music, but for every sad song he wrote one can find a partner to it that is ironic, happy-go-lucky, or often downright funny. "Honky-Tonkin' " and "Hey, Good Lookin' " are as fun-loving as "I'm So Lonesome I Could Cry" or "Lonesome Whistle" are sad and depressing. Even when he recorded as Luke the Drifter, he could go from maudlin ("Men With Broken Hearts" or "Pictures From Life's Other Side") to merry ("Just Waitin' " and "I've Been Down That Road Before").

Hank's love songs also run the spectrum from hopeless (I Can't Escape From You" or "Cold, Cold Heart") to helplessly sad ("I Can't Help It If I'm Still in Love With You" and "Your Cheatin' Heart") to somewhat optimistic ("Half as Much"), to in love ("Baby, We're Really in Love") to wildly, crazily in love ("Howlin' at the Moon"). Then there are those love songs that combine emotions like "Kaw-liga" and "Move It On Over," two hopeless situations that are written and sung with wicked irony.

Many times, I think, Hank wrote songs that are absolutely profound in their expression of emotion. In these songs, he managed to bring together a well of feeling and express it perfectly. For me, two examples of his most mature and sophisticated works are "Ramblin' Man" and "I'm So Lonesome I Could Cry."

Hank ended his life physically wasted and emotionally distraught, and yet, ironically—and apparently true to form—the last months of his life were not only prolific and productive, but most of the songs he wrote were happy, upbeat works, particularly "Jambalaya," "Kaw-liga," and "I'll Never Get Out of This World Alive." Even "Your Cheatin' Heart," written during those last weary months, while not a happy song, is a straightforward, honest, and, in a sense, resigned expression of emotion. And what's more, it turned out to be one of the most successful songs he ever wrote.

I'd like to think that "my comin' " made my daddy happy. I suspect it did, since he wrote a happy song about "Sweet Yvonne" and our "kinfolk comin' by the dozen" to see me. But it didn't work out that way, which, surely, would have made him sad. But as Hank might have said, given all the contradictions, this is "just one of those things that happens that you can't get by."

17
THE WEARY BLUES

Despite my joy at winning the paternity case in October 1987, by late spring 1989, I had begun to despair. Nothing was going right: Our efforts on the two legal fronts were at best out of control and, at worst, fast becoming hopeless. My professional life seemed to be going nowhere. Although my personal life with Keith was as loving as it had always been, my relationship with my adoptive family had turned completely sour.

With regard to our legal battles, nothing had gone right with the exception of the paternity decision. Our New York case, which we had appealed to the Second Circuit Court of Appeals appeared to be in shambles. After we had filed our initial complaint in September 1985, we had amended it several times— adding new defendants and new causes of action—as we discovered more about what had happened. Ultimately, the defendants included: Hank Williams, Jr.; Billie Jean Williams Berlin; Chappell Music Company; Acuff-Rose Opryland Music, Inc.; Wesley H. Rose and Roy Acuff, individually; Fred Rose Music Inc.; and Milene Music, Inc.

In March 1987, the defendants filed a joint motion requesting a "summary judgment," or a court order declaring them the winners of the case without benefit of a trial. They based their arguments on all sorts of complicated legal "wrinkles," but the bottom line was that they were asserting that I had waited too long after learning that I might be Hank Williams' child to file suit. They theorized that I should have hired a lawyer in 1974 at the time my mother told me I might be Hank's daughter; and if not in 1974, then certainly in 1980 when my father offered to help me.

To me, this was absurd. First of all, no one had ever told me, absolutely, that I was Hank's daughter. If anything, I had always been told not only that there was "no proof" but that there was nothing more I could do—or should do—even if I found proof. I certainly was not familiar with the words "copyright renewals"—and knew nothing of my potential claims under federal law—until I met Keith and Mickey Rudin in 1985.

On August 6, 1987, Judge John Keenan of the Federal District Court, Southern District of New York, heard oral arguments on the defendants' motion. It took Judge Keenan thirteen months to think it over, but on September 6, 1988, he handed down an order that declared that I had unreasonably delayed pursuing my claim between 1974 and 1981, and therefore he was throwing my case out in its entirety. While I'm sure he felt he was doing the right thing at the time, to my mind, his position was incredibly unfair. As part of his decision, he wrote:

> An analysis of plaintiff's conduct demonstrates that she ignored facts as early as 1974 that alerted her to the strong possibility that Hank Williams, Sr., was her biological father. Indeed, a cynic might suggest that plaintiff slumbered peacefully and knowingly on her rights until she was awakened by the attractive sound of a ringing cash register.

I was devastated. Once again, I felt like the victim of legal rape. Although his order ran on for thirty-eight pages, he never addressed the merits of what I had done or the complex reasons for my delay. He simply accepted every word the opposition had presented.

Of course, we appealed this decision, but on April 21, 1989, disaster struck again. The Court of Appeals for the Second Circuit affirmed Judge Keenan's opinion, but on different grounds. The Court of Appeals held that my failure to file my complaint between 1974 and 1980 "may well have been entirely excusable under the circumstances"; however, they believed that my delay from December 1980, when Daddy called me, until September 1985, when I filed suit, was without plausible explanation. I had lost again. In view of the many factual errors in the opinion, we filed a motion for a rehearing by the Court of Appeals, but this motion was denied on May 23, 1989.

In Alabama, our case involving the estate of Hank Williams was not going along much better. Although I had won on the paternity issue, I had lost any right to inherit from the estate. The state of Alabama declared that I could not inherit from Hank Williams' estate based on the decision of the 1967 trial, or, in other words, because I had been adopted.

We appealed, and in October 1988, we argued our appeal before a panel of the Alabama Supreme Court. For days before the hearing, David Johnson, our Alabama counsel, and Keith, together with Tom Bowron and Leila Hirayama, two associates from David's office, worked hard to synthesize all the issues involved. They focused on the issue of fraud, based on the assumption that Robert Stewart, the Williamses' lawyer, had been morally and legally obligated to inform me of my rights.

David Johnson argued for our side. He came down hard on the issue of fraud, and also made a strong case based on Keith's pet theory that I wasn't "born adopted," referring to my rights from the moment I was born, and the fact that my subsequent adoption should not nullify those rights.

We left the courtroom feeling optimistic, and expected that the court would rule by the end of the year. However, by May 1989, seven months had gone by, and we were losing hope with every passing day. By late May, when we were denied appeal in New York, I lost hope completely in the Alabama decision.

To add to our problems, by spring 1989, we were involved

in a nasty lawsuit with my Aunt Helen and cousin, Stanley Fountain. In December 1987, my mother had died, after a long and debilitating illness. But the moment she was buried, it was as though history began to repeat itself. I knew when Daddy had died that he had willed everything to Mother, and upon her death, I was to inherit their estate. In other words, my father had made his wishes known—and his wishes included my inheriting his estate.

But it didn't work out that way. Upon Mother's death, I learned that Stanley Fountain had inherited all of Louise Deupree's estate—including Wayne Deupree's money, business, house, and personal effects. I got nothing.

For me, this situation was far more painful than the losses I had endured over Hank's estate. I had known these people—and I had loved them—and I had assumed they loved me. I did not want to sue them, and yet I believed I had no choice—for Daddy's sake and certainly for my own. Keith agreed, and we entered into one more litigation to vindicate my rights. Our trial was set for mid-June 1989 in Mobile and I was dreading it.

Because of all the outstanding legal issues, my singing career was put on hold. Keith—and Owen Bradley—believed that no one in the music industry was going to offer me a recording contract until these legal battles were over. I had been asked to perform publicly at numerous events, but we didn't feel that any of the offers were quite right for my debut.

Every day, I would hole up in the pilothouse of the *Jett Stream* and practice my singing and playing. I had also begun writing a few songs. Nevertheless, I felt very discouraged—and found it difficult to be creative when I felt so down—but I forced myself to keep practicing and writing. Keith kept telling me to be patient—and I never thought I would hear Keith Adkinson extol the virtues of patience—but I was beginning to think patience wasn't the issue. Perhaps we should start rethinking our entire life. We'd been pushing these issues for almost five years, and I was just worn out.

In mid-May 1989, just as I was entertaining the thought of us taking up farming in the Shenandoah Valley, we received a fascinating phone call. It was from a fellow named Ron Taylor from Red Level, Alabama, who was one of the directors of the 16th Annual Hank Williams Memorial Celebration, to be held that year on Sunday, June 4, in Evergreen, Alabama. He wanted to know if I would perform at the celebration.

For years, the Hank Williams Memorial Celebration had been held in and around Mt. Olive, Alabama, where Hank had grown up. The celebrants were mostly local people—"Hank Williams people" from "Hank Williams country"—although hundreds of fans also traveled from Texas, Oklahoma, Tennessee, and other far-flung locations every year just for the show. Hank Jr. had performed at the celebration several times years before, and other big names from the country-western establishment always showed up on the roster as well. Ron told us that this year Michael Twitty (Conway's son) and Charlie McCoy (of "Hee Haw" fame, and perhaps the greatest harmonica player in the world) would be two of the headliners. Also, Jerry Rivers, the fiddler from the original Drifting Cowboys, and Don Helms, Hank's steel guitar player, would be performing. I had never met either Mr. Rivers or Mr. Helms, but I certainly knew who they were, and I was very interested.

I was also flattered that they wanted to include me, and Keith felt immediately that this was the perfect place for me to make my debut as a singing artist and I agreed. We realized that I had less than three weeks to prepare, but I picked up my guitar and went back to the pilothouse and sang my heart out.

Once I got over the initial excitement of being asked to perform at such a special event, I began, naturally, to get very nervous. My fears were exacerbated by Ron's subsequent calls to fill us in on the details. For starters, I was not simply one of the performers—I was to be the star of the show. Also, this year, the Hank Williams Memorial Celebration was serving to kick off the state-sponsored "Alabama Reunion." The state would be playing it up even more than usual in the newspapers in order to generate enthusiasm not only for Hank Williams but for the entire state of Alabama.

The planning committee had decided to resurrect an old

tradition of launching the Memorial Celebration with a wreath-laying ceremony at Hank's grave in Montgomery, scheduled for Friday, June 2. The board asked me if I would lay the wreath and say a few words, and, of course, I agreed. It was beginning to become clear to Keith and me that I was not going to be just the star, but the representative of the Williams family.

Keith and I drove down to Alabama on Wednesday, May 30, and sure enough, in every filling station, restaurant, motel, and shop, we saw a flyer advertising the Memorial Celebration, listing the names of all the performers and stating in big letters "Starring Jett Williams." We picked up a copy of the *Birmingham News* as we drove down I-65, and saw a front-page article headlined HANK'S DAUGHTER COMES HOME TO SING. I had never sung professionally in public, and now I was being billed as the star of the annual tribute to my father, representing the Williams family, standing as a symbol for my home state. I was scared to death.

On Friday morning, we arrived at Oakwood Cemetery Annex for the wreath-laying ceremony. Ron Taylor and Keith Holcomb, another director of the Celebration, met us there with newspaper reporters and television cameras in tow, and escorted us over to Hank's grave. I was nervous but honored, and said as much to the reporters. I noticed Marie Harvell seated on one of the benches at the gravesite. I had not seen her in many months and I went up to greet her, but she responded very coolly to my hello. I noticed that she was wearing a big pin with Hank Jr.'s picture on it, and heard her tell reporters that she came to look out for their interests, which confirmed my belief that Marie had decided which "side" she was rooting for. The next morning, my picture was on the front page of the *Montgomery Advertiser*, and despite Marie's rebuke, I felt very proud and welcome.

To compound my nervousness, I was fearful about the backup band. Needless to say, I did not have a band of my own, so Ron Taylor said he would put together a few of the guys who would be working backup at the concert, and arrange for a practice session on Friday night. We met with them at a school auditorium down in Evergreen for a brief rehearsal. I had planned to sing a couple of Hank Williams songs, "Your Cheatin' Heart" and "Hey, Good Lookin'," as well as two other songs these guys could not possibly know, a song I had written called "Baby Blues" and a song our friend Milton Brown had composed called "Conceived in Love." With so little rehearsal time, there was no way we were going to put on a good show. What's more, this particular band didn't have a steel guitar player or a keyboard, and I wanted both.

On Saturday morning, Keith called Milton Brown in Mobile and asked him for suggestions. Milton knew of a good steel guitar player and a fine keyboard man. He arranged to have them drive up to Fort Deposit, where we were staying at the home of our friend Bill Mixon, to work with me for a couple of hours on Sunday morning before I performed late Sunday afternoon. Ideally, I would have liked five days of rehearsal, but five hours would have to suffice.

As part of the Alabama Reunion festivities, the little town of New Brockton, Alabama, had decided to honor its favorite son, Don Helms, the famed steel guitar player from the original Drifting Cowboys band. Don Helms Day was scheduled for Saturday, June 3, and we felt it was very important that Keith and I go down and pay our respects to Mr. Helms—even though we had never met him and didn't know quite how he felt about me. I knew that Don had not only played with the Drifting Cowboys during Hank's halcyon days but had been a good friend of his since their teens.

Keith and I drove down to New Brockton, which is a two-hour drive southeast of Fort Deposit, and arrived at two in the afternoon. Mr. Helms and fiddler Jerry Rivers were performing on a bandstand in the middle of town when we pulled up. We parked our car, and then joined them on a corner of the "stage," and listened to "the boys," as Hank always called them, play. It was a pleasure to hear my daddy's music played as it was meant to be played. I couldn't help wishing these men were backing me up on Sunday.

When they finished playing, I was introduced to the crowd and said a few words of praise for my daddy's friends and musicians. Keith and I went up and introduced ourselves to Mr. Helms and Mr. Rivers and visited with them briefly. I could tell they were both looking at me sort of strangely, and later Mr. Helms would tell me—as I had been told so many times—how much I looked like Hank.

Both Don and Jerry seemed to genuinely appreciate the effort Keith and I had made to come down to meet them, especially on Don's special day. They introduced us to their wives, Hazel (Helms) and June (Rivers). I liked them both and I hoped we would be able to establish a friendship.

That night, I had trouble sleeping and was up at dawn, cooking breakfast for Keith, Bill Mixon, our host, and various others who were staying at Bill's house for the weekend. The guys from Mobile Milton had found—Rick on steel guitar and Tim on keyboard—arrived at 8:00 A.M., and we started rehearsing. We worked for about five hours, and I was beginning to feel more confident.

The Memorial Celebration was being held in a state park just outside Evergreen, Alabama. It had started about 10:00 A.M. on Sunday morning, but Ron Taylor had said I was not scheduled to appear until around four in the afternoon, so I didn't need to be there until about an hour before showtime. Evergreen is about an hour's drive from Fort Deposit, so we packed up at two o'clock and started down I-65 toward Evergreen.

When we arrived at the gates to the park, I could see that this was not just a little town square but a large, sprawling place with winding roads, a couple of large ponds, rolling hills covered with pine trees—and bumper-to-bumper cars still arriving at 3:00 P.M., although the Celebration had been hopping since morning. (Later I would learn that about five thousand Hank Williams devotees were present that day.) As we circled around the road that led to the bandstand, I could smell pork rinds frying and barbecue roasting, and see that this was a real old-fashioned country picnic, a perfect celebration for Hank and, although I was terrified, the ideal place for my debut. As we got closer to the bandstand, I could see hundreds of people dotting the little rise, all seated on blankets or lawn chairs with their coolers and picnic baskets. Most of these people close to the stage must have been sitting there since 10:00 A.M., and it crossed my mind that they might be a tough, critical audience.

A big air-conditioned motor home was parked to the left of the stage, and all the performers were using it as a dressing room. Keith and I waited in the motor home, but occasionally I would hear Mike Twitty sing or Charlie McCoy play. Everyone was very friendly, and Charlie McCoy paid me a special compliment. He asked if he might play in my backup group, and I was honored. Lanny Hicks, the attractive female vocalist with his group, told me that Charlie was making a "statement" by joining me on stage, and I appreciated both his gesture and her comment about that gesture.

I was also touched because many friends—including Lenore and Sally and their families—came up from Mobile to hear me sing. They positioned themselves so that I could see them from the stage, and it was incredibly reassuring to me to have them there.

The entertainment was running late. I heard Mr. Helms and Mr. Rivers play "Hey, Good Lookin'," "Jambalaya," and "I'm So Lonesome I Could Cry," and it made me want to cry. It also made me even more frightened. How could I possibly follow that act?

At 5:45, Ron Taylor gave me my cue, and Keith opened the trailer door. I put on my cowboy hat, picked up my guitar, and walked out of the cool trailer into a blast of hot air. As I started to walk across the grass toward the steps to the stage, I never felt more lonely in my life. I hadn't really heard Ron Taylor announce my name, but I could see people clapping and hear what I hoped were cheers. I mounted the steps to the stage, and out of the corner of my eye saw my new friends Tim and Rick, the backup boys from Mobile, on my right, and Charlie McCoy, who threw me a reassuring smile, on my left.

As I arrived in the center of the stage, I looked out and saw the most extraordinary sight. These folks who had been sitting in the heat for seven hours were applauding and roaring with encouragement. What's more, they were all beginning to get up and move toward the stage like a gigantic human tidal wave. I didn't know whether to be excited or scared to death.

When I got to the microphone, I adjusted my guitar, gave the boys the sign, and burst into "Your Cheatin' Heart." I had expected silence, but the sea of people before me all seemed to be jumping up and down, dancing, laughing, and crying. I slid into "Hey, Good Lookin' " and then a slower song, "Last Night I Dreamed of Heaven," but I changed it slightly and continued ". . . and saw my daddy there."

As I looked out into the audience, I could see what seemed to be thousands of people, some with broad smiles and some with tears in their eyes. Little children, who had no idea who I was— except that I was Hank's daughter—were dancing along, and everybody was rooting for me. They were with me all the way.

To close, I sang "Conceived in Love," the song our friend Milton Brown had written for me, and I could see Milton and his wife, Margaret, smiling in the crowd. The song is done, in part, as a recitation, Luke the Drifter style, and the words are intensely personal:

> I never knew my daddy,
> But I know my daddy well.
> His life is written in his songs,
> And the stories that they tell.
>
> And through all the controversy,
> There's one thing I am sure of,
> If he had lived, he would have told me
> I was conceived in love.

By the time I got to the first chorus, people were wild with enthusiasm. I sang with all my heart:

> Conceived in love, but treated with shame.
> Denied the right to know my family name.
> But now I know and all the world can see,
> Conceived in love and that's good enough for me.

The last verse of Milton's song says it all, and served as the perfect ending to my debut:

> So let the record show for the world to know,
> What I've known all the while.
> 'Cause that stern old judge looked down and said
> She is Hank Williams' child.

I sang the chorus again, and just wanted to cry as I saw how warmly I was accepted. When I finished, I asked all the entertainers to join me on stage to sing "Jambalaya," and it was an absolute thrill to find myself standing before Hank's people, with Don Helms and Jerry Rivers—as well as some other great country entertainers—beside me. I felt in my heart that I was where I was supposed to be, doing what I was supposed to be doing. I felt like I was Hank's daughter—and that his fans had accepted me.

After the show, I talked with scores of people, many who had come from all over the Southeast just to see me. Old friends of Hank's, like Braxton and Ola Frances Schuffert, had come down from Montgomery; Pappy McCormick had driven up from Florida. Many old friends of mine had come up from Mobile. Later, we drove back to Bill Mixon's house and celebrated with our own barbecue.

That evening, we watched clips from the Celebration on the evening news, and listened to short reviews of my debut. To my relief and joy, they were all positive. Over the next several days, all the newspapers in the region discussed my performance, and I was touched and heartened by the attention. Newspapers from as far away as Atlanta ran stories. Greg Brown, in the *Montgomery Advertiser*, gave me my first professional review. In part, he said:

> As Jett Williams mounted the stage the crowd came to its feet in roaring applause. There was electricity in the air as the people stood and watched Miss Williams sing the songs of her father. Some of the musicians standing near me who knew Mr. Williams Sr. exclaimed, "She even stands like Hank."

She was good. Her performance was strong. As she was singing, everyone around me seemed to think this was just the beginning of a good career. I agree. I think she is going to go places.

For the first time in months, I felt like maybe I was going to go places, too. My weary blues were lifting, and I felt like I'd taken a giant step down a new road. However, before we could begin our travels, we had to settle my outstanding problem with Aunt Helen and Stanley. I dreaded this trial more, perhaps, than anything I had ever faced in my life. But I had to do it.

18
HISTORY REPEATS ITSELF

On a rainy, cool Monday, June 5, 1989, Keith and I bade our friend Bill Mixon thanks and good-bye, got in our truck, and headed down I-65 toward Mobile. I felt good about the events of the day before, but as I had heard people say about Hank, I was experiencing a few pangs of "perfectionism." Apparently, I'd performed well at the Memorial Celebration, but I knew I could do better. I had been incredibly stressed out and nervous—not only because I was performing at all, but because I was performing in public for the first time, to an audience that I feared would be expecting a ghost, with a band that I had not rehearsed with sufficiently. I'd done it, and I'd done it well. But I knew in my heart I could do it better—and now I couldn't wait to get the chance.

In addition, Keith and I were on our way to prepare for a battle I did not want to fight: the trial with Aunt Helen and Stanley. Although the invitation to the Memorial Celebration had cheered me up, I was still upset about the loss in New York and the languishing long-overdue appellate decision in Alabama. Any way you cut it, I didn't need another court battle, and unlike the two we had been fighting for the past four years, this one involved people I had known and loved since I was three years old. To discover that Hank Williams had loved me enough to provide for my care before I was born was indescribably heartwarming. To learn that my Aunt Helen—who I thought had loved me, in whom I had confided since childhood, who was like a second (or third) mother to me—had turned against me was devastating.

This was the situation we faced that rainy morning on the way to Mobile. And in a certain way, I should not have been surprised.

The saga of the estate of Wayne and Louise Deupree is very much in concert with the rest of Mother's affairs. The entire situation had been fraught with ups and downs, warm reunions and cold rejections—just like the rest of my relationship with Mother.

By the time Daddy had called me in December 1980, offering to help me pursue my natural roots, he had already made his own provisions for me as his daughter. In October 1980, he and Mother had executed identical powers of attorney, giving me the authority to manage the affairs of either—or both—of them in the event they became incapacitated. In November 1980, a month later, they executed identical wills. Both of these wills contained the following provision:

> In the event my said wife [or husband] does not survive me for a period of 30 days, or in the event she [he] is deceased at the time of the probate of this will, I give, devise, and bequeath all my property, whether real, personal or mixed, or which I may have power to dispose of at my death, to my daughter, Cathy Louise Mayer, in fee simple and absolutely.

Shortly after the documents were prepared, Daddy handed them to me in Mother's presence. So, at the same time Daddy was encouraging me to pursue my lineage, he was providing for my future security—with my mother's knowledge, support, and participation. Moreover, not only was Daddy providing for me, he was involving me in his business, the Gulf Machinery Company. Over the next several months, he sent me documents such as leases, agreements, and contracts that related to his business.

Shortly before his death in August 1983, Daddy told my cousin (and his nephew) Dana Deupree, that he had his estate in order. He explained to Dana that everything would go to Mother to do with as she pleased until her death, and when she died, everything that remained would come to me. He told Dana at that time that the estate was rather large, so he believed I would be "in good shape" when Mother died.

A week before Daddy died, I visited with him in Mobile, and he gave me a certificate of deposit for $10,000, which was more money than I had ever received at one time in my life. He wanted me to have a little extra "sooner rather than later." He told me that he would give me another one the following weekend, but he was never able to give it to me because he died that week, on August 4, 1983.

Shortly after Daddy's death, I received an official-looking communication from the probate court regarding his estate and requesting my presence at some proceeding. I called Mother to ask her about it, but she said all I needed to do was sign it, return it, and not worry about it. I reminded her that I had copies of their wills and the powers of attorney. She said that Daddy's power of attorney was no longer relevant since he had died, but the wills were good, so I should save them.

After Daddy died, Mother's behavior remained toward me as it had always been—hot one day, cold the next. Sometimes she seemed truly happy to see me or hear from me; on other occasions, she would be distant and often downright mean. However, after Daddy's death, one thing changed. All my life, I had relied on Daddy and Aunt Helen to advise me as to Mom's condition, but now I turned to Aunt Helen exclusively for "reports from the front lines." After I moved to Washington, in January 1985, I relied on Aunt Helen even more. Mother never passed judgment on my move to Washington—at least not to me—and Aunt Helen was openly understanding and supportive. I trusted her totally.

After I moved, I called both Mother and Aunt Helen regularly. At times Mother was friendly and loving, and at other times she would reduce me to tears. It didn't take Keith long to figure out the dynamics of my relationship with her—he considered her "an emotional terrorist"—but he believed I should try to sustain some sort of relationship with her.

In May 1985, over a period of several days, I tried to call Mother and got no answer. I became concerned and called Aunt Helen, who, for the first time, seemed evasive and vague. Finally, she admitted that Mother was in the hospital. The doctors had diagnosed ovarian cancer, which they had operated on, and she was starting radiation treatments and chemotherapy.

I wanted to go to Mobile immediately to see her, but Aunt Helen insisted that Mother did not want to see anyone right now, so instead of paying a visit in person, I called Aunt Helen and Mother regularly on the telephone. But then Mother began experiencing severe physical reactions to the treatments, and for weeks at a time would often refuse to speak with me. I told Aunt Helen that I was very upset about this, but Aunt Helen assured me that Mother was not speaking to anyone, so I should not feel that her rejection was personal.

Nevertheless, on other occasions, Mother would go out of her way to show interest in my welfare. In January 1986, I had an appendicitis attack, and was rushed to the hospital in the middle of the night. Mother was in the midst of her chemotherapy, so I left a message with her maid and then I called Aunt Helen. Later that day, after my surgery, Keith received a call from Mother. She was very concerned, and wanted a complete description of the hospital, the doctors, and my condition. She also wanted to know if I had enough health insurance, and offered to pay for the entire operation if that was necessary. Her concern made me feel very good, but since she expressed it so rarely, I could never really count on it.

In June 1986, the moment for an inevitable and dramatic crossing of the many tracks of my life arrived. We were in the midst of the "discovery" period of our case, and Hank Jr.'s lawyers said that they wanted to take Mother's deposition in Mobile. Of course,

I understood that they wanted and needed to know what I knew and when I knew it. However, they did not understand the fragility of my mother's personality, and that questioning her about my natural parents could press her toward another suicide attempt. They were not aware that she had been hospitalized suffering from depression after I had gone to the Cooks' fiftieth wedding anniversary party. If such a benign event would throw her off, what would a summons to a legal deposition do? What's more, as a result of her cancer and of chemotherapy, she was in a more fragile state than usual.

As it turned out, Hank Jr.'s lawyers had somehow gotten their hands on a memo Keith had written months before—a summary of my life story that was meant to be used for securing a book or movie interest. It depicted Mother's mental and emotional history, and described in some detail the abuse I had endured as a result of her addictions. In some ways their discovery helped the situation. One reason I had not searched for my roots, after first being told that I might be Hank's daughter, was my concern with my mother's vulnerability. I did not want to hurt her, but Junior's lawyers made it clear that they were going to question Mother closely regarding the memo. Keith believed they were taking a hard line with regard to Mother to embarrass me and hopefully dampen my enthusiasm for proceeding with the lawsuit. In a certain way, they were right. I was sure Mother would be very upset, and I was almost hysterical.

By the time we learned that Junior's lawyers had the memo, Mother had already been summoned and knew that she would be deposed on Monday, June 16, 1986, in Mobile. To my amazement, Mother didn't seem to mind getting involved; in fact, she appeared to enjoy the attention. Keith and I had told her that we could make arrangements for the lawyers to come to her home, but she said she was looking forward to dressing up and coming downtown to "tell it like it was."

We realized that there was no way we were going to block the introduction of the memo into her deposition, and Keith reasoned that the only way to handle the situation was to prepare her. "People hate surprises," he said. "If we can't avoid the problem, we at least must tell her about it so that she will not be caught off guard." I knew he was right, but naturally I dreaded this confrontation.

We were in Nashville deposing Owen Bradley when we learned of the opposition's plans, so immediately after the proceedings we drove to Mobile, arriving on Friday afternoon, June 13. (It didn't escape my notice that probably the most difficult meeting I would ever encounter with my mother was landing on Friday the thirteenth.) Some years before, Daddy and Mother had moved from the house in Spring Hill where I had grown up to a house on Dauphin Street that was nearer to Aunt Helen. I had never felt particularly comfortable in this house, and on this ominous Friday the thirteenth, I felt even more like an intruding stranger.

Mother was waiting for us in the living room, smoking a cigarette and looking weary and ill. She must have seen the worried expression on my face, because her first words were: "It's the drugs, honey. They make me swell up fat as a tick, don't they?"

Keith immediately began explaining to her the situation surrounding the deposition, the sort of information the opposition was looking for and why, and finally the details they had gleaned about her condition from the memo. Mother sat there, nodding, taking in everything Keith was saying. I sat there, feeling as if I was in the midst of a Fellini-esque nightmare, floating in a kaleidoscope of painful images from my past.

Suddenly Mother burst out laughing.

"Hell, Keith," she said, "all that's true."

I could see that Keith was as disconcerted as I was by her response.

"Yes, ma'am," he replied. "But it's unfortunate that they might bring this information up at your deposition on Monday."

"Well, honey," she said, "after all I've been through, those sons of bitches can't hurt me."

She laughed again, and we all sat there for a moment, wondering what to do next.

"There is one thing, though," she added. "If you do a book or movie, would you call those suicide attempts 'accidental overdoses'? It sounds better, don't you think?"

Then she paused for a moment. "Hell," she continued. "Say what you want to say—just tell the truth. I'm not proud of it— but I'm not ashamed of it either."

I felt incredibly relieved. The unspeakable had been spoken, we had confronted the problem, and Mother seemed prepared for her deposition. All three of us realized that something significant had taken place that evening.

On Monday morning at 9:45, Louise walked into the lawyers' office in downtown Mobile. She was dressed to the hilt and had driven herself there without assistance. Joe Matranga, Daddy's lawyer and a family friend, arrived to represent her, and six other lawyers from both sides were present to depose her.

Calmly, Mother told her story. She related that she had come up to the University of Alabama on my twenty-first birthday to tell me that I might be Hank's daughter and that a two-thousand-dollar check from the estate of Lillian Williams Stone was waiting for me in Montgomery. She told that she had explained that my birth father could be a famous singer from Alabama, and then asked me if I knew who my natural father might be. She recalled that I had said "Louis Armstrong" and laughed as she told the story, although she got the joke wrong. (I had guessed Nat King Cole.) She also got certain other facts confused because she tended to merge information she learned later with facts she knew in 1974. But she did not reveal any earth-shattering or embarrassing tidbits, she didn't get rattled or flustered, and I was proud of her. In spite of her physical condition and heavy medication, she had gotten through the ordeal.

Hank Jr.'s lawyers did not seem to be having nearly as much fun with Mother as they had expected. Finally, one of the lawyers pulled out Keith's memo and asked Mother: "Would you like to hear how your daughter will portray you in any book she might write or movie she might make?"

"No thank you, honey," Mother said. "That won't be necessary."

After the deposition, Mother insisted on taking Keith and me to lunch at another of her favorite Mobile restaurants, the

All Seasons on Airport Boulevard. She didn't know how much longer she would be able to dress up and drive herself, and she wanted to enjoy herself while she could. Lunch was nothing short of delightful. We made easy small talk and shared happy memories. For a few hours, we could all forget Mother's cancer and all pain—past and present.

After lunch, Mother looked at Keith and said, "Sugar, I want to talk to Cathy alone, if that's all right. I think we'll just go sit in my car for a little while." Keith said he had scores of telephone calls to make, so while he went to the pay phone, Mother and I walked out to her car.

For the next hour, to my amazement, Mother put into words—and tears—all the hurts, fears, and pains of our past. To my surprise, she understood about much of the pain I had experienced as a result of her drinking and her breakdowns.

"I know I was awful to you," she said. "I was a terrible mother and I was mean," she sobbed.

She talked about her alcoholism, her addiction, and finally her fear of losing her battle with cancer. When she began talking about death, she told me that she had made provisions for me and that, after she died, I would be well fixed, and would never have to worry about financial security. She sounded sincere, and I believed her.

Although Mother had not been well enough to attend our wedding in September 1986, in December of that year, she said she was feeling much better and wanted to come for a visit—she was curious about our boat and wanted to get better acquainted with Keith. Then she mentioned that she did not want Aunt Helen to come with her—indeed, she did not want Aunt Helen to even know she was coming.

I was elated. Keith and I cleared our schedules, made reservations for her at a nearby hotel, and planned a tour of Washington we knew she would enjoy. Two days before she was scheduled to arrive, the telephone rang. To my surprise, it was Aunt Helen.

"She's not coming," Aunt Helen said.

"What do you mean?" I asked, confused not only by her announcement but by the fact that she knew anything about the trip.

"She's changed her mind," Aunt Helen said. "She decided to go to California." As it turned out, Mother had indeed gone to California to visit a relative, and once again I felt the familiar hurt wash over me.

Over the next several months, we talked to Mother on the telephone fairly regularly. As in the past, she would be hot or cold, depending on her mood. Moreover, she was frequently very ill. In late December 1986, she was diagnosed with lung cancer, and again was treated with chemotherapy. When I would call, she would often slur her words and was sometimes incapable of concentrating long enough to finish a sentence or a thought. Once, in the spring, we made a trip to Mobile especially to see her—at her request—but when we arrived she told us she was too sick to visit with us.

In August 1987, we were in Mobile again and I called Mother and told her we wanted to stop by. This time she agreed. She was in a great mood and looked surprisingly well. She asked all about the "Hank Williams project," and even reminded me that she had ordered an extra twelve copies of *Southern Magazine*, which had published a feature story on me in December 1986. Mother said that the photograph of me on the cover was the best picture of me she had ever seen.

By this time, Mother was virtually bedridden, but when we arrived she was dressed and sitting in the living room. She got up, walked over to a table, and picked up an envelope that she handed to me. Inside was a beautiful card, signed "I love you, Mom." Inside the envelope was a check for one thousand dollars. She wanted me to buy some nice clothes to wear during the upcoming trials. She also insisted that we come over the next day for lunch. She said that she had a special menu, and she was proud that she was able to fix the meal herself.

Although her birthday was a few days away, Keith and I decided that we would make the lunch a birthday celebration. We loaded up with a birthday cake, cards, balloons, and flowers. She was thrilled with the attention, and proud that she had remembered that the lunch she had planned—shrimp salad and macaroni and cheese—was a special favorite of mine.

A few days later, on August 21, I telephoned Mother to wish her a happy birthday. This time, Aunt Helen answered the telephone. She was very cool, and told me that they had just taken Mother to the emergency room because of severe chest pains, but the hospital had released her and she was resting.

Between August and November 1987, much happened with regard to our cases. The paternity trial was held in September, and on October 26, Judge Kennedy issued his order stating that Hank Williams was, in fact, my father. As a result of all the publicity, I was frequently interviewed in newspapers and on radio and television. My relationship with Mother, although still not perfect, had improved so much that I tried to make a point of addressing the positive aspects of adoption, and publicly praised my adoptive parents frequently.

In early November, we were scheduled to be in Mobile again as part of a media tour. I called Aunt Helen as soon as we got to town, and she informed me that she was bringing Mother to her house, and that we should come over there for a visit. When we arrived at Aunt Helen's about noon, Mother was already there. She needed to have oxygen tanks near her at all times, and the sight of them distressed me. Nevertheless, she seemed glad to see us.

As soon as I walked in the door, she handed me a small box that contained a diamond wristwatch that Daddy had given her years earlier. It was a lovely gesture, but I was a bit disconcerted when I overheard Mother ask Aunt Helen: "Should I give it to her?" and Helen answer: "Do what you want, but I don't want to hear about it tomorrow."

I told her that I also had a surprise for her. I had decided that I wanted to stage a little "concert" for her, so Keith and I had brought along a tape player with musical tracks of songs I wanted to share with her. I started with "Your Cheatin' Heart" and then moved on to "What'll I Do," telling her the story of Keith playing it over and over the night we originally recorded it. Then I sang "Crazy" and three or four other songs. I could see she was proud of me. Finally I said, "Now I have a very special story and song for you."

Then I told her my memory of a Mardi Gras ball she, Daddy, and I had attended when I was in college. On the way to the ball, Mother had told me I was in for a special treat—Harry James and his band would be playing that night. As I recalled it, I didn't know who Harry James was, and Mother had been disgusted with me.

As the night had worn on, Mother and Daddy got into their cups and lost each other in the crowd. At one point I found Daddy, who then sent me to find Mother. Finally—to my horror—I heard a familiar voice from the stage. I looked up, and there was Mother with her arms around Harry James, singing her favorite song, "You Made Me Love You." With that, in Aunt Helen's kitchen, I belted out, "You made me love you, I didn't want to do it, I didn't want to do it." I thought Mother would laugh, but instead she just stared at me for a moment, then broke into tears. I will never know how I completed that song, but I did. By then, Aunt Helen and Keith were also crying.

Later that afternoon, I did a live radio talk show in Mobile. I had told Mother I would be talking right to her—and I did. Once again, I tried to emphasize the positive aspects of my life as the adopted daughter of Wayne and Louise Deupree. I felt good about the show and was delighted to learn from Aunt Helen that she and Mother had listened to it together and had loved it.

Mother invited us over for lunch the next day, saying specifically that she wanted to spend some time with me without interruptions. When we arrived, Mother's insurance agent was there, and Mother explained that she wanted to give us what she called "cancer insurance," and that she was going to pay for one year's premiums. We spent the next hour filling out the forms, and then Mother handed her agent a check to pay for the first year's premiums on Keith's and my insurance.

Shortly after the agent left, Aunt Helen and Stanley arrived. We talked for a few minutes, and then Mother told them that she wanted to spend some time with me alone. We talked for the rest of the afternoon in a warm, easy, and loving way. Again, she mentioned her will and told us that I was to receive her estate when she died. In fact, she wanted me to take whatever I wanted from the house right then and there. When I declined, she insisted that I take a couple of special pictures, some records, and some little mementos.

We left about 6:00 P.M. to drive to Montgomery. Mother wanted to know where we were staying because she said she worried about me when we traveled. I gave her the number of the Prattville Holiday Inn, where we always stayed, but since she had never concerned herself about me in her life, I certainly did not expect her to call. However, no sooner had we checked in to our room when the phone rang. Indeed, it was Mother making sure we had arrived safely.

"You get a good night's sleep, sugar," she said. "Remember, I love you and everything is going to be all right. Everything is going to be fine."

"I love you, too, Mom," I said.

This was one of the last coherent conversations I ever had with my mother. Shortly after we got home to Washington, I received a certified letter from Mother in the mail, dated just a couple of days after we had left. It came in a typed envelope, addressed only to me. It read:

> My purpose in writing to you now is to let you know that I am leaving everything to my nephew, Stanley Fountain. I have reflected back on what you have received over the years and it is my judgment that you have already received from me and Wayne your share of our combined assets and I have therefore left you nothing in my will. I do hope you understand. If you get in a situation where you need funds, you might give Stanley a call, and if he so desires, he may help you, although I make it clear he is under no obligation to do so.
>
> Joe Matranga, who you know, has prepared my will according to my instructions. Stanley has a copy and at my death, I have instructed him to contact Mr. Matranga. I am sending a copy of this letter to Mr. Matranga for his files. If you have any questions concerning the contents of this letter feel free to call Stanley or Mr. Matranga. Stanley also has a copy of this letter.

The letter was signed: "Love, Louise Deupree."

I was dumbstruck. My mind raced over the shared memories and tears. I remembered the warm dinners we'd had together and the thoughtful gifts she had given me—the thousand dollars for clothes, the watch, and the cancer insurance she insisted on buying. Most of all, I remembered her unsolicited statements that I would always be financially secure. Something was very, very wrong.

Keith read the letter carefully. He had witnessed many of our poignant moments, and he instantly saw the obvious: My mother had not written this letter, a lawyer had. In fact, at the bottom of the letter were the initials of the secretary who had typed it. It had been mailed from Gulf Shores, Alabama—where Stanley lived—not Mobile. In addition, it made reference to things like "combined assets," which was not Mother's way of expressing things and was probably a reference to the joint wills that my parents had executed in 1980.

I immediately called Aunt Helen, hoping that she would know what was going on. She did—and she said it just broke her heart.

"Don't pay any attention to that letter," she said. "Just throw it in the trash can." She repeated this phrase over and over, and finally said, "You know how your mom is. She'll probably change her mind tomorrow."

But then she added something else that I found very strange. She said: "Besides, Stanley hasn't got a selfish bone in his body. God forbid it ends like this, but if it does, you know he will be fair with you."

Fair with me? I could not understand what she was talking about. It was as if the past weeks and months were slipping through my fingers like sand—as though the heartfelt reunions with my mother had never happened.

After I called Aunt Helen, I called Mother. When she answered the telephone, she said, "I wasn't sure you would ever call me again." Her words were slurred, and, of course, I knew she was very ill. Indeed, I was surprised she was able to speak on the telephone at all.

"I love you, Mom," I said. "But what's going on?"

She could not even articulate an answer. She was heavily medicated, and light-years away from the woman I had visited with less than a week before.

My mind turned to the painkillers on the table by her bed. Several times over the next few weeks, I tried to speak to my mother—but usually communication was limited. On some occasions when I called, her maid would tell me she was unable to talk to me. I knew she was ravaged with cancer and pain, and this time, when she turned to drugs, I felt it was okay.

At 10:00 P.M. on December 27, 1987, Aunt Helen called to tell me Mother had died.

"I'm going to bury her tomorrow," Helen said.

"What are you talking about?" I said. I was indignant. I wanted to be at her funeral and I simply could not get to Mobile by the following morning. Finally, Aunt Helen agreed to put off the funeral for a day, but she said she was carrying out my mother's specific wishes regarding the funeral arrangements. Her attitude was cold and businesslike; she did not seem at all the warm, supportive aunt I had known most of my life.

Keith and I arrived in Mobile and we went straight to Aunt Helen's house and from there to the funeral home. Several of Mother's friends were at the service, but they were outraged because they had not been called and had found out about the funeral only by accident at the last minute. It reminded me of Daddy's funeral.

After the burial, Keith and I returned to Aunt Helen's house. Stanley was there also, and he and Aunt Helen began talking to each other as though we weren't present. To make matters worse, they began discussing my mother's possessions—her house, her fur coats, her jewelry. I asked Aunt Helen about Mother's diamond earrings, and Helen told me that Mother had given her all her jewelry shortly before she died.

"And the house?" I asked.

"Oh, she gave that to Stanley years ago," Helen answered.

At first, neither Stanley or Helen would look me in the eye. Neither one even tried to comfort me, nor would they accept any sympathy from me. Finally, after a couple of tense and painful hours, Stanley looked directly at me, and as though he had finally mustered the fortitude to take his "inheritance," he said something that shot through my heart.

"I can't help it if she always loved me more than you."

I knew that if I didn't leave I would burst into tears, and I did not want to lose my pride in front of them. Keith and I just looked at each other and left.

Of course, the moment we got into the car I fell apart. I cried for hours. My mother had just died, and my aunt, whom I had loved, was cold as ice. What's more, her son, Stanley, now had all of my parents' estate for himself.

Keith was furious, and although we were still fighting the Williams situation on two fronts, he started digging with the same fury he had used to probe for Hank and Bobbie's contract. Within weeks, he was able to discover that Joe Matranga, my mother's lawyer, had prepared the certified letter I had received in late November, and Stanley, as we had suspected, had mailed it. At the same time he wrote the letter, Matranga had prepared a will for my mother, dated November 24, 1987, disinheriting me and leaving everything to Stanley, with Aunt Helen as alternate beneficiary and executor.

Keith also discovered that, over the years, my mother had also prepared three other wills—wills I had known nothing about. The first one was dated August 11, 1983 (one week after Daddy's death), and left virtually everything to Stanley and did not mention me; the second was a codicil to that will that specifically disinherited me; and the third was a will dated August 1986, that again left virtually everything to Stanley and specifically disinherited me and my lineal descendants. During these years, Stanley had kept all her books, written all her checks, and administered all of her medication—for which he was paid a salary.

Keith was also able to put together a detailed account of my mother's medical history. Although I knew she had suffered, I had no idea how many shock treatments, suicide attempts, hospital stays, and illnesses my mother had endured until I saw the report. Of course, I knew she had a lifelong history of depression, but we discovered that she had been hospitalized more than a dozen times for long periods, beginning in 1959 and continuing at about two-year intervals until 1981. In 1959 (the year I was legally adopted) she endured a series of electroshock treatments, which were repeated in March 1963 and January 1964. She was hospitalized for suicide attempts twice, in 1971 and in 1981, and I remembered other occasions that were not reported. Over the years, she had been treated with various drugs for her depression—Valium, Elavil, Prednisone, Mellaril, Dalmane, Sinequan—many of which were addictive.

To compound her problems, she was diagnosed with rheumatoid arthritis in 1970, ovarian cancer in 1985, and lung cancer in 1986. Her doctors also recorded their recognition of her alcohol abuse, but apparently they focused on her depression and on her physical problems and never dealt with the alcoholism.

By the time Keith finished compiling Mother's medical history, it was clear to us that my mother—before Daddy's death, and certainly after it—with the onset of cancer and her increased drug use, was particularly susceptible to manipulation. It was equally clear that Aunt Helen and Stanley had the opportunity to exercise undue influence for their personal gain.

Keith explained to me carefully that breaking a will was extremely difficult, and probably impossible. Still, I begged him to set this record straight, too, regardless of whether or not we won. He agreed, and brought in David Johnson's firm in Birmingham to serve as Alabama counsel. David was only lukewarm about the entire situation, but I didn't care. I was angry and I was hurt. We charged Stanley Fountain with fraud and undue influence, preying upon my mother's drug dependency and mental incompetency, and filed suit in the spring of 1988.

The trial was finally scheduled for June 26, 1989. We all arrived in the courtroom, and Helen and Stanley sat directly behind me. Repeatedly, I thought of the old cliché "If looks could kill, I'd be dead," and although I caught them "looking at me," we never spoke.

They brought Mother's psychologist as well as her banker, her accountant, and a few of her personal friends as witnesses. The psychologist stated that Mother's mental and physical condition had been deteriorating since 1978, and, even then, she was susceptible to the influence of others. An associate of Joe Matranga's testified that Aunt Helen had driven Mother to Joe Matranga's office in order to execute the final will on November 24, 1987. Mother was so ill at the time that she was unable to leave the car, and the document had to be brought to her for her signature. In a way, this testimony worked on our behalf.

Nevertheless, some of the testimony was very hurtful to me—particularly the testimony of Mother's personal friends. One woman said she believed that I had "slammed the door in my adoptive parents' faces" by pursuing my roots, and that I had "killed my parents," which distressed me no end.

However, by the afternoon of the second day, I was convinced we had won. Keith was a little less enthusiastic, but felt strongly that the jury was moving in our favor. David Johnson was totally negative, and was sure we were losing. Suddenly the judge demanded a conference of all lawyers, Stanley, and me in his chambers. Keith was not present because he and David had agreed that the jury might react negatively to his presence due to his high profile in the Hank Williams cases.

The judge, Joe Matranga (Stanley's lawyer), David Johnson, and Stanley all felt we should settle. After a few minutes, they left me alone with David and his associate, Steve Mobley, and the two of them persuaded me to settle. They assured me that in their professional opinion I could never win. I could hear Keith's words ringing in my ears—"Do what you have to do, but I wouldn't settle—we've won it"—but I accepted, and regretted my decision from the moment the words passed my lips. To make matters worse, as I walked out of the judge's chambers, a court official handed me a note saying, "The jury was with you all the way."

Needless to say, our trial was another media event in Alabama. The parallels between my case against Aunt Helen and Stanley and my case against Hank Williams Jr. et al. had not escaped local reporters any more than they had eluded me. My adoptive daddy had planned for my care and security just as my natural daddy had done. And his wishes had been thwarted, too.

As I walked out of the courtroom I was deluged by newspaper reporters, microphones, and cameras.

"Who won?" was, of course, the obvious question. And I answered from my heart:

"In a situation like this, there are no winners or losers." Then I walked outside and dissolved into tears.

My portion of the settlement was not insignificant and served as a vindication of my position, but still it didn't give me much solace. The next morning, we drove over to Joe Matranga's office and I picked up a few of my childhood pictures and some porcelain plates that came from the Deupree side of the family that I had promised to my cousin Dana. Beyond that, I received nothing personal—none of my mother's jewelry, none of the furniture or mementos that I had grown up with, not even a few additional family pictures that I desperately wanted—virtually nothing of personal significance or value. Stanley got it all.

Now Stanley was probably Mobile's newest millionaire, and Aunt Helen could retire from her hairdressing business—which she did. For me, it was as though my years as the "daughter" of Wayne and Louise Deupree had never happened—or worse, didn't matter.

19

SETTING THE
RECORD STRAIGHT

By the time the Fountain trial was over, we had been away from home for almost five weeks. I was emotionally exhausted, so when my friend Lenore Johnston and her husband, Butch, asked Keith and me if we wanted to join them for the Fourth of July weekend, we accepted. Lenore and Butch had rented a beachfront house at Gulf Shores, and the idea of soaking up some sun, playing with their kids, and just relaxing sounded fantastic.

Although our days with the Johnstons were ideal, we were both upset to receive a call from my half sister, Jo. My half brother Ronnie Tippins, age twenty-eight, had fallen off a cliff while he was out hiking over the weekend, and the fall had left him on a life-support system with no hope of recovery. Jo, in her grief, wanted to check with me before the doctors disconnected the life-support system and, amazingly, tracked us down in the middle of the night in Gulf Shores. I was very upset and frustrated because there was little I could do to help her, but I loved her for calling me and including me in such an important and disturbing family decision. Ronnie's death made me wonder, too, if this wasn't a sign that we were in for still more unhappiness.

On July 5, we headed for home. We drove for a few hours, but, at about 4:00 P.M., decided to spend the night at our "home away from home," the Prattville Holiday Inn, nine miles north of Montgomery. When we got to our room, I checked our message machine at home one last time for the day and was shocked to discover we had many messages—all from various reporters asking for my reaction to the "Supreme Court ruling."

My heart stopped. It had been almost nine months since we'd argued our appeal of the estate case before the Alabama Supreme Court panel and, given the excitement of the Evergreen performance and the devastation of the trial against Aunt Helen, I had put my worries over the Supreme Court decision in the back of my mind.

One of the calls had been from a UPI reporter in Montgomery, so I took down his number and gave it to Keith. As I paced up and down the room, Keith called the reporter back. I could hear only Keith's side of the conversation, and I was close to dying, but suddenly Keith gave me a big smile and a thumbs-up sign.

"We won!" Keith yelled as he put down the phone, grabbed me, and swung me in the air. "The reporter said the opinion was forty pages long and complicated, but he understood enough to know we knocked them dead." We decided to drive down to the courthouse and get a copy of the decision immediately.

We ran out to the truck and started speeding down the highway toward Montgomery. We had almost decided not to stay in Montgomery that night—and I couldn't help but believe that fate had placed us here. That old double rainbow again. We parked near the courthouse and raced up the long marble steps. Inside the lobby, we found the clerk who handed out the court's opinions. We told her that I was Cathy Stone, the plaintiff in the "*Cathy Stone* v. *Hank Williams* matter," and she handed us the thick document with a smile and a "Congratulations."

We ran out to the truck and drove around for a couple of minutes to find a quiet parking space away from the courthouse. We pulled up by a nickel-meter space on Dexter Avenue, right in front of an old-fashioned hotdog joint, just the type of place I'm sure Hank must have frequented. I knew I was going to enjoy reading this order, but I was trembling all over. Keith held it between us so we could both read, but he was so excited that he began reading it aloud, so I gazed out of the window and just listened.

In a remarkable forty-four-page document, the justices of the Supreme Court of Alabama confirmed everything we had been contending for the past four years. What's more, they even added a couple of opinions in our favor that we had not considered. They declared that the prior rulings (with the exception, of course, of the paternity ruling) with regard to my position as to the estate of Hank Williams were null and void, not only because I had been defrauded, but because the court had also been defrauded from the start. They also agreed to reopen my daddy's estate and make me an heir.

They began with a "Statement of the Facts," including, in its entirety, the contract Hank Williams and Bobbie Jett agreed to in October 1952. They emphasized the detailed plans Hank and Bobbie had made for my custody and care, the fact that Hank would have had complete custody and control of me from age three to age five (after which time they would begin to share custody), and that Hank had agreed to support me at all times. They also highlighted the three separate occasions when Hank was specifically referred to as "the father."

They then outlined the various issues that they had addressed in order to come to their conclusions:

- Whether the judgments rendered in the 1967 and 1968 proceedings involving my right to share in the estate could be reopened by reason of legal fraud on the court;
- Whether the administratrix (Irene Williams Smith) or the attorney (Robert Stewart) had a duty to notify the court of my existence;
- Whether the court's failure in 1967 and 1968 to grant my guardian ad litem (Drayton Hamilton) permission to appeal the rulings constituted an error of law sufficient to warrant changing these orders;

and finally,

- Whether I, as an illegitimate child, should be entitled to inherit from my natural father.

The justices started out with a bang. After outlining their rationale, they went forward with power and indignation. Regarding the issue of legal fraud, they said:

> . . . Stone argues that . . . the evidence shows that they [the defendants] fraudulently conspired to keep certain facts relating to her existence, identity, and potential claim to the estate of Hank Williams concealed from the court. We agree.

"We agree"! Never had two such simple words sounded so beautiful.

Then, the judges went on to support their "agreement" with detailed descriptions of the complicated machinations that had gone on between Robert Stewart and Irene Smith with regard to me. They began by mentioning some sensitive legal issues, including the fact that Bobbie Jett and I had not been represented by legal counsel at the time of the preparation of Hank and Bobbie's agreement, as well as the point that I was not mentioned in the original letters of administration for Lillian Stone. As a lawyer, Stewart should have known that it was unethical for Bobbie not to be represented by counsel. Further, after I was born and with full knowledge of my existence, he did not include me as a potential heir in the letters of administration—although he did list Billie Jean. The judges carefully outlined Stewart's complex role:

> Over the course of 22 years following the death of Hank Williams, Stewart remained actively involved in the affairs of the Williams family. Throughout the years 1953 to 1975, Stewart served as attorney for the estate, and from 1969 through 1975 he also served as the administrator of the estate. In 1953, Stewart even acted as Lillian Stone's attorney in her action to adopt the child.

The justices then quoted page after page from my adoption records, and noted the numerous times Mrs. Stone had stated that her son was my father, such as ". . . and that the father of the child is her son, Hank Williams, deceased . . ." or that "while crying, [Mrs. Stone] stated that she knew that this [my adoption] is what her son would want her to do."

They described Robert Stewart's two-faced and deceitful behavior with regard to my adoption by Mrs. Stone. They noted that he served as Mrs. Stone's lawyer for the adoption, yet simultaneously carried on a fascinating correspondence with Irene Smith. They included in detail a letter dated April 6, 1953, from Irene Smith to Robert Stewart. This letter was written just three months after Hank's death and my birth, but already Irene was worried about her share of both her mother's estate and Hank's royalties. It also portrays dramatically both Irene's and Stewart's sophisticated understanding of the situation:

Dear Mr. Stewart:
 . . . Thanks for sending the royalties check. It sure came in handy . . . I want to thank you again for looking out for me. You know if mother adopts that child there will be a new will. Tee [Smith's husband] says that if she adopts it and then can't take care of it, he is not going to let me take it. Keep this under your hat, mabey [sic] it will never be necessary for me to have the child at all. I feel that the poor child would have a lot better chance in this life if it were adopted by someone that would never know of its origin at all. It won't be three years before someone will start telling it that it isn't exactly like other children. Oh, I guess I sound like I just don't want mother to change her will but really that isn't it at all. I don't want a thing that we don't work for ourselves and whether or not I get that house or not doesn't bother me in the least. I am only thinking about that child. It may be the one thing that will help Mother live to be a hundred[;] Lets hope so. She seems to love it very much and will perhaps give it a wonderful chance.

I loved the fact that Irene had said that she was "only thinking about that child," yet insisted upon referring to me as "it" throughout her entire tirade. The court, however, paid attention to the legal issue—the fact that after my grandmother died, Irene had refused to fulfill her commitment to care for me and immediately initiated procedures to make me a ward of the state. Again, quoting extensively from my adoption records, the Supreme Court also illustrated the great extent to which Robert Stewart was involved in getting me out of the way. They noted that on April 22, 1955, less than two months after my grandmother's death, I was legally made a ward of the state.

Brick by brick, the Supreme Court laid a firm foundation for ruling that Irene Smith and Robert Stewart had committed fraud. The judges reasoned that I had a strong claim based on Hank and Bobbie's agreement alone. They believed Stewart, as the attorney for Hank's estate, and Irene, as its administrator, deliberately set out to exclude me "despite their intimate knowledge of . . . [my] claims as a potential heir to the estate and as a possible creditor under the terms of the agreement to provide support . . ." Keith had always held that I had a claim against the estate on the basis of Hank and Bobbie's agreement alone; now the Supreme Court of Alabama confirmed it.

To support their assertion of fraud, the court zeroed in on two letters. The first letter, dated February 28, 1962, was written to Stewart from Harold Orenstein, legal counsel for Wesley Rose, and showed clearly Stewart's (not to mention Wesley Rose's) knowledge of my potential rights to share in my father's copyright renewals:

> . . . from the documents which you have furnished to me, Catherine Yvone Stone (born Antha Belle Jett) was returned to the State of Alabama Welfare department after the death of Lillian Stone, and then re-adopted by persons unknown. Nowhere in the documents is there an indication of the names of the natural parents of Catherine Yvone Stone. We assume that these documents were the ones that you mentioned had been sealed and could never be re-opened.

Clearly, however, Mr. Orenstein knew precisely who the parents—or at least the father—was. In 1962, as Wesley Rose and Irene were beginning their conversations regarding renewing the copyrights, Mr. Orenstein apparently wanted to deal with the potential problem created by "this child." Later in the letter he said:

> It would seem that some token payment to the State of Alabama Welfare Department again on behalf of this child may or may not be indicated (depending upon your viewing of Alabama law). There is no way of evaluating now what a share of the renewal copyrights would be worth and no one could predict their valuation. We feel that a nominal payment might forever cut off the right of this child to the renewals. We should like to have further comment from you . . .

Stewart responded to the issue in a letter dated July 5, 1962. He acknowledged that I had a right to a share of the copyright renewals, and that I might well create a serious legal situation:

> . . . Since the statutory right of the child comes to it through its father, and since the federal courts have held this right belongs to an illegitimate, we may be faced with a difficult problem, and certainly one we would not want to litigate.
>
> As possible alternatives we can:
>
> a. Consider that by the adoption all rights under the renewal statutes have been lost;
>
> b. Try to explain the matter to our Welfare Department which does not want the child ever to know its background, but which would probably feel a duty to protect any right the child might have, and hope for a cooperative settlement and court approval;
>
> c. Petition the court for approval of an agreement between Acuff-Rose and the Guardian, requesting that a guardian ad litem be appointed for Randall and another for all other possible minors who might claim a similar renewal right. If we use this procedure, the guardian ad litem will have to be told what we are talking about and might be vigorous in asserting this right. Much would depend on the person appointed, over which we have no control.
>
> I do not believe we can make a token payment to the Welfare Department since any payment which would bar a later claim

would have to be made with an understanding of the facts by the court. My alternatives are not much better, but perhaps you can improve on them with a little thought.

The court went on to observe that no proceedings concerning the estate of Hank Williams were ever instituted on my behalf. However, in 1967, when Audrey Williams petitioned the court for a final settlement of the estate on behalf of Randall, Irene Smith, as administratrix, finally advised the court that an illegitimate child of Hank's might exist somewhere. The court then appointed Drayton Hamilton to again serve as my guardian ad litem.

The court noted that during the 1967 proceedings, Hamilton called Stewart to testify concerning his knowledge of my claim. As the court observed, despite Stewart's extensive knowledge of these circumstances from his involvement with my father, mother, grandmother, and aunt, he revealed nothing, with the sole exception of producing the original custody and support agreement. Certainly he did not reveal the contents of all the correspondence and information he knew concerning my adoption and the information furnished to the Department of Pensions and Security. The court further noted that Irene Smith, aside from advising the court of my existence, "remained silent about what she knew."

The court concluded that Drayton Hamilton had been vigorous in asserting my right to the copyright renewals. (I was not totally convinced, but I was willing to let this point go.) They said that Mr. Hamilton "argued that Hank Williams had accepted the child as his own and had made legal arrangements to have full custody and control of the child, and that if the law did not recognize her right to inherit simply because she was illegitimate, then the law was unconstitutional and should be changed." (In another one of its footnotes, the court then noted that the U.S. Supreme Court, within four months of the judge's denying Mr. Hamilton permission to appeal, basically agreed in another case that an illegitimate child could not be denied rights merely because of birth out of wedlock.)

The court then observed that despite the rulings against me in 1967 and 1968, Stewart (who became the administrator in 1969) began setting aside a share of the estate for me:

> . . . in a series of letters to the attorney for Williams, Jr., Stewart wrote that "the last two distributions to Randall . . . were actually an encroachment on the one-half of the Estate which could conceivably be claimed by the child." Stewart's concealment with regard to the Stone child continued and in April, 1974, he wrote counsel for Williams, Jr., that Stone had traveled to Montgomery and claimed her homestead that had been set aside for her in the Lillian Stone estate. Stewart wrote: "[Her] ancestry may well be reasonably obvious to her, and further trouble may ensue."

I had always found this point amusing. Stewart and the others had gone to so much trouble to make sure I was not able to inherit, yet he still allowed money to be put aside for me. I thought this was one of the most telling facts of all. (As a side note, Hank Williams, Sr.'s, estate was kept open until 1975, which was one year after I turned twenty-one—not when Junior turned twenty-one, which would have been the normal procedure. Of course, the portion that Stewart "held" for me until that time was given to Hank Jr. in 1975.)

After defining the various dimensions of legal fraud, the court found that it had been defrauded by Stewart and Smith, for the following reasons:

—. . . that as an attorney, Stewart had a fiduciary relationship with the estate of Hank Williams, his client, is elementary . . .

—. . . Stewart, as administrator and Smith, as administratrix, held the position of a trustee, and their administration of the estate was that of a trust.

—This Court has held that an administrator who knowingly and willingly conceals from the court administering an estate the name of an heir or distributee, is guilty of such a fraud on the court as to authorize a court of equity to set the decree of settlement aside.

In other words, the court found that Robert Stewart and Irene Smith had committed fraud and wanted the old rulings set aside. After concluding that these actions "constituted legal fraud," the court took the time to observe that although Irene Smith revealed my existence, she did it for the express purpose of proving that I did not have a right to share in the estate. This was the "straw man" theory that Keith had surmised years before—that Irene had mentioned me only to support her own case for giving Acuff-Rose the copyright renewals early and at a low fee.

Thus, the court had found fraud, and decided that Robert Stewart and Irene Smith were responsible. Now the justices moved to their third issue, that being whether or not the judge's failure to permit Drayton Hamilton to appeal the ruling against me constituted an error of law. On this point, they nailed Judge Emmet, who had presided over the 1967–68 proceedings and who had ordered Hamilton not to appeal. They said:

> . . . there can be no question that the trial court's refusal to allow Stone to utilize her right to appeal constituted an error of law, especially when the judge's order that disallowed her claim stated on its face that he did not consider it to be in her best interest.

They went on to conclude that even if the 1967–68 proceeding had not been tainted with fraud, given the actions by both Robert Stewart and Irene Smith, the error of law committed by Judge Emmet and the trial court compelled them to reconsider the judgments. They carried their opinion one step further by saying that the "error" was compounded by the fact that the "beneficiaries" of his decree were the same individuals who were attempting to now bar any right to share in the copyright renewals.

The court also spent time analyzing the issue of "what I knew and when I knew it," an issue that was particularly important to me. I was relieved and vindicated because they understood completely my position that there was no proof that Hank Williams was my father and, apparently, no way for me to confirm or deny it. They noted that Mother's statements to me suggesting that Hank could be my father appeared "to have been presented merely as theory or speculation." The court then waded in and stated their acceptance of my position:

> The record . . . shows that at the early age of three, Stone had been transferred from Montgomery, permanently, to an adoptive home in Mobile, which effectively removed her from any persons who might have known her identity. In addition . . . the record is quite clear that the attorney and administratrix of the estate and others did all they could, including committing legal fraud, to ensure that she never discover her identity or any facts material to her claim, and the record shows that the State of Alabama, acting through the Department of Pensions and Security, and the courts essentially contributed to the concealment of her parenthood, although aware of it. Any public record or documents that might have led to her discovery of her paternity at an earlier date had been ordered sealed by the court from the time that she was a small child. Upon retrieving these sealed documents in 1985, Stone promptly made a demand for her share, and the plaintiffs instituted this action for a determination of her rights in view of the prior judgments. Based on all of these considerations, we conclude that her attack on, and request for relief from, the prior judgments rendered in this matter are not time-barred.

This statement delighted me, since I had been so disturbed by the New York opinion that I had "slumbered peacefully" on my rights until I was "awakened by the attractive sound of a ringing cash register." The New York court had thrown my case out on precisely this issue, but the Alabama court saw the reality of the situation, and it was heartwarming.

The court then addressed an issue that was dear to Keith's legal heart. The court noted that "Williams, Jr., Acuff and Rose are the parties who initiated litigation from which this appeal arose, and who, themselves sought a resolution of the matter of Stone's rights in the estate of Hank Williams."

In other words, back in 1985, it was Randall, Roy Acuff, and Wesley Rose who had brought the initial suit, and in their pleading, had asked for a judicial determination that Junior was the "sole heir" and the "sole child" of Hank Williams. In 1987,

Judge Mark Kennedy had decided that Junior was the "sole heir," but held a trial whereby it was determined that he in fact was not the "sole child"—that I was the natural child of Hank Williams.

At that time, Keith had hoped that the court would focus on the rest of the "relief" sought by Junior (and the others) in their original complaint. They had asked that if the court "alters, modifies or otherwise changes the [1967 and 1968] orders, that the court determine the rights of the parties hereto with regard to the Estate of Hiriam 'Hank' Williams and the copyrights and the renewal copyright interest of the musical compositions of Hiriam 'Hank' Williams." In other words, if they changed the orders—which the lower court had done by declaring that Junior was not the sole child—Junior wanted the court to reopen Hank's estate and thoroughly judge all claims to it. It was their language, their choice.

Keith had maintained all along that this language would come back and bite them just as fiercely as their request that a court decide that Randall was the "sole child." Sure enough, it did. The Supreme Court of Alabama now decided that the estate should be reopened.

Finally, the court addressed the issue of my "legitimacy." For years, I had joked that I thought my real name was Alleged, since in all the newspaper and magazine articles about me, the reporters insisted on referring to me as the "alleged daughter of Hank Williams." After I won the paternity trial, "alleged" was changed to "illegitimate," which didn't make me particularly happy. Both Keith and I believed that Hank and Bobbie's contract, in fact, had legitimated me, and the Supreme Court concurred with us on this issue as well:

> It is quite possible that the 1952 custody and support agreement would have been sufficient to legitimate Stone if Stewart, the child's mother, or other parties, including the State of Alabama, had attempted to utilize this method.

They then concluded that "under the law as it exists today, there can be no question that where, as in this case, paternity has been established by clear and convincing evidence, the law recognizes the right of the child to inherit through intestate succession." They listed six points which, to them, confirmed paternity:

1. The 1952 agreement referred to Hank Williams throughout as "the father."
2. The 1952 agreement required that my mother relinquish all rights.
3. The 1952 agreement provided that I should live with Hank Williams' mother for two years, during which time he would fully support me.
4. The agreement provided that at the age of three I was to live with Hank Williams continuously and be wholly and completely supported by him.
5. Lillian Stone, Irene Smith, and other family members acknowledged and publicly held me out as the daughter of Hank Williams.
6. The records of the Montgomery County Department of Public Welfare repeatedly documented that Hank Williams was my natural father.

The court even went so far as to note that "Williams, Jr., did not live with his father, but rather, lived in Tennessee with his mother, Audrey Williams." In an observation that made me want to hug each and every one of the justices, the court stated: "It appears then that Hank Williams attempted to provide the opportunity for a closer parent-child relationship with Stone, who was to live with him, than that being enjoyed by his other child . . ."

Finally, they closed by saying that "unlike many cases in which the alleged father denies paternity and wishes to have nothing to do with the child, this is a case in which the father not only wished to accept responsibility for the child, but convinced the mother to give the child up, so that it might live with him and be reared by him."

Over those long months and years—particularly when I was so roundly rejected by the New York court—I questioned the fairness and humanity of the judicial system. With these statements, I not only felt completely vindicated but I sensed that real people with real emotions had decided my fate with both meticulous legal thought and humanity.

To conclude, the justices needed to address the much-argued point of my right to inherit even though I had been adopted. Again, this was one of Keith's pet theories: He believed I had not been "born adopted." Keith maintained that Judge Emmet had been wrong in the 1967–68 proceedings when he decided that I was denied rights to inheritance because I had been adopted; and what's more, Judge Kennedy had been shortsighted in 1987 when he upheld that decision. Keith, David Johnson (our counsel in Alabama), and Jim Goodman (the lawyer from Mr. Rudin's firm who had worked on the New York suit) all believed that my rights had vested the moment I drew breath. Again, the Alabama Supreme Court agreed, and said:

> The trial court in the 1968 proceedings was erroneously of the opinion that the fact that Stone had twice been adopted acted as a bar to her recovery . . . . The crucial fact that the trial court failed to recognize in this case was that Stone had not been adopted at the time of her natural father's death. Therefore, any right that she had to inherit from his estate would have vested at the time of his death and would not have been affected by her subsequent adoption some two years later.

The judges concluded by ruling that—given all the evidence that Robert Stewart and Irene Smith had concealed my claims to the estate and that the state agencies and the court had failed to protect my rights—the 1967 and 1968 decrees with regard to me be set aside, and the estate be reopened. As they put it:

> Accordingly, in order to balance all of the equities involved in this case . . . we order that the 1967 and 1968 judgments rendered in this matter be set aside, in part, and that Stone is entitled to receive her proportionate share of any proceeds of the estate of her natural father, Hank Williams, including any income or interest, and of any copyright royalties, but prospectively

only, from the date that she gave notice of her claim, August 5, 1985.

By making this conclusion, the Supreme Court had gone far beyond the point we had originally anticipated and had taken an unexpected—and totally appropriate—step. We would have been pleased if they had returned the case to a lower court for a trial to prove fraud. Instead, since the entire record was before them, they had taken care of the decision themselves. They even decided the point from which they believed I should receive "relief": August 5, 1985, the day on which my attorneys first made a written demand for my share. They then stated that our case be "remanded for a full hearing and settlement in a manner consistent with this opinion." Implicit in this decision, Keith believed, was the notion that since an Alabama judicial system had messed up years before—an Alabama court had better straighten it out. Now, all that was left to be done was an accounting.

I could not have been happier. After nine years of struggle —five of them working with Keith almost full-time—the record was finally straight. After all of the heartache, tears, and sweat, we had won and it had been worth it. Keith and I had no doubt that Hank Jr. and "his boys" would appeal this decision, but as we pulled out of that parking space and started back to our motel, Keith couldn't help say—with a smile—"There are some real unhappy sons of bitches in Nashville tonight."

Yea, I thought. Absolutely.

20
JAMBALAYA

The next day, my victory was all over the news. In July 1989, *USA Today* ran an interesting article. In their Lifeline Section, they said: "The illegitimate daughter of the late Hank Williams Sr. should share in the country music legend's songwriting royalties. Cathy Deupree Adkinson—a singer whose stage name is Jett Williams—can share in the estate . . . worth more than $500,000 a year . . . from the time she filed her initial claim in 1985."

Keith and I chuckled when we read the figures. All we knew was that we had spent money—big money—to vindicate my claims. We had no idea what we might ultimately receive because Hank Jr. had consistently refused to give an accounting. His lawyers had said from the start that first we had to prove we were entitled to anything—then they might let us have a peek at how much.

When we got home to Washington on Saturday, July 8, we found an especially interesting letter among the overwhelming stack of mail we picked up from the post office. It was a note from Jerry Rivers, my daddy's old friend and the fiddler from the Drifting Cowboys. He began by saying how much he had enjoyed meeting us in New Brockton and Evergreen, but then he got down to business. Based on certain comments Keith had made to him, he wondered if we might be interested in a "marriage" between Jett Williams and the Drifting Cowboys band. The Drifting Cowboys had remained active on and off for the thirty-six years since my father's death. At the time of Jerry's letter, the band included Jerry, Don Helms on steel, Frank Evans on guitar, Bob Andrews on bass and vocals, and Jimmy Heap, Jr., on drums.

Both Keith and I thought the idea made perfect sense—and we were even more gratified when we noticed that the letter was postmarked before the July 5 Supreme Court ruling. Jerry and Don had been part of my father's original band, and what's more, they had been his friends. Everyone we had talked to said that Don and Jerry were totally straight-arrow—everyone spoke highly of them. They had been playing my daddy's songs for forty years. We, of course, had heard Jerry and Don perform in New Brockton and Evergreen, but we had never heard the entire band play.

Jerry had anticipated this response from us, and when we called, he told us the band was scheduled to perform on July 17 in Cordorus, Pennsylvania, and invited us up for the show. The idea of having a band of my own and going on the road was truly heady stuff for me. Before the Memorial Celebration, I had been having my doubts about my career, but after I'd seen the faces of the fans, I knew I had to stay with it. I felt I was destined to sing.

On July 17, Keith and I drove to Cordorus and arrived about an hour before the show. We chatted a bit with Don and Jerry and met the rest of the band members. I was very impressed with their show—Jerry's fiddle seemed to jump to life, and Don made his steel guitar wail just the way he had forty years before with my daddy. Their show ran with precision—no stumbling around, no hunting for a note. These men were professionals; they knew exactly what they were doing.

Jerry introduced me to the audience, and the Pennsylvania fans responded as strongly as the Alabama folks had. I didn't sing that day, although I was dying to belt out a few of my daddy's songs—I knew I was ready. The fact that the crowd had accepted me without hearing me sing a note was encouraging.

We left Cordorus with a handshake and a "done deal." After the contract and a few other details were figured out, we would have a new act: Jett Williams and the Drifting Cowboys Band. The Drifting Cowboys were booked through Buddy Lee Attractions, Inc., a Nashville firm that represented not only the Drifting Cowboys but some of Nashville's biggest stars, including Willie Nelson, Ricky Van Shelton, Emmy Lou Harris, and, at one time, Hank Williams, Jr. We agreed that Buddy Lee would become the booking agent for our new act as well. The band had old bookings into early October, the last one in Round Rock, Texas, on October 5, 1989, so we decided that we would make ourselves available from October 15—and give ourselves three months of rehearsal time.

Nevertheless, now that we were playing with the band and had a booking agent, I began to feel frightened. Performing as Jett Williams, the daughter of Hank Williams, had its up side— and its down side. As Owen Bradley had told me, I could draw a crowd at least once, but I had better give a little something "extra."

In early August, Keith and I traveled to Nashville to sign with Buddy Lee and begin rehearsals with the band. Buddy Lee turned out to be an unforgettable character, a powerful personality, and a friend. He told us that he had known about me for a number of years and had followed my saga in detail. Keith liked the fact that Buddy did not strike him as a man easily intimidated by anything—not the ghost of Hank Sr. or the displeasure of Hank Jr., whom Buddy had represented years before.

Not only did we get a fair amount of rehearsing done while in Nashville, we also earned ourselves a few more "family" members. Within days, Don Helms and Jerry Rivers became "Uncle Don" and "Uncle Jerry," and their wives, their children, and their grandchildren quickly became surrogate aunts and cousins.

But no sooner did I begin to feel comfortable with the band than I started dreaming. I knew we would begin performing sometime after October 15, but nothing would have made

311

me happier than to debut with the band in my home state of Alabama—ideally, Mobile. Apparently, I wasn't the only one dreaming, because within weeks Jerry had managed to book us on Saturday, October 7, at the Greater Gulf State Fair in Mobile.

By August 1989, the entire "pot" of my life was at a full boil. Less than three months before, I had been ready to take up farming or sail away on the *Jett Stream.* I appeared to be losing in the courts, my singing career was at a dead end, and I was in despair. Now everything had shifted. I had made my professional debut as a singer, had done well, and now had a band—and it wasn't just any old band; it was my daddy's band. We were listed with a Nashville booking agent, and not only were the show dates coming in, the first one had come from my hometown.

The legal machines in Alabama and New York were moving along—not necessarily at top speed, but they were making progress. Of course, we had secured our major win in Alabama on July 5, when the Alabama Supreme Court decided that fraud had been committed and the estate of Hank Williams, Sr., would be opened and a settlement would be made on my behalf.

Naturally, Hank Jr.'s bunch had screamed bloody murder and filed for a rehearing. As a result, they would have to "brief" their position (that is, explain it to the court in a long written document), and we would have to brief ours. Then, apparently, the Alabama Supreme Court would have to rule again.

This situation was complicated by events in the New York case. I considered New York lost, but Keith, thank God, never gave up the ghost. First, after we had lost in May, Keith and Mr. Rudin had filed to have our appeal heard by the U.S. Supreme Court. Then, after we won in Alabama, we had filed a motion in New York asking the appellate court to recall its order, which would give us the opportunity to petition for another hearing. To my amazement, they agreed to recall their decision, and in August we were told that we would be able to file another brief in New York explaining our position.

By August, all the legal motions, petitions, and briefs were flying—creating incredible confusion, even for us. For example, New York's recall of the decision made our appeal to the U.S.

Supreme Court superfluous—since now there was no decision to appeal. Obviously, New York was watching what Alabama did—and vice versa. I could see the entire situation jamming up, and I feared it would all just come to a crashing halt. We would file our brief in New York, and then New York would sit on it until they saw what Alabama decided, and all of this would take so much time!

Although August 1989 brought with it much action and happiness, we did suffer one more tragedy: My old Irish setter, Tooley, died. I believe God gives and he takes away—and by August, God was giving me plenty, so I guess He felt I needed to be reminded of life's fragility.

We buried Tooley at Larry and Connie Finks' farm in the Shenandoah Valley on the most beautiful corner of the property with a "big sky" view. Larry had made a wooden cross with Tooley's name on it, and we placed Tooley in the earth, feeling as though we'd lost our son.

In the midst of my grief over Tooley, I discovered yet another disturbing problem—a lump on my breast. I was still feeling fragile and fatalistic, and although my doctor assured me that he was 99-percent certain it was benign, I couldn't help but focus on the 1-percent chance that it was not. I was operated on on September 18, and fortunately my doctor was correct—the tumor was benign.

By the end of September, I realized that my life had changed completely in just a few short months. I love to cook, and all this activity reminded me of making a stew. It takes hours to prepare all the ingredients, and then more time for them to sit in the pot and simmer. Then suddenly it all comes together. My life had been simmering for years, and now I sensed we were about to feast on a big pot of jambalaya.

On our wedding anniversary, September 28, Keith took me to dinner at the Jockey Club in Washington, one of our favorite restaurants. They have the best crab cakes in town, in my opinion—and my opinion is reliable when it comes to crab cakes—so we celebrated not only three happy years of marriage, but toasted to a happy future. Toward the end of dinner, Keith had arranged for a florist to deliver eight long-stemmed red roses with a note saying "I love you." He also gave me an antique garnet pin in the shape of a horseshoe. "Old luck is best," Keith insisted, and he wanted me to wear it during every performance.

On September 29, we left Washington for a swing into Texas to meet with the band, and then on for our trip to Mobile for the debut at the Gulf State Fair. We were also going to stop in Dallas, to visit with a high school friend, Dottie Vielle, and her husband, Dickie Boykin. Dottie had gone into the costume-designing business in Dallas. We had been talking to her for weeks about creating something special for me to wear in Mobile. Since I had selected white as a signature color, Dottie had designed a white sequined shirt she knew we would love—and we did. We completed the outfit with white pants, belt, boots, and a new Stetson. Keith even insisted on buying me a white guitar, which made it all perfect.

On Thursday, October 5, I made a "surprise" appearance with the Drifting Cowboys in Round Rock, Texas. I had felt a need to perform once publicly with the band before we met with all the publicity on October 7 in Mobile, and, as it turned out, I was glad we had gone to the trouble. The crowd loved the show, to my relief, and I felt in my bones that Mobile would be a success.

We left Round Rock at midnight on the fifth, drove for four or five hours, crashed for a few hours, then drove on toward Mobile, where we arrived at 5:00 P.M. on October 6. Several television interviews had been set up for me, the first being that evening on a local program called "The Uncle Henry Show." A limousine picked us up at 7:00, but by now I was on automatic pilot.

That evening we had a relaxing dinner at Ruth Chris's Steak House with a few friends from Atlanta who had come especially for my debut with the Drifting Cowboys. Early the next day, I did two interviews with local network news programs, talked with reporter Jeffrey Frank, who was writing a piece on me for the *Washington Post* magazine, and chatted with scores of friends who dropped by our hotel room to wish me well. My automatic pilot was turned high—but I was still scared to death.

At 5:30, we drove out to the fairgrounds. The show was scheduled for 7:00, and at 6:45 the heavens opened and it poured. But luck was with us. At exactly 7:00, the rain stopped, the crowds started gathering, and the band started playing on schedule to hundreds of enthusiastic fans.

I sat behind the stage in a dressing room, listening to the band—particularly Don and Jerry—bring my daddy's music alive. I could almost feel Hank's presence. Visions of Bobbie Jett raced through my mind, too, and I wondered if she wasn't in "God's heaven" watching over me. I even felt Daddy's and Mother's presence, and wondered how they would respond were they here this night. I even felt old Tooley was by my side.

At 7:45, Keith led me through the maze of equipment that dotted the back of the stage. Phil Fajardo, the drummer who was working for us that night, was beating the introduction to "Kaw-liga," and as I looked out to the audience, I could see Lenore waving a "We Love You, Jett" sign, and Sally waving a bouquet of roses. Out of the corner of my eye, I saw Hazel Helms, June Rivers, and a whole generation of Drifting Cowboys grandchildren, who had come from Nashville for the show. Instead of feeling lonely—as I had felt in Evergreen—I felt like my old life and my new life had come together—blended in a truly wonderful way. Even at Evergreen, despite my fear, I knew I was destined to sing, and now I saw that everybody—old friends and new—agreed with me. I sang twelve songs, and when we finished with "I Saw the Light" I knew we'd done well.

We received a number of fine reviews, but the one by Mignon Kilday in the *Azalea City News* was long and especially gratifying. She wrote: ". . . when that spotlight hit her, she eclipsed the golden moon. From then on, everything and everyone else was forgotten as she performed." Mignon went on to say: "Truth to tell, we expected an untrained, somewhat weak presentation. Boy were we ever knocked over by a wonderfully clear, clean, strong, pure sound. Another generation of Hank Williams and now Jett Williams fans is born." She closed her article with a touching remark: "That wasn't a quarter moon up there, it was old Hank grinning with pride—just like we were."

When we left Mobile the next day, I was both exhausted and elated. And by the following Thursday, when "the boys" and I did another performance in Birmingham, I was beginning to feel like an old pro. It was working.

And so was the judicial process. In early November, we had to fight off some bad press when it was reported that the U.S. Supreme Court had declined to hear our case. We knew that this was not terribly significant because the New York Court of Appeals had recalled its decision, but, not surprisingly, few others understood all these machinations.

On November 9, the Alabama Supreme Court responded to Hank Jr.'s request for a rehearing. Again, the legal dance was complicated, but basically the Alabama Supreme Court reaffirmed its July 5, 1989, decision and we won again. The estate of Hank Williams was, indeed, reopened. And just to make its position absolutely clear, the Supreme Court added another ten pages to its opinion, clarifying certain points.

As Keith had surmised, it seemed that the Court of Appeals for the Second Circuit in New York had waited to make sure that the Alabama Supreme Court ruling was final before it took action. Within a month of the Alabama reaffirmation, on December 5, the United States Court of Appeals issued its opinion, beginning with an acknowledgment of the Alabama case:

> At the time of plaintiff's appeal before us, she also had pending an appeal to the Supreme Court of Alabama where she sought to have her father's estate opened and to obtain her proportionate share of that estate.

The Appellate judges then went on to reiterate the Alabama findings in great detail, focusing primarily on their conclusion that fraud had been committed and their belief that, given the actions of Robert Stewart and Irene Smith, I had acted in a timely manner. As a result, they found that:

Although not bound by the decision of the Alabama Supreme Court . . . its decision involved different parties and applicable law . . . we believe that its finding of fraud required a reappraisal of our decision made before that court ruled.

I had won! New York was going to reconsider their position. The Court of Appeals had based its previous decision on the lower court's finding that I had "slumbered peacefully" on my rights—I had waited too long—or, in legal terms, I was subject to an unwritten statute of limitations known as "laches." As a result of its being in agreement with the Alabama Supreme Court ruling, New York concluded that:

> . . . the evidence of fraud, which the Alabama Supreme Court found persuasive, makes summary judgment dismissing plaintiff's claim on the grounds of laches inappropriate. The figure representing justice is blindfolded so that the scales are held even, but justice is not blind to reality. Plaintiff therefore should have her day in court and an opportunity to have a jury determine the merits of her claim.

Keith and I were home on the *Jett Stream* on that freezing cold December day when we got the call that, at last, I would have an opportunity to explain my position in a court of law to a jury of my peers.

When I read those words, "justice is not blind to reality," I felt a warm surge of joy flow through me. Yes, I was excited—but it wasn't the thrill I had experienced in July when the Supreme Court of Alabama set the record straight. Like the performance in Mobile, this legal decision made me feel calm and complete. It was a warm, happy feeling, a sense that, at last, all was "right" with the world.

EPILOGUE

Shortly after my suit against Stanley and Aunt Helen was settled, my uncle Bill Deupree said to me: "Honey, a lot of rain has fallen on your life."

Obviously, this was true. My daddy died just five days before I was born. My mother, for her own reasons, found it necessary to give me up. My grandmother died, after months of negotiations to adopt me, just as I turned two. I was tossed out to become a ward of the state, and then placed in a home with two parents who found the complexities of my life—not to mention their own—simply too difficult to handle.

From day one—January 6, 1953—I have been fighting. And not only have I been battling against the cannonballs fate shot right in my face, I've been struggling with a number of snipers who were hiding in the bushes of my life, concealing themselves—and me—from all that was just.

Apparently many people presume that Keith and I fought this battle for the most vulgar of all reasons: money. Certainly, I'm human and like to live well. And part of our "reality" is that

Keith and I have rung up hundreds of thousands of dollars of debt in our little war. In truth, if we ultimately receive some money from all of this, it will be welcome.

But, for me, money was never the issue. Justice, blind justice, was my cause—from the start. As we uncovered all the facts of the case of "Baby Jett" and I knew what my daddy intended for me, my urge to make things right grew and grew—to the point where, at times, I found myself in a perpetual state of rage. Not only did I believe in my heart that I deserved a fair shake, I also realized that I needed to fight for the rights of Hank Williams, Bobbie Jett, Lillian Stone, and Wayne and Louise Deupree. It is astonishing to me that Robert Stewart, Irene Smith, the Acuff-Rose firm, and any number of lawyers and businessmen could wreak such havoc. Certainly they were not fighting for justice or the rights of a fatherless baby girl. They were fighting for one reason—and one reason only: money.

It is strange, but despite the rage I often feel toward Hank Williams, Jr., I sometimes feel sorry we are so at odds. Just as I was a fatherless child, so was he. Like me, he too has had his struggles with the ghost of Hank Williams. Like me, he was also manipulated by people who were interested in their own agendas, not his. His rights were impinged upon—at times even by the same folks who brought you the saga of "Baby Jett."

At his deposition, Hank Jr. denied repeatedly that he knew anything about me, and recently we have heard rumors that he says that my name will never cross his lips. But, of course, he did know about me, and certainly he knows about me now. Yet I recognize that in those early years, he was just a child. He had nothing to do with Irene Smith placing me into the welfare system, Judge Richard Emmet declaring that I was unable to inherit because I was adopted, or Robert Stewart hiding the truth from me and my adoptive parents. He might have agreed with them then, and probably still does—but it is unfortunate.

I wonder sometimes, as I watch him accepting his third Country Music Entertainer of the Year Award or winning his Grammy for the "Tear in My Beer" video, if he feels vindicated as a result of his own talent and success. Surely, he is not happy about the results of our "battles," but I wonder if he will ever want to really set things right—for Hank's sake—and meet his little sister. I hope so. God knows, stranger things have happened.

Despite the "rain" that has fallen on my life, I can't help but feel I've been blessed. It seems to me that whenever I was dealt a blow by fate, someone was always beside me to cushion the shock. My grandmother, Lillie, who was sick and experiencing her own deepest sorrow, agreed to take me as an infant and raise me. Mama and Daddy Cook provided love and devotion to a little girl who was just a ward of the state. Betty Rogers, Anita Gadel O'Toole, and Mary Lee Glover recognized that I was starved for love and affection, and they provided it, not only when I was a child but to this day. Sally Rogers O'Donnell and Lenore Gadel Johnston have stuck by me through thick and thin and remain the dearest of friends.

As I dug back into my deeper roots, I could see that I was loved—and wanted—from the start by an incredible assortment of special people: Henry and Ilda Mae Cook, Pappy McCormick, Connie and Bob Helton, and even Marie Harvell. They all considered adopting me when my grandmother died, but were told that I could not go with anyone who knew my "origins."

From the moment I made my midnight call that August night in 1981, the Jetts have accepted me with open arms. I know in the beginning, Willard found it difficult to acknowledge Bobbie's "illegitimate" daughter, especially one who was fathered by such a well-known celebrity. But he swallowed his pride and opened his heart to me. Sadly, Willard died in 1986, and Patsy passed away in 1989, but I will forever appreciate their acceptance of me.

The same was true of all my half brothers and sisters. Many times Jo has said to me, "You are a big part of our hearts and we're proud of you." When I have asked Jo if my existence was difficult for her, she has said "No!" in her special, enthusiastic way. She told me from the beginning that she and our brothers and sisters felt that since Bobbie wasn't there, they had to stand in. And they love me as she would have loved me.

Through all the Tippins kids, I have come to know Bobbie

and feel Bobbie's love. Frankly, for many years, I found it terribly difficult to accept her rejection of me, but as a result of the love I have received from all the Jetts, I now know that she, too, carried a heavy burden of grief because I was "lost" to her just as she was "lost" to me.

Life is not perfect, and my loss of Aunt Helen's love and friendship is very painful to me. But in one of those great ironies of life, as a result of the trial, I became much closer to the Deuprees, and enjoy a very special relationship with that side of my adoptive family—especially my uncle Bill and my cousin Dana.

If life is not perfect, sometimes it comes pretty close. I find myself saying so often, "I know who I am, I know what I want—and I know who I belong to." And, of course, "who I belong to" is Keith Adkinson. I truly was blessed the moment he came into my life, and I know I always will be blessed because of him.

And there is one other person who blessed me, who was there in the beginning trying to "cushion the shock," and who I know is there now, rooting me on. I can't help but believe he would be angered to know that his "Sweet Yvonne" was treated so shabbily by people he trusted. Yet today, as I stand up and sing the songs he wrote, backed up by Jerry and Don, "the boys" who helped create his inimitable sound, I know he would be proud. Kinfolk are comin' by the dozen not only to see Yvone, but to hear ole Hank's music. And that's what he wanted most in the world.

Uncle Bill was right—it has rained much in my life. Perhaps that's why I continue to see those double rainbows. Or maybe it was all just meant to be.

CHRONOLOGY

12 August 1898   Jessie Lillie Belle Skipper [Lillian Skipper Williams Stone], mother of Hank Williams, born in Butler County, Alabama.

12 November 1916   Jessie Lillie Belle Skipper and Elonzo Williams are married.

5 October 1922   Bobbie Webb Jett is born in Nashville, Tennessee.

17 September 1923   Hiriam "Hank" Williams is born to Lillie and Lon Williams in Mt. Olive, Alabama.

10 July 1937   Williams family moves to Montgomery, Alabama.

Fall 1937   Hank Williams begins to perform professionally in Montgomery.

10 July 1942   Lillian Williams divorces Elonzo H. Williams in Montgomery, Alabama.

15 December 1944   Hank Williams marries Audrey Mae Sheppard Guy in Andalusia, Alabama.

1944–1948   Hank performs regularly on WSFA in Montgomery and tours with the Drifting Cowboys.

14 September 1946   Hank and Audrey travel to Nashville to meet Fred and Wesley Rose and establish Hank's songwriting and recording career.

1 March 1947   Lillian Williams marries William Wallace Stone.

26 May 1948   Audrey divorces Hank for the first time, in Montgomery, Alabama.

August 1948   Hank becomes a regular on the Louisiana Hayride.

22 December 1948   Hank records "Lovesick Blues" in Cincinnati, Ohio.

25 February 1949   MGM releases "Lovesick Blues" which becomes *Billboard*'s number-one hit of 1949.

26 May 1949   Randall Hank Williams is born in Shreveport, Louisiana.

11 June 1949   Hank makes his debut on the Grand Ole Opry to six encores.

9 August 1949   Hank and Audrey's 1948 divorce is amended nunc pro tunc.

1950   Hank has three songs on *Billboard*'s yearly retail sales chart: "Why Don't You Love Me," "Long Gone Lonesome Blues," and "Moanin' the Blues."

1951   Hank has three songs on *Billboard*'s yearly retail sales chart: "Cold, Cold Heart," "Hey, Good Lookin'," and "Crazy Heart."

Hank meets Bobbie Webb Jett in Nashville.

13 December 1951   Hank's back is operated on in Nashville.

3 January 1952   Hank moves out of the Franklin Road house.

10 January 1952   Audrey files for separate maintenance.

February 1952   Bobbie Jett visits Hank in Montgomery, where he is staying with his mother at 318 McDonough Street.

April 1952   Bobbie Jett becomes pregnant.

29 May 1952   Hank and Audrey's divorce is final.

13 June 1952   Hank records "Jambalaya," "Settin' the Woods on Fire," and "I'll Never Get Out of This World Alive" in Nashville.

Summer 1952   Hank evidently meets Billie Jean Jones Eshliman.

11 August 1952   Hank is fired from the Grand Ole Opry.

15 August 1952   Hank and Bobbie go to Lake Martin, near the town of Kowaliga, Alabama. Hank writes "Kaw-Liga."

Bobbie Jett and her three-year-old daughter, Jo, move into Lillian Williams' boardinghouse at 320 McDonough Street in Montgomery.

23 September 1952   In Nashville, Hank records "Your Cheatin' Heart," "Kaw-Liga," and "Take These Chains From My Heart." This is Hank's last recording session.

13 October 1952   Hank Williams and Billie Jean Jones Eshliman secure a marriage license in Bossier City, Louisiana.

15 October 1952   Hank Williams and Bobbie Jett sign a contract regarding the care of their unborn child.

18 October 1952   Hank Williams and Billie Jean Eshliman are married by a justice of the peace in Minden, Louisiana.

19 October 1952   Hank Williams and Billie Jean Jones Eshliman are married publicly twice at performances in New Orleans, Louisiana.

28 October 1952   Billie Jean's divorce from Harrison Eshliman, whom she married in 1949, becomes final.

30 December 1952   Hank leaves Montgomery for a performance in Canton, Ohio.

1 January 1953   Hank Williams is pronounced dead on arrival at the Oak Hill, West Virginia, hospital.

4 January 1953   Hank's funeral is held at the Montgomery City Auditorium, and he is buried at the Oakwood Cemetery Annex.

6 January 1953   Bobbie Jett gives birth to me at St. Margaret's Hospital in Montgomery, and names me Antha Belle.

Robert B. Stewart brings Lillian Stone letters of administration (of Hank's estate) to sign. Stewart also drafts a short will for Lillian.

14 January 1953   Lillian Williams Stone takes me, eight days old, into her home and calls me Cathy. Bobbie Jett has already returned to her uncle's home in Nashville, Tennessee, with her other daughter, Jo.

28 January 1953   Lillian Stone has her first meeting with the Montgomery County Department of Public Welfare.

January 1953 – December 1954   Lillian Stone represented by Robert B. Stewart goes to great lengths to adopt me.

18 June 1953   Bobbie Jett signs "consent of parents to adoption" form in Davidson County, Tennessee, allowing the Stones to adopt me.

8 July 1953   William Wallace Stone and Lillian W. Stone file petition to adopt me.

31 August 1953   Bobbie Jett provides a handwritten note acknowledging that Hank Williams is my father.

18 September 1953   Telegram and letter from Virginia authorities to Alabama Department of Public Welfare stating that Irene Williams Smith accepts responsibility for me should her mother die before I am grown.

21 September 1953   Interlocutory Order of Adoption issued to Mr. and Mrs. W. W. Stone.

27 April 1954   Lillian Stone is divorced from W. W. Stone, and is awarded custody of me.

23 December 1954   My adoption by Lillian Stone is finalized, and my name is legally changed to Cathy Yvone Stone.

26 February 1955   Lillian Williams Stone dies of heart failure at age fifty-seven.

10 March 1955   Irene Williams Smith advises the Alabama Department of Pensions and Security that she does not want me.

11 March 1955   W. W. Stone reluctantly agrees to have me turned over to the state as a ward.

15 March 1955   I am turned over to the Montgomery County Department of Public Welfare, and am taken into a licensed boarding home.

15 March 1955 – 21 February 1956   I live at the home of Mr. and Mrs. Henry Cook in Pine Level, Alabama.

20 February 1956   I meet Wayne and Louise Deupree, my adoptive parents, for the first time.

21 February 1956   I am taken by the Deuprees to their home in Mobile, Alabama.

22 March 1956   The Supreme Court of Alabama rules against me in a case involving the estate of Lillian Williams Stone.

23 April 1959   Final decree of adoption of Catherine Yvone Stone is issued to Wayne and Louise Deupree, and my name is changed legally to Cathy Louise Deupree.

1963   Irene Williams Smith sells renewal copyrights to Hank Williams' songs to Acuff-Rose Publishers.

1967   Audrey Williams and Randall Hank Williams sue Irene Smith to void the 1963 renewal contract with Acuff-Rose and to close the estate of Hank Williams, Sr.

June 1967   My guardian ad litem, Drayton Hamilton, petitions court to surrender contract between Hank Williams and Bobbie Jett, dated October 15, 1952.

18 August 1967   A hearing is held in Judge Richard Emmet's chambers to discuss the October 15, 1952, contract. Emmet orders the contract and the notes on the hearing sealed by the court.

12 September 1967 Drayton Hamilton, my guardian ad litem, argues in a petition to the court that I am a legitimate heir of Hank Williams, Sr., and entitled to share in his estate and royalties.

13 September 1967 Drayton Hamilton seeks an order compelling Robert Stewart to produce all correspondence Stewart holds regarding the relationship between Hank Williams, Sr., and all parties involved in my birth.

27 September 1967 A *Montgomery Advertiser* article reports that Maury Smith, lawyer for Acuff-Rose, says that Hank Williams had recognized "in a written contract" that a child had been born to a woman in Montgomery.

1 December 1967 Judge Richard Emmet rules that Randall Hank Williams is the sole heir to the estate of Hank Williams, Sr.

30 January 1968 Judge Emmet rules in favor of Acuff-Rose and Irene Smith.

8 April 1968 Handwritten letter from Drayton Hamilton to Wayne Deupree requesting advice about appealing decision regarding me. The Deuprees do not want Hamilton to appeal.

5 May 1972 Billie Jean Williams Berlin files a suit in Atlanta against MGM with regard to the movie *Your Cheatin' Heart*.

5 January 1974 Louise Deupree tells me that I might be Hank Williams' child, and that I have been left about $2,000 from Lillian Stone's estate.

7 January 1974 I pick up the check from the estate of Lillian Williams Stone in Montgomery.

4 April 1974 Robert Stewart sends a letter to Richard Frank (Hank Jr.'s lawyer in Nashville) informing him that I have picked up my check from the Lillian Stone estate.

15 April 1974   Richard Frank sends a letter to Robert Stewart acknowledging his "disturbing" letter, and stating that I am probably "aware of my ancestry."

17 April 1974   Bobbie Webb Jett dies in Norwalk, California, at age fifty-one.

May 1975   I graduate from University of Alabama and marry Michael Mayer. We move to Montgomery, where I get a job at a community center.

August 1975   The estate of Hank Williams, Sr., is closed.

22 October 1975   A Nashville judge rules that Billie Jean Williams Berlin was the common-law wife of Hank Williams at the time of his death, and therefore is entitled to participate in the copyright renewal royalties.

4 November 1975   Audrey Williams dies in Nashville at the age of fifty-three.

October 1980   Wayne and Louise Deupree execute identical wills and powers of attorney leaving their combined assets to each other and then to me.

December 1980   Wayne Deupree tells me he thinks he was misled in 1967 with regard to the proceedings. He sends me the few papers regarding my past that he has in his possession.

20 January 1981   I reestablish contact with my foster parents, Henry and Ilda Mae Cook.

March 1981   I find Marie Harvell, Hank Williams' cousin, in Montgomery. I visit her many times over the next two or three years.

April 1981   I go to the Bureau of Vital Statistics and view my birth certificate, which states that my mother is Bobbie Webb Jett from Nashville, Tennessee.

August 1981 After learning his name from Marie Harvell, I call Willard Jett, Bobbie's uncle, in Nashville.

September 1981 I meet Patsy Jett in Montgomery.

October 1981 I meet Jo Jett Tanguay and my other half siblings in California.

4 August 1983 Wayne Deupree dies.

September 1984 I meet Keith Adkinson, a Washington lawyer.

15 – 19 October 1984 I fly to Washington to discuss my legal situation and make a demo tape.

December 1984 Keith and I go to Nashville and meet with several people in the music business, including Roy Acuff, Wesley Rose, and Owen Bradley.

7 January 1985 Keith and I go to Nashville again, and Owen Bradley agrees to work with me on my singing.

10 January 1985 Department of Pensions and Security agrees to read to me the entire file regarding my adoption by Mrs. Stone.

20 January 1985 I go to Washington to work on my career, my case, and to be with Keith.

Late February 1985 Keith meets with Milton A. Rudin, who agrees to join him in pursuing my copyright renewal interests.

March – September 1985 We move to a farm outside Nashville, Tennessee, to work with Owen Bradley on my music career.

11 July 1985 Keith sues the Alabama Department of Pensions and Security and the Bureau of Vital Statistics for my files and holds a press conference.

12 August 1985   All records from Pensions and Security and the Bureau of Vital Statistics are turned over to us.

11 September 1985   I am sued by Hank Williams, Jr., and others. I receive the "sealed file," which includes the original contract between Hank and Bobbie from the Montgomery County court.

12 September 1985   A complaint is filed on my behalf in Federal Court in New York.

24 October 1986   My suit in the New York Federal Court against the holders of the copyright renewals is amended. We now allege fraud.

March 1987   Defendants in federal copyright case request a "summary judgment," declaring them the winners.

July 1987   Judge Mark Kennedy, in the suit pending in Alabama, rules that Hank Williams, Jr., is the sole heir to the estate of Hank Williams, Sr.; however, he orders a trial on the issue of whether or not Hank Williams, Jr., is the sole child.

6 August 1987   In New York, Judge John Keenan of the federal court hears oral arguments on the "summary judgment" motion filed by the defendants.

2 September 1987   In Alabama, a trial is held to discern if Hank Williams, Jr., is or is not the sole child of Hank Williams, Sr.

26 October 1987   In Alabama, Judge Mark Kennedy rules that I am Hank Williams' natural child.

October 1987   We file our appeal of the July decision of the Alabama court that I could not inherit from the estate of Hank Williams, Sr., because I was adopted.

25 November 1987   Louise Deupree executes a will naming Stanley Fountain as beneficiary and executor with small bequests to others. Louise sends me a letter telling me I am disinherited.

27 December 1987   Louise Deupree, age sixty-five, dies. Most of her estate is left to Stanley Fountain; I receive nothing.

6 September 1988   In New York, Judge Keenan of the federal court throws my case out in its entirety reasoning that I had delayed pursuing my claim.

October 1988   We argue our appeal of Judge Kennedy's Alabama estate decision (the part denying my ability to inherit from Hank Williams' estate) before a panel of the Alabama Supreme Court.

21 April 1989   In New York, the Court of Appeals for the Second Circuit affirms Judge Keenan's September 1988 opinion that I had waited too long to pursue my claims. I lose again.

May 1989   We file a motion for a rehearing by the Court of Appeals of the Second Circuit, and are denied. Keith and Mickey Rudin file for an appeal with the U.S. Supreme Court.

4 June 1989   I make my debut as a singer at the 16th Annual Hank Williams Memorial Celebration in Evergreen, Alabama.

26–27 June 1989   Two-day trial on an action I brought with regard to Louise Deupree's estate and my disinheritance.

5 July 1989   The Supreme Court of Alabama rules in my favor, deciding that fraud had been committed against me. The decision is appealed by Hank Williams, Jr.

Midsummer 1989   In New York, the Court of Appeals for the Second Circuit recalls its April 1989 decision.

August 1989   I join forces with Don Helms and Jerry Rivers, who had played with my father, and we form Jett Williams and the Drifting Cowboys Band.

7 October 1989   I debut in Mobile with my new band.

9 November 1989   The Supreme Court of Alabama reaffirms their July 5, 1989, decision and deny the rehearing requests filed by Hank Jr. and others.

5 December 1989   In New York, the U.S. Court of Appeals rules in my favor and orders Judge Keenan to give me a trial by jury.

ACKNOWLEDGMENTS

Like many other aspects of my life story the publication of this book has been serendipitous. We had long thought my story would make an interesting book, but we had not actively sought a book contract. Nevertheless, a book contract came looking for me. An article about me appeared in *Southern Magazine* in December 1986, and a few months later, my husband and I got a call from David Vigliano, a literary agent in New York who introduced us to Harcourt Brace Jovanovich, Publishers. We were very impressed with HBJ, especially the intelligence and quality of the books they published. We made a deal with them, and have appreciated the support and encouragement they have given us during the preparation of the manuscript and the publication of this book. Particularly, we appreciate the vision, support, and editorial guidance and skill of Claire Wachtel, the enthusiasm of Leigh Haber and Dori Weintraub, and the labors of others whom we never met but who clearly worked hard to bring my story to publication.

Of course, the good work of Pamela Thomas was essential

to getting this book out. Pam not only brought the professionalism, dedication, and commitment required to assist me in reducing my saga to writing, she went that "extra mile." Pam put her heart into the project and an extra measure of effort above and beyond the call of duty. She traveled throughout Alabama and Tennessee, to my old haunts and those of the other principals. She developed an appreciation for our values and a deep respect for my father's legend.

We consulted several books in order to put together the brief biography of my father that is included in these pages. *Sing a Sad Song* by Roger M. Williams was the first book about Hank Williams I ever read. (By the way, Roger M. Williams is not related to Hank Williams.) This is the book I looked through on the afternoon of my twenty-first birthday, just hours after my adoptive mother told me I might be Hank's child. In it, I found references to "the child, a girl," and I was so haunted by them that I couldn't bring myself to actually read Mr. Williams' book from cover to cover until the mid-1980s. This book obviously holds a special place for me, and I leaned on Mr. Williams' interpretation of Hank's life—and quote from him frequently—in these pages.

The other biography of Hank I looked to for an objective and complete view of his life—both professionally and personally—is *Hank Williams: A Bio-Bibliography* by George William Koon. Both my husband and I believe that Bill Koon's biography of Hank is one of the best ever written, and I particularly appreciate Bill's permission to quote extensively from his book with regard to the issues surrounding Hank's death.

Other books we refer to and would like to acknowledge are: *The Man Behind the Scenes*, by Juanealyn McCormick Sutton; *Your Cheatin' Heart: A Biography of Hank Williams*, by Chet Flippo; and *Hank Williams: From Life to Legend*, by Jerry Rivers.

We also looked to Bill C. Malone's remarkable book *Country Music U.S.A.* for a general history of country music, and to *Grand Ole Opry*, by Chet Hagan, for a fascinating history of that American musical institution. In addition, we read *Behind Closed Doors: Talking with the Legends of Country Music*, by Alanna Nash. Her talks with various country music stars were helpful, and her interview with my half brother, Hank Williams, Jr., was especially informative.

We also consulted a very special book called *Lost & Found: The Adoption Experience*, by Betty Jean Lifton, which provided a marvelous insight into my own background, as well as a confirmation of feelings I had long held about the circumstances of my own life. This book was given to me by Martha Hume, the author of an article about me that appeared in the December 1986 issue of *Southern Magazine*, and I thank Martha for her special interest in me and my story.

During the research and preparation of the manuscript, many people gave of their time, energy, and memories. I want to thank Mrs. Ilda Mae Cook, Jimmy Cook, and Jewel Cook Smith for sharing their memories of the year I spent with them. I also want to thank Sally Rogers O'Donnell, Betty Rogers Mathews, Lee Rogers Ward, Mary Lee Glover, Lenore Gadel Johnston, and Anita Gadel O'Toole for sharing their memories of my adoptive parents, Wayne and Louise Deupree, and my youth in Mobile.

Among the people who knew my father, Hank Williams, and came to me with their stories and their truth, I would like to thank Connie and Bob Helton, Ola Frances and Braxton Schuffert, Neal (Pappy) McCormick, Bob Pinson, Jerry and June Rivers, Don and Hazel Helms, and Owen Bradley.

In addition, I would like to thank Jerry, Don, Owen, and Buddy Lee, for their guidance and support with regard to my singing career. Needless to say, I also appreciate the support of the rest of the Drifting Cowboys band—Bobby Andrews (vocals and bass), Frank Evans (guitar), and Jimmy Heap, Jr. (drums)—as we work on our concert tours. I want to extend special thanks to Jim Morris of Washington, D.C., for appreciating my talent early on, for helping me in the very beginning, and for taking the time to be interviewed for this book.

Over the last several years, many people have shared with me their memories of my mother, Bobbie Jett. Particularly, I am grateful to Virginia Harpst; Jeannie Jett Byrne; Mickey Jett; and my half brothers and sisters Richard, John, Linda, Melissa, and especially Jo Tippins Tanguay. I also want to remember Willard and Patsy Jett and Ronnie Tippins, who although they are no longer with us, added to my life, and to my knowledge of my mother.

I also want to thank my old friends Connie and Jim Buckalew and Kemper and Mike Franklin—as well as many others too numerous to mention—for their support, love, and encouragement during the long years of my search. Over the past five years, many "newer" friends also sustained me in innumerable ways. In particular, I would like to thank Connie and Larry Finks and Clifton and Vicky Dinneen.

I want to thank my adoptive family, the Deuprees—especially William L. Deupree and his son, Dr. Dana Deupree—for their unwavering support of my initiatives in searching for my natural parents and for their willingness to come forward in my struggle over the estate of my adoptive mother.

Special appreciation must also go to Keith's mother, Pauline Adkinson, for her continuing interest, and to his aunt, Irene Ruffner, for her unwavering, uncritical, and wholehearted support of all of our undertakings, from chasing our dreams to buying the *Jett Stream*. Aunt Irene, at eighty, matched us every step of the way with enthusiasm and commitment.

Finally the person who deserves most of the credit is my husband, F. Keith Adkinson, and I want to thank him for devoting his life and his career to making my dream come true. Keith devoted many hours, days, and months to organizing, writing, and rewriting *Ain't Nothin' as Sweet as My Baby*; without his time and effort this book would never have been written. More than that, without his love, friendship, support, and legal talent, I would have never found out who my father was, what happened to his wishes and my life; I could never have set the record straight, nor would I have had a singing career. Keith never once wavered; he invested all his love, energy, and financial wherewithal to support my cause. For this, I want to thank him with my whole heart. Without Keith, there would have been no Jett Williams—and there would be no story to share.